TEXTUAL TRAFFIC

SUNY series

EXPLORATIONS

in

POSTCOLONIAL STUDIES

Emmanuel C. Eze, editor

TEXTUAL

TRAFFIC

Colonialism, Modernity, and the

Economy of the Text

S. SHANKAR

STATE UNIVERSITY OF NEW YORK PRESS

Published by
STATE UNIVERSITY OF NEW YORK PRESS, ALBANY

© 2001 State University of New York

For information, address State University of New York Press,
90 State Street, Suite 700, Albany, NY 12207

Production, Cathleen Collins
Marketing, Dana Yanulavich

Library of Congress Cataloging-in-Publication Data

Shankar, Subramanian, 1962–
    Textual traffic : colonialism, modernity, and the economy of the text / S. Shankar.
        p. cm. — (SUNY series, explorations in postcolonial studies)
    Includes bibliographical references and index.
    ISBN 0-7914-4991-2 (alk. paper) — ISBN 0-7914-4992-0 (pbk. : alk. paper)
        1. Travelers' writings, American—History and criticism. 2. American literature—20th
century—History and criticism. 3. English literature—20th century—History and criticism.
4. Travelers' writings, English—History and criticism. 5. Modernism
(Literature)—English-speaking countries. 6. Postcolonialism—English-speaking
countries. 7. Colonies in literature. 8. Travel in literature. I. Title. II. Series.

PS366.T73 S53 2001
810.9'355—dc21

                                                                            00-058791

            10   9   8   7   6   5   4   3   2   1

For my parents

K. S. Subramanian and K. S. Champakam

To be colonized is to be removed from history, except in the most passive sense. A striking illustration of the fact that colonial Africa was a passive object is seen in its attraction for white anthropologists, who came to study "primitive society." Colonialism determined that Africans were no more makers of history than were beetles—objects to be looked at under a microscope and examined for unusual features.

—Walter Rodney, *How Europe Underdeveloped Africa*

Contents

ACKNOWLEDGMENTS

In the years it has taken me to write this book, many debts have been incurred. Barbara Harlow was her customary self in reading and rereading through the many stages of this book: critical and exacting in her assessment, constructive and helpful in her responses. At Rutgers University (Newark), Barbara Foley has repeatedly amazed me by her generosity with her time in the midst of a busy schedule of work. Other colleagues at Newark have exemplified for me much of what is good in academic work. Fran Bartkowski, Belinda Edmondson, H. Bruce Franklin, Rachel Hadas, Gabriel Miller, and many others have helped make Rutgers (Newark) a stimulating and supportive environment. Thanks are also due to Ann Cvetkovich, Lester Faigley, José Limón, and Anne Norton for their early advice on the manuscript. Hosam Aboul-Ela, Purnima Bose, Luc Fanou, Rachel Jennings, Laura Lyons, Luis Marentes, Louis Mendoza, and Supriya Nair read initial drafts and helped push the book in directions it needed to go. Through a few crucial years of learning and writing, they and other friends in Austin, Texas, provided a community of intellectual companionship that remains valuable to this day.

A seminar on the aesthetic at the Center for the Critical Analysis of Contemporary Culture in New Brunswick generated ideas that made their way into the first chapter, though unknown to other participants. I would like to thank the participants and especially George Levine, the director, for an instructive year of discussions.

I would also like to take this opportunity to thank the following friends, collaborators, and teachers (some of whom invited me to make presentations from the work in progress): Meena Alexander, Agha Shahid Ali, Vik Bahl, Jane Bai, Srimati Basu, Moustafa Bayoumi, Tim Brennan, Kanishka Chowdhury, Shamita Das Dasgupta, Gaurav Desai, V. Geetha, Zulfikar Ghose, Paul Greenough, Kathy Hansen, Jonathan

Haynes, Andy Hsiao, Nalini Iyer, Neil Larsen, Vincent Leitch, Sunaina
Maira, Michael Moffat, Chandra Talpade Mohanty, Satya Mohanty,
Kirin Narayan, Peter Osborne, V. Padma, Carla Petievich, R. Radhakr-
ishnan, N. Ram, Rajeswari Sunder Rajan, Raj Rao, Josna Rege, Bruce
Robbins, P. Sainath, Ramón Saldívar, Louisa Schein, Nirmal Selvamony,
Asha Sen, Vijay Seshadri, Yumna Siddiqi, Alexandra Seung Hye Suh,
Gayatri Chakravorty Spivak, Rajni Srikanth, Eric Tang, Shashi Tharoor,
Susie Tharu, and Ved Prakash Vatuk.

   I am grateful to Lalitha Dharini for providing me with the picture on
the book's cover, which depicts a scene from Komal Swaminathan's Tamil
play *Oru Indhiya Kanavu* (*An Indian Dream*). Swaminathan's later plays
share some general "theoretical" ground with my argument in this book
regarding a "cultural politics of praxis." Lalitha Dharini, the daughter of
Swaminathan, was enthusiastic and helpful during the time spent translating her father's most important play *Thaneer, Thaneer* (*Water!*).

   For helping to provide me with a community of friends and family on two continents, thanks are also due to the following: Girija,
Raman, Shekar, Lakshmi, Amitava, Jael, Anjana, and Mr. and Mrs.
Bhattacharjee; Neena Das, Dermot Dix, Mini Liu, Tina Malaney, Debi
Rai Chaudhuri, and Helio San Miguel; and Aniruddha Das, Satinder
Jawanda, and Chandana Mathur (all three founding or long-term mem-
bers of the SAMAR Collective). Outside the academic world, my
notions of a cultural politics of praxis have found opportunities as well
as instructive limits in the work of the SAMAR Collective, a left South
Asian alternative media resource based in New York.

   My deepest debt, my most important acknowledgment, is to Anannya Bhattacharjee, who shares willingly in so many more aspects of my life
than is necessary or seems possible. Her work over the years in a variety of
organizations (including the SAMAR Collective) has been exemplary to me
above all for its commitment and sense of personal and political integrity.
And Ujay is the greatest wonder and joy to me every day.

   It remains only to conclude by thanking Jane Bunker, my editor at
SUNY Press, for her capable and considerate handling of this project
and the anonymous readers for their detailed and helpful critiques. Of
course, the responsibility for any oversight or weakness in the argument
of the book is solely mine.

   With love, this book is dedicated to my parents, whose hand in it
is perhaps the most indirect, but not therefore the least important.

PREFACE

Colonial Modernity, Textual Economics, and Travel Narratives

The concerns of this book are indicated by the title to the preface. The aptness of calling a book on travel narratives "Textual Traffic" must be immediately evident. At the same time, the book title is intended to allude to the manner in which a text, as a part of a textual economy, "traffics" in meaning. Thus, it identifies an argument regarding literary and cultural criticism. The allusion to the historical argument regarding colonial modernity lies, perhaps more distantly, in the power of "traffic," in the sense of the kind of mobility that sent metropolitan travelers into the colonial world (and vice versa), to signify modernity.

How are our notions of modernity and postmodernity clarified by an attention to the history of colonialism? In pursuing an answer to this question, the book subjects the relationship between colonialism and modernity—and postmodernity—to a sustained analysis. Recent work in postcolonial studies has turned increasingly to the issue of this relationship. Some of this valuable work is reviewed in the following pages, while the thrust of the argument is to focus attention on the mutually constitutive nature of the relationship and on the notions of "value" encoded within such a term as *modernity*. The substance of the book is an argument regarding the enduring relationship of (neo)colonialism to modernity, but it is impossible in the current moment to comment on this relationship without settling accounts with the powerful claims that have been made on behalf of a certain idea of *post*modernity. Influential arguments have been made that we have passed from the age of modernity to the age of postmodernity. This book, however, takes up contemporary texts (among others) to argue for their modernity—and so the engagement with postmodernity in a book on colonial modernity. Indeed, as the first chapter reveals, it is by way of such an engagement that the argument originally arrived at "colonial modernity."

By "colonial modernity" the colonial dimensions of modernity (the ways in which the origins of what is conventionally regarded as modernity include colonialism) rather than the dimensions of modernity in a colonized area are identified. The parallel construction here would be what is conventionally called "capitalist modernity" (one example is David Harvey in *The Condition of Postmodernity*; see, for example, page 108). Certainly, there is potential for confusion here because "colonial modernity" is sometimes used (e.g., in the work of the subalternist historians in India) to refer precisely to the characteristics of modernity in a colonized area, a related but distinct concern. However, there does not seem to be any more convenient way, especially when a comparison is intended with such a construction as capitalist modernity, to capture what is meant by the colonial dimensions of modernity. Hence, my decision to retain "colonial modernity." What is labeled colonial modernity in subalternist historiography is referred to in this book as the modernity of the colonized.

Intimately connected to the notions of value alluded to above is the argument made in this book for the recuperation of the category of "praxis" for cultural criticism. Praxis has many meanings. Often, it is taken to mean politically conscious action. But, at its broadest, within certain traditions of thought, it refers to a specifically human mode of being in the world. "Praxis" is used most often in the second sense in this book. At the end of a significant work of historiography, Guyanese historian Walter Rodney wrote of "the element of *conscious activity* that signifies the ability to make history, by grappling with the heritage of objective material conditions and social relations" (*How Europe Underdeveloped Africa* 280, italics in text). This I take to be praxis in the second sense. Occasionally, in my argument, there are also references to "practice," a word that cannot but be touched by the meanings of "praxis" in the context of the argument. It has been retained for those places in the book where a more modest term than "praxis"—so burdened, after all, by specific usages—seemed to be called for.

At the level of critical methodology, this turn to "praxis" is the main contribution of the book. Exhaustive attention has been bestowed in the last thirty years on "discourse" and "text" as useful critical terms.

"Praxis" foregrounds a different set of concerns. It suggests a different manner of approach to cultural questions. While sensitive to the useful critical elaborations of "discourse" and "text," the argument in this book recognizes their limitations and explores the alternative proffered by a countervailing interest in a "cultural politics of praxis." Needless to say, this exploration cannot be said to have been exhausted here.

The notion of a "textual economics" advanced in this book is most useful, then, in directing critical attention to the category of praxis. Writing about a kind of literature explored in detail by her in an important book, Barbara Harlow observes, "Resistance literature calls attention to itself, and to literature in general, as a political and politicized activity" (*Resistance Literature* 28). Although it is not related specifically to resistance literature, "textual economics" is an attempt to explore this insight into "literature in general" in a systematic manner. In arguing for a textual economics, it is suggested that it is relevant to speak of a "textual economy" that produces and distributes "value." The model here is Karl Marx's analysis of the political economy of capitalism as the production and distribution of a particular kind of "value." The argument for a textual economy invites us to consider both how a specific text is the expression of a specific praxis and how praxis is thematized within a text. Of course, expression and thematization are linked to each other; and so the argument regarding colonial modernity here proceeds partly by uncovering the thematization of various kinds of praxis in various texts. The comments on praxis and textual economics in this book emerge out of the discussion of travel narratives and a colonial modernity, but the scope of the comments is far more general and not restricted to "postcolonial studies."

The third thematic concern of the book is with the genre of the travel narrative produced in the colonial and post-/neocolonial contexts. Narratives of travel written in these contexts, as many scholars have argued, mediate between representations of the colonizer and the colonized through different narrative strategies. The typical colonialist narrative of travel effectively encodes the colonial relationship as a confrontation between the colonizer (as traveler), on the one hand, and the colonized (as "native"), on the other. However, the protocols of such a narrative are also transformed and subverted in various other deployments. The burgeoning critical commentary on travel narratives has only fitfully recognized this latter point. The argument in this book attempts to remedy this situation by directing attention to a wide vari-

ety of travel narratives. Furthermore, the travel narrative written in a
(neo)colonial context is especially well-suited for a discussion of colonial
modernity. It stages in an especially overt way the relationship between
(metropolitan) traveler and (colonial) "native." In the process, it reveals
for our analysis the contours of a colonial modernity. I should also note
that my concern is with the (neo)colonialist travel narrative as a single
genre of writing. As this book makes clear, there are of course many differences between a colonialist and a neocolonialist travel narrative. I
hope, however, this book also makes clear that there are enough continuities to warrant the approach adopted, which is to have recourse to
one of the two usages depending on the context but without abandoning the larger generic framework.

The argument summarized above is presented in two parts. This
presentation attempts to capture the history of the project: the identification of a set of questions—a theoretical conundrum—and the subsequent elaboration of an answer. Thus, Part I (Prologue to an Argument)
introduces the subject of the book and discusses questions of methodology (first chapter) and genre (second chapter). The discussion of modernity and its relationship to colonialism, introduced in the first part, is the
chief concern of Part II (Colonialism and Modernity). What is the relationship of colonialism to modernity? As suggested above, an answer to
the question is valuable both in itself and for what it can tell us about
contemporary formulations of postmodernity. The question is taken up
in earnest in chapter 3 (especially toward the end), dealt with substan-
tially in chapter 4, and brought to a conclusion in chapter 5. And so the
final chapter completes the circle and returns to the questions and texts
introduced in the first.

The period covered in the book is from the high colonialism of the
end of the nineteenth century to the neocolonialism of today, from Joseph
Conrad's *Heart of Darkness* to Steven Spielberg's *Indiana Jones and the
Temple of Doom*. Within the cogency of this twentieth century (whose
broad contours are becoming clearer and clearer to us as it recedes into
the past), the discussion concerns itself with Africa, India, and Afro-
America. The comparativism enabled by references to these carefully chosen locations is, I believe, crucial to the argument regarding colonial
modernity because it permits us to scrutinize the universalist pretensions
of such a modernity. Such important—and different—works of cultural
criticism as Barbara Harlow's *Resistance Literature*, Edward Said's *Culture and Imperialism* and Mary Louise Pratt's *Imperial Eyes* have illus-

trated the value of a similar enabling comparativism, and their lead has been followed here. It may be asked how it is that the black South during segregation finds a place in this context. The argument is that the segregated black South bears similarities to the colonial world. A particular tradition of African-American thought has argued the approximate homology of black America and the (post)colonial world. Chapter 3 offers many reasons why this may be appropriate. While the homology is only approximate, to overlook similarities is to be a poor student of history. Thus, the comparativism of the argument in this book allows us to recognize a certain thematic commonality in travel narratives emerging out of different cultural contexts during a coherent period ranging from the moment of high colonialism to the moment of neocolonialism. As will become clear in the first chapter, such comparativism accordingly finds methodological justification in the specific kind of attention to "praxis" as a critical category that is being advocated here.

Jonathan Swift's *Gulliver's Travels*, the only "literary text" discussed in detail that does not fall within the above period, finds a place in the book chiefly as a percipient critique of the generic protocols of the colonialist travel narrative. Of course, to approach *Gulliver's Travels* chiefly as critical commentary is to transgress the boundary separating primary from secondary text. Hopefully, it is not the only fruitful transgression in the book.

PART ONE

PROLOGUE TO AN ARGUMENT

CHAPTER ONE

INTRODUCTION

Textual Economics, the Modern, and the Postmodern

Many years ago, I read the East Indian epic *The Ramayana* with my students. The version we read was the novelist R. K. Narayan's highly accessible rendering based on the canonical Tamil *Ramayana* of Kamban. On the day we took up the text, the discussion soon turned to the portrayal of the heroine Sita as virtuous and obedient; indeed, as a heroine whose virtue consisted of her obedience—to her father, her husband's father, and above all, her husband. Inevitably, a number of students took this portrayal of Sita to be representative of the status of women in Hindu culture. I had taken pains to establish the contemporaneity of the epic and its status as a living scripture for many Hindus. Hence, some students decided, this was what Indian culture was all about. The distinction between Indian and Hindu was not one familiar to them (which is not to say that it is any more familiar to Indians in general).

I worked to undo this easy equation of all of Indian culture with one text, albeit a text as significant as *The Ramayana*. Was it intellectually responsible, I asked, to generalize in this fashion? What would one make of someone who generalized about contemporary American culture based solely on the evidence of the Bible? I observed that there were alternatives to Sita in Hindu culture and tried to illustrate my point by bringing up the example of the goddess Kali, whose symbolic cultural associations are quite the opposite to those of Sita. No sooner

3

had I finished than the hand of a young woman who had been one of the most vocal regarding the representativeness of *The Ramayana* as an Indian text went up. She demanded to know, with some visible anger, whether Kali was not an "evil demoness."

I had to ask, Where had she learnt such a thing about Kali?

From the film *Indiana Jones and the Temple of Doom*, came the reply! Most of the other students had also seen the film. Many of them agreed, based on the film, that they got the impression Kali was a demoness. They were surprised to learn that that is not the way Kali is understood in Hindu culture.

The classroom incident took place at an opportune moment. I had been reading, viewing, and writing about a variety of travel narratives having to do with Africa and India. One of them was the ever-popular *Indiana Jones and the Temple of Doom* (henceforth *Temple* when abbreviated).

I was interested in *Temple* precisely because it was such a popular contemporary representation of India. The film—directed by Steven Spielberg, story written by George Lucas—is set in 1935. It begins in Shanghai where Indy Jones (played by Harrison Ford) is found negotiating over a diamond with the villainous Lao Che. He escapes from Lao Che only after a series of miraculous scrapes, including a fall from a pilotless plane in an inflatable boat. At the end of the fall, presumably over the foothills of the Himalayas, Jones finds himself in an Indian village with his sidekick (a Chinese boy of ten called Short Round, played by Ke Huy Quan) and an American singer Willie Scott (played by Kate Capshaw) whom Jones is forced to take with him in Shanghai.

In the Indian village, the peasants implore Jones—in crowded scenes of outstretched hands reminiscent of the reified images of "Third World" poverty put out by "charitable" organizations on television—to save their children who have been enslaved by Mola Ram, the evil priest of Kali (played by well-known Indian actor Amrish Puri). Mola Ram is in the process of rebuilding the "thuggee" cult that the British had eradicated a century earlier and Jones must counter the evil magical powers of Mola Ram, who is misusing the sacred Shankara stones, to save the children. This he does through a series of spectacular exploits and the children are finally reunited with their parents, who signify their gratitude to the intrepid Jones in more crowded scenes, but now of folded hands.

In thinking about *Temple* as a travel narrative, I felt the ideological force of such a mass cultural (as opposed to popular cultural) expression of neocolonial discourse should not be underestimated.[1] As Salman Rushdie notes in an essay that discusses the Raj revival films (he touches on *Temple* also), "I should be happier about this, the quietist option . . . if I did not believe that it matters, it always matters, to name rubbish as rubbish; that to do otherwise is to legitimize it" ("Outside the Whale" 16). At the same time, I was aware that *Temple* might be seen by many critics as a postmodern text—as it has been, for example, by Kenneth Von Gunden in a book entitled *Postmodern Auteurs: Coppola, Lucas, De Palma, Spielberg and Scorcese*.[2] The sheer volume and influence of the discourse on postmodernity made it impossible for me to ignore the possibility that the movie, such a successful and popular cultural product of the so-called postmodern age,[3] was a dizzying spectacle of discursive self-referentiality only incidentally about a historically particular entity called India. It has become common in critical practice to regard texts that function (or are perceived by critics to function) under the sign of the postmodern as constitutively self-ironic. Yet, I continued to feel, we should not overestimate the self-ironization of a movie like *Temple*.

The student's remark and the ensuing discussion crystallized for me later as a question. If it was indeed postmodern irony that was on view on the screen, what sense were we to make of the remarks of the students? In the case of *Temple*, I realized, a full engagement with postmodernism could not be avoided. My project was really concerned with the relationship between colonialism and modernity; but, by now, so close is the association between modernity and postmodernity in the universe of theoretical issues—as indeed I discovered in presentations that I made about the film to academic audiences—that it is impossible to discuss one without the other. At the end of the engagement, which took the form of a many-staged inquiry carried out over a period of time, the chief issues that interested me in the travel narratives that I had already been considering would finally be clarified. This chapter introduces the chief issues as they emerged out of the engagement. Some of the issues had to do with questions of methodology (to which I turn first) and others with the plausibility of regarding *Temple* as a postmodern text. In the latter case, I approach *Temple* as an example of immensely influential contemporary cultural narratives. While *Temple* is certainly a film and exploits many resources uniquely available to cinema, such narratives are not to be found only in films. The discussion that follows, then, touches on some of the specifically filmic characteristics of *Temple*, but focuses attention on narratival features.

I turn first however to questions of methodology, to an exploration of what it means to refer to "the economy of the text." This is mainly a matter of convenience and clarity, for it is not as if questions of methodology were solved first, to be succeeded then by other questions. Indeed, my concern with the economy of the text is a consequence of my explorations of such narratives of travel as *Temple*. The more I thought about such narratives, the more I grew interested in the notion of a textual economy; and the more I elaborated such a notion, the more it clarified for me the thematic issues with which I was concerned with regard to travel narratives. The kind of organization best suited to a book can only do approximate justice to such a process of discovery and elaboration.

ECONOMY AND VALUE

We may begin with one of the definitions for "economy" presented in the *Oxford English Dictionary*: "The structure, arrangement, or proportion of parts, of any product of human design." Another definition, "in a wider sense," describes "economy" as "The organization, internal constitution, apportionment of functions, of any complex unity." Under the first of the two definitions given above, the dictionary in fact goes on to specify and give examples of usage (the economy "of a poem, play, etc.") in a literary context. This conventional literary understanding of economy as "structure, arrangement" "of a poem, play, etc." is transformed when we consider other definitions of "economy" as "The administration of the concerns and resources of any community or establishment with a view to orderly conduct and productiveness; the art or science of such administration" or, in the specific phrase "political economy," as "originally the art or practical science of managing the resources of a nation so as to increase its material prosperity; in more recent use, the theoretical science dealing with the laws that regulate the production and distribution of wealth" (*OED*). It is in the two latter meanings of "economy" that an interest in value attains paramount position, but it is easy to see how the latter meanings are closely related to the idea of economy as "structure, arrangement." A reading of *Temple* as the cryptic narrative of a particular production and distribution of value—to anticipate an argument that will be elaborated below—brings these different meanings of the word "economy," linked historically, back together and asks how it is that "value" might be said to be produced and distributed with regard to "a poem, play, etc."

Two definitions of "value" as a noun suggested by the *Oxford English Dictionary* are relevant here: "A standard of estimation or exchange; an amount or sum reckoned in terms of this; a thing regarded as worth having" and "The quality of a thing considered in respect of its power and validity for a specified purpose or effect." As a verb, to "value" is well known as "To estimate or regard as having a certain value or worth" and "To consider of worth or importance; to rate high; to esteem; to set store by." These definitions of value suggest the hierarchy hidden in the word.

Definitions drawn from a dictionary can be suggestive but not adequate for a full analysis of these terms.[4] In *Capital*, Karl Marx explores the meanings of "economy" and "value" in illustrative detail. Marx's concern is with one kind of economy—capitalism—whose origins are in the very "cell-form" of the system (the commodity form) and which is organized around the idea of the marketplace (*Capital*, vol. 1, 90). The idea of "textual economy" put forward here is indebted to Marx's example, hence the extensive review that follows; but it serves no purpose to force direct correspondences between Marx's critique of *political* economy in his work and the critique of *textual* economy here. The objective here is simply to trace the general trajectory of Marx's argument in *Capital* and elsewhere to learn from it a useful way to approach the task of critically analyzing texts. As Ernest Mandel notes in his introduction to the first volume of *Capital*, Marx is not laying out universal economic laws in *Capital* but rather examining one historically specific mode of economic organization (12–13).

In the three volumes of *Capital*, Marx sets out in detail what he perceives to be the fundamental mechanisms of the economy of capitalism. Marx shows that this economy can be examined from many different perspectives. In its highest form, in its form as industrial capital, the extraction and distribution of "value" in a capitalist economy involves the conjoining of labor-power with means of production in a unique productive process. The objective of the productive process is the creation of commodities whose value is greater than that of the commodities (labor-power and means of production) that went into the process. Where does the increased value come from? Marx asserts that it comes from labor power, the only commodity from which labor, as activity capable of generating value, can be extracted:

> A use-value, or useful article, therefore, has value only because
> abstract human labour is objectified [vergegenstandlicht] or materi-
> alized in it. How, then, is the magnitude of this value to be mea-
> sured? By means of the quantity of the "value forming substance,"
> the labor contained in the article. (*Capital*, vol. 1, 129)

Although Marx asserts that the origins of economic value lie in labor, he
acknowledges that this value is *realized* only through the process of
exchange—"Money [that which mediates exchange] as a measure of
value is the necessary form of appearance of the measure of value which
is immanent in commodities, namely labour-time" (*Capital*, vol. 1,
188).[5] It is only when the commodity that is the product of the joining
together of labor-power and means of production enters into a relationship of exchange with another commodity that its value becomes visible
(expressed in money in the example above).

Put in this way, we may now view the transactions of exchange
under capitalism as a process through which the value of the commodity is revealed. This discovery of value is, of course, not innocent, for it
is simultaneously the process which allows the capitalist to complete the
expropriation of surplus value. To put it in yet another way, we may say
that it is in the realm of exchange and circulation that the concentration
of value in the hands of the capitalist is brought to a closure. The corollary of this terminus is that the commodity can no longer subsist in the
domain of exchange. Referring to this aspect of the life of the commodity, Marx writes, "Once a commodity has arrived at a situation in which
it can serve as a use-value, it falls out of the sphere of exchange into that
of consumption" (*Capital*, vol. 1, 198). And so finally, after the commodity has passed through the realm of exchange (in however many
stages), it enters the realm of use through an act of consumption.

Seen from the aspect of Marx's analysis here, it would be appropriate to summarize the processes of exchange under capitalism as a
ceaseless movement of objects from the realm of potential use-value
(where the object has potential to satisfy some human want) through
the realm of exchange-value to the realm of use-value (where the potential is finally realized). Put in a different way: under capitalist processes
of exchange, objects which possess unutilized use-value are made to
enter the realm of exchange but only to return to the realm of use-
value, this time with their use-value fully prepared for consumption by
the individuals who acquire the objects. Indeed, if we were to view cap-

italism from an even more generalized perspective, it is not only from the point of view of exchange that such a movement is visible. What is the process of capitalism as a whole, including both the circulation and production of commodities, but the ceaseless, complex and transformative circular movement from (potential) use-value through exchange-value to use-value? It is this process of travel and return that unveils the value (not use-value) that lies hidden in the object as commodity. Viewed in this fashion, the immensely complex process of the alienation of different objects from the realm of (potential) use to the realm of exchange until their final return (even if only as a part of something else) to the realm of use is nothing less than of fundamental importance in the operation of the economy of capitalism. Without such a process of displacement or alienation, no value would emerge to be appropriated: "Capital . . . is a movement, a circulatory process through different stages. . . . [V]alue passes through different forms, different movements in which it is both preserved and increases, is valorized" (*Capital*, vol. 2, 185). Indeed, as is most clearly visible from the second volume of *Capital*, the processes of capitalism are reiteratively characterized, as our vantage point shifts, by this feature of circular but transformative travel. Thus, in the three circuits of capital described in the second volume, the movement is from M to M', C to C', and P to P' (standing respectively for money capital, commodity capital and productive capital). The concluding terms of these circuits represent greater values than the initial terms. Commodities in capitalism *must* describe such circular and transformative journeys so that value may be appropriated by the capitalist.

Does not this represent a capitalist travel narrative, the travel account of a commodity? Is not the commodity then a kind of traveler? I ask these questions in preparation for the argument regarding the economy of the text that will emerge later in this chapter.

ECONOMICS AND PRAXIS

If there is an economy, there is also a corresponding economics—that is, a methodological attitude, elaborated through a process of generalization and abstraction, that is attentive to the notion of an economy. Karl Marx discusses such procedures of generalization and abstraction in the introduction to the *Grundrisse* when he considers whether there is any such thing as production in general—that is, whether any universal laws pertaining to all modes of production throughout history can be summarized. He writes:

> [A]ll epochs of production have certain common traits, common characteristics. *Production in general* is an abstraction, but a rational abstraction in so far as it really brings out and fixes the common element and thus saves repetition. Still, this *general* category, this common element sifted out by comparison, is itself segmented many times over and splits into different determinations. Some determinations belong to all epochs, others only to a few. . . . [T]he elements which are not general and common, must be separated from the determinations valid for production as such, so that in their unity . . . their essential difference is not forgotten. (224, italics in original)

Later, Marx puts the matter even more succinctly when he writes, "To summarize: There are characteristics which all stages of production have in common, and which are established as general ones by the mind; but the so-called *general preconditions* of all production are nothing more than these abstract moments with which no real historical stage of production can be grasped" (226, italics in original). In the ensuing pages of the introduction to the *Grundrisse*, Marx specifies the details of production in general only in the most broad terms. Similarly, an economy of the text can be generalized—as will be done below—only so far before we are led back to the many variations actually existing. What can be generalized with a greater degree of comfort is a general form of analysis that we might call "economics"—understood here as the analysis of systems of production and distribution of value, an eminently (as we shall see) political form of analysis, for the pursuit of an economics in this context ultimately leads us to the category of "praxis."[6]

There is much to be unpacked in the reference to the category of praxis in this context. If the immediate "content" of value in a political economy is objectified labor, the ultimate "content" is nothing else than praxis. It is possible to argue that, in Marx, "labor," the activity understood as the production of items for human consumption in a political economy, is one of the manifestations of praxis, understood as a more general human activity that finds expression in the purposeful organization of the world and in the unavoidably social nature of human existence. In the first of his "Theses on Feurbach," Marx suggests that "practice" be understood as, simply, *human sensuous activity* and, again, in the eighth thesis, "Social life is essentially *practical*" (143 and 145, italics in original). Praxis or "practice" is set forward here as a central element in Marx's materialist attitude to history. It is this orientation in Marx that permits Antonio Gramsci to refer to Marxism as a "philosophy of praxis" when he is interested in dissociating it from its deterministic elements. And Lukacs, noting that "Marx, more concrete and logical than Hegel, effected the transition from the question of existence and its hierarchy of meanings to the plane of historical reality and praxis," examines the historical valence of this praxis for the proletariat in "Reification and the Consciousness of the Proletariat" (127). "[I]n his mature works [Marx's] *method* always operates," Lukacs continues on this theme, "with concepts of existence graduated according to the various levels of praxis" (127–28, italics in original).

"Labor" is one of the manifestations of praxis. It is the specific expression of praxis in a *political* economy. In a late essay, "Freedom and the Historical Imperative," Herbert Marcuse defines praxis in a way that would seem to support such a broad understanding. Praxis, in this essay, is "supra-individual action" (211); and "freedom originates indeed in the mind of man [*sic*], in his ability (or rather in his need and desire) to comprehend his world, and this comprehension is *praxis* in as much as it establishes a specific order of facts, a specific organization of the data of experience" (217).[7] In an early essay "On the Philosophical Foundation of the Concept of Labor in Economics," on the other hand, Marcuse is interested in questioning the tendency within political economic theory "to conceive of labor only as economic activity: the praxis within the economic dimension" (9). Labor to Marcuse "is an ontological concept of human existence as such" (11) and "the specific praxis of human existence in the world" (13); yet, he does want to maintain the distinction between "praxis" and "labor." Labor is a fundamental and definitive feature of human existence; but this does not mean that it is coterminous with "praxis" in its meaning. Douglas Kellner in his book-length review of Marcuse's career suggests that for Marcuse, in this essay, "[w]hat must be shown is that economic activity is rooted in the practice through which the human species constitutes its social-historical world and its own unique way of life" (88). Marcuse's way of making a distinction between "praxis" and "labor," even while asserting the centrality of "labor" to the human condition, is questionable. It involves, for example, a facile proposition that "primitive" peoples are outside of history because they do not labor as "so-called civilized people" do (28).

All the details of his arguments in this essay cannot be endorsed, but in his attempt to make a distinction between praxis and labor, which he defines as "a mode of human praxis," Marcuse is mostly justified (28).

Another sustained treatment of Marx's concept of praxis is to be found in Richard Bernstein's *Praxis and Action*. Summarizing his survey of the theme of praxis in Marx, Bernstein writes: "[w]hat might at first seem to be a chaotic array of meanings—*praxis* as human activity, production, labor, alienation, relentless criticism, and revolutionary practice—are aspects of a single, comprehensive and coherent theory of man [*sic*] and his world" (76, italics in original). This theory of the human is what Bernstein has defined as Marx's "radical 'anthropology'" (76). Through such an anthropology, Bernstein suggests, Marx aims to offer a systematic description of the alienated condition of human beings and a path out of this condition. And so he writes: "Marx had a profound understanding of the ways in which men *are* what they *do*, of how their social *praxis* shapes and is shaped by the complex web of historical institutions and practices within which they function and work" (306, italics in original). Bernstein makes a convincing case for the centrality of the theme of praxis in Marx's work.[8]

Praxis identifies a fundamental characteristic of humanity. Praxis, as the term for *human* activity, the term for the way in which human beings as a collectivity of individuals interact with one another and their environment, does not make sense otherwise. Such a position need not be understood as anything more than a minimal humanism that while recognizing a feature shared by all human beings does not, therefore, become insensitive to the point that the ways in which human beings interact with one another and with their environment can be dramatically varied. A minimal humanism need not be disrespectful of the legitimate claims of difference. Indeed, it could be argued that at least as great a danger lies in the philosophies of difference that have in recent years been guilty of a rash insensitivity to the claims of a shared humanity. The need to specify the minimal characteristics of a shared humanity according to ideas of "rationality" and "agency" is indeed the burden of Satya Mohanty's critique of contemporary (postmodernist) relativisms in *Literary Theory and the Claims of History*:

> I intend to show why we need a more precise definition of rationality than either [of two versions of relativism] offers. It would be seriously debilitating for critical analysis to confuse a minimal notion of rationality as a cognitive and practical human capacity with the

grand a priori foundational structure that has traditionally been
called reason. Indeed, as we seek now to understand the colonial
encounters which have shaped our historical modernity and to
extend or radically revise our current notions of philosophical and
cultural "conversation," the task of elaborating a positive but non-
idealized conception of the "human" can be seen as tied to this spec-
ification of a minimal rationality. (117)

Praxis, then, is being advanced here as the general term for an active,
human mode of being in the world. Furthermore, it is being argued that
notions of "economy" in whatever area of discussion bear a close relationship to such an idea of praxis. Indeed, one of the useful aspects of
an attention to "economy" is its ability to identify the relevance of the
category of "praxis."

TEXTUAL ECONOMY AND TEXTUAL ECONOMICS

Does not—to return to a question already posed in anticipation of the
discussion that will be undertaken in this section—the summary of the
processes of capitalism above—the circular movement of the commodity from M to M', C to C', and P to P'—represent a capitalist travel narrative, the travel account of a commodity? Is not the commodity also a
kind of traveler? My purpose in asking these questions is to illustrate
how a text such as *Indiana Jones and the Temple of Doom* is also an
economy. Temporarily alienated from his place of primary identification
(U.S./metropolis), Indy Jones is displaced to India (colony/proto-"Third
World") through the narrative of travel. In the process, as we will see
below, value is realized and assigned to the traveling protagonist of the
narrative and to the site from which the protagonist set out, the United
States. The realization and expropriation of this value simultaneously
devalues India in relationship to the United States.

This is a summary of an argument that will be elaborated later in
this chapter. But to make such an argument regarding *Temple* is to arrive
at an expanded understanding of "economy"—an understanding for
which Gayatri Chakravorty Spivak's comments on value are exemplary.[9]
In these comments, Spivak demonstrates the extraordinary capacity of
"value" to clarify different forms of relationship. Her references to
patriarchy as "traffic in affective value coding," for example, effectively

capture the economy of patriarchy ("Poststructuralism, Marginality, Post-coloniality and Value" 238). These comments are suggestive both for an understanding of patriarchy and an understanding of "textual economy."

An attention to praxis, whose relevant meanings have been reviewed above, helps us account for the "value" present in the text in particular ways. "Value" in the text is similar to but distinguished from "value" in a political economy, explainable in the first instance by recourse to "labor" (in the final instance, of course, here too we are led back to praxis). If we were to pursue the "value" present in the text through the different forms of its appearance in an attempt to explain it, we would arrive, finally, at praxis.

A textual economics is, then, antiformalist. An approach to a text that looks at it "economically" cannot be content with a narrow analysis of the text itself. Such an approach cannot be happy with tracing simply the particular ways in which a text—for example *Temple* through the mechanisms summarized above—distributes and organizes "value." It must also be concerned with the "content" of this value and with questions regarding where this value arises. Such an approach cannot isolate, in other words, questions regarding the *structure* of the text but must also be properly attentive to the full implications of the *evaluative structure* (structure of evaluation) and *economy* of the text and to the ways in which the latter lead to questions of praxis. In their turn, these questions point not only to the way the text originates in praxis but also to the way in which "praxis" itself comes to be represented and evaluated in a variety of ways in the text. This last concern will be of especial importance to the discussion of modernity in this book.

A textual economics—an economics of the text, an attitude to a text that is attentive to its appearance as an economy—therefore, impels us to dissent from the following assertion made by William Wimsatt and Monroe Beardsley in "The Intentional Fallacy," one of the most famous manifestoes of formalist aesthetics:

> There is a gross body of life, of sensory and mental experience, which lies behind and in some sense causes every poem, but can never be and need not be known in the verbal and hence intellectual composition which is the poem. For all the objects of our manifold experience, for every unity, there is an action of the mind which cuts off roots, melts away context—or indeed we should never have objects or ideas or anything to talk about. (12)

An economics of the text, a methodological recognition of the economy that is the text, suggests otherwise. Even at the time of New Critical hegemony when this passage was written, R. S. Crane and the Neoaristotelians expressed a qualified opposition to such a position. Thus, Crane in *The Languages of Criticism and the Structure of Poetry* makes a pluralist argument for a diversity of critical approaches and acknowledges the utility of historical criticism. He notes, "I have as fond a regard for Longinus and for the masters of historical criticism as I have for Aristotle, and as strong a conviction of their continuing utility" (193). Crane's idea of structure is indeed more dynamic and less dogmatically committed to a formalist aesthetic than the criticism of Wimsatt and Beardsley. However, Crane's acknowledgment of the utility of a historical criticism is a part of his generally pluralistic approach to intellectual matters. Nothing in his "more adequate criticism" of poetic structure *necessitates* a reference to history. Indeed, Crane himself writes that his critical practice "is a method, above all, that necessarily abstracts from history and hence requires to be supplemented by other very different procedures if we are to replace the works we study in the circumstances and temper of their times and see them as expressions and forces as well as objects of art" (192). Thus, as Vincent Leitch points out, the interest of the Neoaristotelians in structure remains bound very much by a formalist understanding of poetics.[10]

Drawing on Fredric Jameson's apt distinction between history and historicism (see *Political Unconscious* 18), we might say a textual economics has nothing to do with such a supplementary and historicist nod toward history. It insists, on the contrary, that the verbal and intellectual composition which is the poem (to echo the words of Wimsatt and Beardsley above) can only be properly comprehended in its articulation with a context around it, in the manner of its transposition of elements received from outside the text into particular evaluative structures. Form, in textual economics, then, is nothing more than a convenient term for the conceptualization of an element that mediates between an inside and an outside while, in fact, being constituted by the very interaction of an inside and an outside. The idea of a textual economy circumvents the problematic of form and its relationship to content by translating that entire problematic into more productive terms.

And so it follows that a textual economy is not a closed system. Rather, its currents of meaning—its structures of value—flow into the surrounding sea of human praxis which is, as Lukacs reminds us, history itself (see "Reification and the Consciousness of the Proletariat" 185–86). At the same time, currents from the surrounding sea flow into it and determine its structures of value. It is in the realm of praxis, the sea of history, that the evaluative structures and the value that they distribute have their origin. In this context, it is appropriate to regard "historical context" as a "practical context." The text is submerged in the domain of praxis—its practical context—and *textual economy* is simply the term used to indicate the totality of the relationships discussed above. Correspondingly, "textual economics" is simply the critical attitude commensurate with the notion of a textual economy.

Toward a Cultural Politics of Praxis

At the same time, of course, textual economics is itself a form of praxis. The argument for it is advanced at a particular time within particular institutions. Inescapably, it is offered as a supplement or critique or refinement of certain other critical practices. To clarify textual economics as a form of critical practice requires attention to these other critical practices. Textual economics has already been described as a kind of antiformalism. It is, clearly, closer to the critical practices of discourse analysis and ideology critique (which takes ideology as the governing category in the analysis of culture). These, among the most influential contemporary modes of cultural criticism, approach culture as an inescapably social phenomenon. It remains for us to consider in greater detail the relationship of textual economics to ideology critique and discourse analysis, before we turn to an illustrative exploration of *Temple*.

"Ideology" did not begin as a Marxist term, and it does not exist today exclusively as a Marxist term; but a great deal of the debate around the proper use of it certainly revolves around Marxist understandings. Ideology is by now a crucial term in Marxist accounts of cultural phenomena. "Discourse," again an old term, has achieved new currency under the impact of poststructuralist accounts of culture. Both have become such capacious terms as to subsume the entire sphere of culture within themselves. Indeed, in the case of discourse, in extreme forms the very distinction between a discursive and nondiscursive reality disappears.

The tendency on the part of the theorists of discourse to collapse such a distinction is attributable to the idealist origins of contemporary theories of discourse. An instructive illustration is offered in the case of

Richard Terdiman's powerful exploration of discourse analysis in *Discourse/Counter-Discourse*. Terdiman draws extensively on Marxist writers (especially Antonio Gramsci) to formulate his ideas of the discursive. He is aware, therefore, of the distinction between a nondiscursive reality and discourse that remains fundamental to most Marxist theorizations of culture. He is able to contrast a literary "revolution" (his inverted commas) to "more material arenas of productive activity and human struggle" (80).

Yet, at an earlier point, he is able to cite a well-known passage in which Michel Foucault wrote, "Discourse is not simply that which expresses struggles or systems of domination, but that for which, and by which, one struggles; it is the power which one is trying to seize," and find in it a "reminiscence of Marx's description of ideology in the 1859 preface to *A Contribution to the Critique of Political Economy*" (qtd. in Terdiman 55). The passage from Marx that Terdiman cites as evidence for his claim reads as follows (with his interjection):

> In studying such [revolutionary] transformations, it is always necessary to distinguish between the material transformation of the economic conditions of production, which can be determined with the precision of natural science, and the legal, political, religious, artistic or philosophic—in short, ideological forms in which men become conscious of this conflict and fight it out. (qtd. in Terdiman 55)

While the idea that discourse, like ideology, is a site of struggle is indeed reminiscent of Marx, Marx and Foucault diverge dramatically in the evaluation of ideology and discourse respectively in their systems of thought. For Foucault, discourse "is the power which one is striving to seize," but for Marx ideology cannot enjoy a similar status. The power one is trying to seize cannot be limited to ideology; indeed, any seizure of power must necessarily target the means and conditions of production themselves. Terdiman thus passes over in his assessment of these two passages what may be a fundamental incommensurability of "discourse" and "ideology" in much contemporary usage.

In *Theories of Discourse*, Diane Macdonell comments on discourse in a manner similar to Terdiman, suggesting as he does an agonistic discursive terrain in which different discourses face off against one another and contest the social production of meaning. At the same time, she is far more sensitive to the dangers of idealism inherent in certain understandings of "discourse," and careful to reflect on the relationship between "ideology" and "discourse" at some length. "What has been argued of ideology and discourse . . . [earlier in the book]," she writes, summarizing her position at one point, "allows one to say that ideologies have a material existence, discourses are part of the ideological sphere, and ideologies are practices which subject" (100). Early in the book, she has declared that "It is probably the case that no real advance is made by extending the conception of discourse too far beyond processes of speech and writing" (4).

Macdonell clearly recognizes how slippery the terrain can be in a pursuit of "discourse." That way leads to an idealist privileging of thought over being—she approvingly cites Althusser's thesis of "the primacy of being over thought" (qtd. in Macdonell 78). Thus, she subordinates discourse to ideology. A theory of discourse for her is part of a theory of ideology and her approach to ideology is essentially Althusserian, despite her criticism of some of Althusser's arguments. "Ideologies," she suggests by paraphrasing Althusser, "are systems of meaning that install everybody in imaginary relations to the real relations in which they live" (27). Furthermore, every ideology, for her, exists in struggle with other ideologies. In a book that is an introduction to theories of discourse, then, ideology does the work of locating discourse within a historical and materialist paradigm.

For their part, theories of ideology have been reviewed at length by Terry Eagleton in *Ideology: An Introduction*.[11] Early in the book, Eagleton lists sixteen different "definitions of ideology currently in circulation" (1–2). What follows in the book is a lengthy exploration of these meanings through an engagement with the works of various writers. At the end of the book, Eagleton does not offer a final definition of ideology, because no such definition is possible. He begins the first chapter of the book by writing:

> Nobody has yet come up with a single adequate definition of ideology, and this book will be no exception. This is . . . because the term "ideology" has a whole range of useful meanings, not all of which are compatible with each other. To try to compress this wealth of meaning into a single comprehensive definition would thus be unhelpful even if it were possible. . . . [I]t is probably more important to assess what is valuable or can be discarded in each of these lineages than to merge them forcibly into some Grand Global Theory. (1)

By the time we reach the conclusion of his book, Eagleton has picked out what seem to be the two most important candidates for the definition of ideology:

> Very often, [ideology] refers to the ways in which signs, meanings and values help to reproduce a dominant social power; but it can also denote any significant conjuncture between discourse and political interests. From a radical standpoint, the former meaning is pejorative, while the latter is more neutral. My own view is that both of these senses of the term have their uses, but that a good deal of confusion has arisen from the failure to disentangle them. (221)

The review of Terdiman, Macdonnel, and Eagleton above shows how vexed the question of the relationship of discourse to ideology can be. A capacious view of discourse as any signifying system and the foundational constituent of power itself (a not unconventional position in contemporary cultural criticism) is incompatible with certain aspirations for a materialist cultural theory. Taking recourse to the term "ideology" to escape the idealism inherent in "discourse" leaves us, however, with a different problem. While such recourse leads us into a terrain that is very productive for cultural theory, it also leaves us with a frustrating lack of clarity on several key questions.

Textual economics is a preliminary exploration of a form of cultural criticism that takes "discourse" and "ideology" as points of departure as well as reference, having recourse to them when necessary. It is an attempt to escape some of the limits of discourse analysis. If a sufficiently broad view of ideology critique is taken, it may be possible to subsume textual economics within it. Textual economics explores some of the same terrain as ideology critique to reach some of the same conclusions; but from a fresh direction. Its chief utility is in recovering the category of "praxis" for cultural criticism. The most important of the critical positions represented by "textual economics" is this insistence on the relevance of the category of praxis—an insistence also given recent expression, albeit in a different manner, by E. San Juan.[12]

Textual economics attempts to circumvent the inadequacy of the contemporary "cultural politics of representation" (How often have we not heard or read this phrase in announcements for conferences, papers, books, journals?) by counterposing to it what may be called a cultural politics of praxis. It challenges what Aijaz Ahmad in *In Theory* has

argued has been "in more recent years . . . the centrality of reading as
the appropriate form of politics" and seeks to shift the emphasis from
representation to praxis (3). This putative challenge to a cultural politics
of representation is indeed concerned mostly with emphasis; for, certainly, an attention to action, many will claim, is a part of the contemporary cultural politics of representation (as an attention to
representation would remain part of what is being called here a cultural
politics of praxis). Furthermore, there is a great deal to the argument
that there can be no *easy* separation of representation and action as
mutually exclusive terms. Indeed, the territory between the two is a continuum and *finally* representation can be seen as a form of action and
action as a form of representation. Yet, the manner in which we formulate our cultural politics can be of immense importance. If speaking and
writing are the exemplary modes of human existence implicit in a cultural politics of representation, doing and feeling are the exemplary
modes implicit in a cultural politics of praxis. A textual economics, making a cultural politics of praxis its object of inquiry at the same time that
it itself aspires to engage in a cultural politics of praxis, does not aban-
don the domain of representation (it is "textual") but orients itself to the
domain of praxis. At the end of *How Europe Underdeveloped Africa*,
Walter Rodney wrote, as he concluded a monumental and practical
work of historiography, of "the element of *conscious activity* that signifies the ability to make history, by grappling with the heritage of objective material conditions and social relations" (280, italics in text). If it is
conceded that "conscious enunciation," thoughtful speech, is the model
of culture that lies encrypted within a cultural politics of representation,
a cultural politics of praxis follows Rodney's lead and orients itself to
culture as conscious activity, as the ability to *make* history in a thoughtful (not to be confused with reasonable) way.

It may be argued that "making" an economy out of a text itself
moves in the direction of an idealism that ignores the materiality of what
is conventionally understood as an economy, what has been referred to
above by the classical term "political economy." Certainly, it is not being
argued here that a textual economy is any less material than a political
economy. This does not mean, however, that all distinctions between a
textual and a political economy can be erased. To assert that both are
equally material phenomena does not mean that we cannot hold that
there are different spheres of materiality, distinguishable, as the discussion above of labor and its relationship to praxis suggests, by different

modes of praxis. At issue here is a notion of "materialism" centered on the category of "praxis" rather than "matter"—what Marx once referred to as "the establishment of *true materialism*" based "on the social relationship 'of man to man [sic]'" (108, italics in original).[13]

Furthermore, a demonstration that a text is an economy goes a long way toward "materializing" the text by showing how it is amenable to questions and modes of inquiry similar to those that are usually reserved for domains generally regarded as more material. It is possible to understand a textual economics, then, not as a disguised regression to a kind of idealism but rather as the introduction of a materialist mode of analysis (that is, focussed on the category of praxis) to domains often separated out as not material. It embodies a more thoroughgoing materialism than a vulgar separation of the base as material from the superstructure as ideal.

Another objection that might be made to a textual economics is that, in the form being elaborated in this book, it is really a type of narratology. Such an objection—made perhaps on reaching the end of the book—might observe that textual economics here has mostly concerned questions of narrative, indeed narratives of travel or displacement, as exemplified in this chapter by *Temple*. Is a textual economics nothing more than a narrative economics or, even more narrowly, an economics of the *travel* narrative? Is it simply an argument about texts in general extrapolated from an argument regarding travel narratives? Certainly, the idea of a textual economics emerged from an interest in *Temple* and the other travel narratives discussed in this book. Also, much of the discussion in this book, because of the nature of its subject, will take the form of analyzing narratival and thematic structure. However, the production of value and its transfer (which makes the value visible), so vividly discernible in *Temple* because of its overt representation of displacement or movement (as will be shown below), is not unique to it or to other travel narratives like it. "Transfer" alludes to a spatialized trope and narratives of displacement are therefore especially well disposed to reveal the existence of transfer, but this does not mean that such transfer of value is not to be found in other texts.

And so we are led—in order to illustrate the point—to an analysis of a text that is not a travel narrative, indeed not even a narrative as conventionally understood; we are led to a postcard. The postcard is a picture of graffiti on a wall. Some of the words of the graffiti record a famous exchange between M. K. Gandhi and a reporter.[14] The reporter asks Gandhi, "Mr. Gandhi, what do you think of Western Civilization?" Gandhi replies, "I think it would be a good idea!" These words, in white lettering, are placed on a brick wall. The legend "No Ball Playing," also in white lettering but much smaller, appears directly beneath the exchange between Gandhi and reporter. Below the legend is a confusion of scribbles, erased graffiti and torn-off bills. High on one side is a barred window. On the other side is a gate. These two apertures into the wall frame the exchange between Gandhi and the reporter.

How is this postcard to be understood from the perspective of a textual economics?

We could begin our analysis of the postcard with the evaluative structure—structure of evaluation, structure through which value is distributed within the text—of the exchange itself and note the movement of language from the reporter to Mr. Gandhi and back to the reporter. In this movement, the status of the West is subverted because of Gandhi's refusal to allow the verbal circuit to be completed in a predictable way. Instead of allowing value to move to the site signified as West (as it does in *Temple*), Gandhi redirects the movement of value. In what direction? It is not immediately clear, but certainly what we recognize in the exchange is the wittiness of Gandhi's repartee. The ship of language moves from the reporter to Gandhi and again to the reporter but does not carry any freight back with it. Good nationalist that he is, Gandhi practices swadeshi and keeps value within his own realm by denying it to the West. In doing so, Gandhi reveals that irony can be one mode of subverting an evaluative structure. Gandhi's practice of irony here redirects value to, we can now recognize, the Other of Western Civilization in this context—Indian civilization.

Next, we could move to a consideration of the visual evaluative structure of the postcard and note the rather obvious fact of the location of the lettering that represents the exchange between the reporter and Gandhi in the center of the postcard. What passes between this lettering and the margins of the postcard is everything that lies between. Thus, this postcard, like countless millions of other pictures in the history of humanity, draws on a conventional visual evaluative structure (and we might think of John Berger's *Ways of Seeing* in this context) that organizes space in such a way as to direct value to the center of a picture and to drain it from the margins. Perhaps we could characterize the process of visual cognition in this way: the eye locates the center of the picture, and then recognizes the margins, but only to move back to the center. In the process, visual value is transferred to the center. In the case of this postcard, the white border at the margins and the placement of the bold lettering at the center of the postcard reinforces this *conventional* structure of pictorial space. Thus, we see how two different evaluative structures are conjoined in this postcard (much, as we shall see below, as in the case of *Temple*).

If we were to enter the postcard now and continue our analysis of the formal qualities of the arrangement of the lettering on the wall, we might want to note the contrast of the white lettering on the dark wall made by the passage of the paint (or some other such material) between the wall and the verbal evaluative structure noted above. In this fashion, we might suggest, the evaluative structure of the exchange itself is assigned value over the wall by the application of paint of a particular color. Pursuit of this line of inquiry, however, takes us directly to questions of praxis (this is not the only way we are led to such questions), for we are encouraged to consider now the human hand that was instrumental in the application of the paint on the wall. We recognize that at the root of the many different assignations of value we have noted thus far lies human agency. We recognize that the postcard is a textual *economy*, not just a bundle of evaluative structures.

And so we might be led to consider questions regarding the specific nature of this human agency and the (social and political) economies within which it subsists. In the postcard, there are some clues for the pursuit of this inquiry. Two such clues are the identification of Gandhi as "Mr. Gandhi" and the legend "No Ball Playing." Both these clues suggest that these graffiti are located in some Western English-speaking country, probably in North America. The graffiti are thus part of social commentary in the very belly of the whale. We may explore here the processes by which an anticolonial sentiment expressed in India in the early part of the twentieth century is relocated in a different, if allied, historical situation (which we should have learned by now to gloss also as a *practical* context). The specific features of this different situation are not fully discernible within the postcard, and we can only speculate in the broadest terms regarding the praxis that is represented by the lettering on the wall. However, even if we find our opening only in speculation, such speculation can lead us to productive questions regarding the way in which the context appears within the text.

Yet another line of inquiry regarding the textual economics of this postcard would lead us to consider its status as a commodity. The postcard is after all an object produced to be sold for profit. What is the relationship of the commodity-character of the postcard to its textual economy? What is the relationship of the postcard's existence as a cell-form of a capitalist economy to the evaluative structures that are part of its textual economy? Ultimately, such questions are resolvable only by reference to praxis. We are thus led not only to questions regarding the economic processes involved in the production and distribution of the postcard as a physical object but also to questions regarding intellectual property and the commodification of intellectual work under capitalism. In what directions is value transferred in such cases? In what ways do the values configured by the evaluative structures of the postcard's textual economy have their origins in the political economy represented by its commodity character (and vice versa)? Such questions take us in the direction of exploring the ways in which an economy of commodification (a political economy, in the classical sense of the term) relates to a textual economy. They demonstrate to us how a textual economy is connected to other economies. Finally, a postcard is, of course, an object that is meant for travel. The person who buys the postcard is meant to place a stamp on it and send it on its way to a recipient, who (it is expected) will not only read the news on the postcard but will also appreciate the writing on the wall. The postcard thus enters other historical contexts, other contexts of praxis, and encounters other economies.

The questions that have been raised about the postcard do not exhaust all possible questions that might be asked regarding it. They simply illustrate some of the possibilities present in textual economics as a methodology. The case for a textual economics lies in its ability to pose questions regarding context in a novel and urgent way and in its ability to relocate the terminology of "privilege" and "marginality," so pervasive in contemporary cultural and social criticism, back within a methodology that is not happy to recognize discourse as a self-sufficient universe. At its broadest, a textual economics departs from a cultural politics of representation, of reading, and initiates an engagement with a cultural politics of praxis, of doing.

Finally, a clarification regarding the use of the term "praxis" in this book might be in order. "Praxis," in the critical traditions invoked in this book, refers both to politically conscious action and, at its broadest, to a specifically human mode of being in the world. "Praxis" is used most often in the second sense in this book; rather than have recourse to awkward constructions, I have relied on the context to convey which meaning is intended. In addition, there are occasional references to "practice"—for example, "literary critical practice"—which resonates with "praxis" in the context of the argument. The resonance is intentional. Practice is supposed to suggest praxis without being subsumed by it. I have retained it for those places where a more modest term seemed to be called for.

It bears repeating here that the notion of a textual economics is mainly useful in directing critical attention to the category of praxis. It should make criticism regard praxis at many different levels—not only at how a specific text is the expression of a specific praxis, but also at how praxis is thematized within a text. Of course, expression and thematization are intimately linked to each other. Often, we learn about the former through analysis of the latter. This is certainly the case with regard to the argument about modernity in this book.

Furthermore, the specific kind of attention to "praxis" being advocated here presumes a specific kind of historical methodology. The argument in this book is resolutely comparativist. This critical posture is the result of the conviction that in certain respects the explorations of colonialism and modernity undertaken here are best served by reference to more than one historical context, for in this fashion we can scrutinize the universalist practical pretensions of "colonial modernity" more adequately. The comparativism, in other words, matches the broad conceptual terrain opened for us by the idea of praxis being invoked here.

The notions of textual economy, value, evaluative structure and cultural politics of praxis elaborated above emerged, as I have noted before, out of my explorations of *Temple* and the other travel narratives examined in this book, even as they have helped to clarify an understanding of such narratives of travel. It is time to turn, then, from this preliminary consideration of terms which will be essential to the argument in this book to a more substantive discussion of *Temple*. Such a discussion may begin by taking up a question broached at the very outset of this chapter—the apparent postmodernity of *Temple*, argued for by such critics as Kenneth Von Gunden.

HISTORY AND THE POSTMODERN

Neither "postmodernism" nor "postmodernity" can be said to be an uncomplicated term in contemporary critical usage. As John Carlos

Rowe writes in "Postmodern Studies," "the ambiguity of the postmodern is a consequence of the different ways the term has been used to characterize a wide range of social, aesthetic, economic and political phenomena" (179). Relevant to our inquiry into the considerable mass-cultural significance of *Temple* noted at the beginning of this chapter are those usages that tend to see "the postmodern" as indicative of a broad historical condition. If many viewers are inclined to see *Temple* as a "postmodern" text, what can this immensely successful film tell us about the "postmodern" age? In the pages that follow, it is such broad usages of the postmodern—which make of it a label for a historical condition—that are referred to and interrogated.

In *The Postmodern Condition*, one of the most influential of such considerations of postmodernity, Jean-François Lyotard begins by suggesting that the "modern" is characterized by a belief in the efficacy of metadiscourses and grand narratives: "I will use the term *modern* to designate any science that legitimates itself with reference to a metadiscourse . . . making an explicit appeal to some grand narrative, such as the dialectics of Spirit, the hermeneutics of meaning, the emancipation of the rational or working subject, or the criterion of wealth" (xxiii, italics in text). For Lyotard, such a belief is opposed to the "postmodern," which signifies an age of narratival crisis: the difference between the modern and the postmodern is the result of a contemporary crisis arising out of technological transformations of knowledge systems. Lyotard argues that the modern period found a belief in truth viable. Such viability has been made impossible in the era of the postmodern. Now "efficiency" replaces "truth" as the criterion of legitimation. The ultimate effect of the critique of modernity made from Lyotard's position is to throw the baby of revolutionary struggle and guided social reform ("the emancipation of the rational or working subject") out with the bathwater of grand narratives in general. Thus, a deeply conservative political agenda underlies this influential perspective on postmodernity, a point that has already been sufficiently well made by such writers as Terry Eagleton.[15]

While it is indeed true that all contemporary commentary on the postmodern as a historical condition cannot be collapsed into Lyotard's argument, there is a curiously uncritical consensus around some of his assertions, chiefly that the postmodern condition is characterized by a suspicion of grand narratives and metadiscourses in general. Whether this suspicion is endorsed or not, it seems to have been taken for granted that a crisis of grand narratives does indeed exist. Thus, even Fredric Jameson, whose brilliant work has done so much to elucidate the relationship between culture and history (including, as will become clear below, in ways directly relevant to the argument in this book) and who remains committed to the kind of politics of liberation and of epistemology of totality that Lyotard derides, is only able to contest Lyotard by suggesting "not the disappearance of the great master-narratives, but their passage underground as it were, their continuing but now *unconscious* effectivity as a way of 'thinking about' and acting in our current situation" (xii, Foreword, *The Postmodern Condition*, italics in original). The choice then seems to be only between a total disappearance of grand narratives and the retreat of such narratives into a political unconscious.

History, Jameson argues, is no longer in fashion in such an age. Instead of history, we have historicism. In postmodern times, Jameson notes in *Postmodernism, or the Cultural Logic of Late Capitalism*, cultural producers have nowhere to turn to but the past now that the uniqueness of individual production that modernism believed in has become impossible (17–18). This turn to the past is not a turn to history (understood in a properly materialist way) but to a "'historicism,' namely, the random cannibalization of all the styles of the past, the play of random stylistic allusion" (18). Later, Jameson compares this historicism to "nostalgia," taking as his example the "nostalgia film" (19).[16] The import of Jameson's discussion of postmodernism's relationship to the past is to foreground the ahistoricity of postmodernism, to suggest that it is, despite its almost compulsive allusion to the past, particularly insensitive to history as a dialectical and conflictual process. "[A] genuine philosophy of history," Jameson has noted in an insightful passage from *The Political Unconscious* discussing the difference between historicism and history, "is capable of respecting the specificity and radical difference of the social and cultural past while disclosing the solidarity of its polemics and passions, its forms, structures, experiences, and struggles, with those of the present day" (18). This is what the historicism of postmodernism apparently does not do.

It may be argued that this description of the postmodern text's relationship to the past fits the case of *Temple*. J. Hoberman has noted how *Temple* draws explicitly on cinematic exotica, especially Hollywood adventure films, from the thirties and forties and from the Saturday afternoon serials and adventure television shows George Lucas enjoyed as a boy (63).[17] As James Monaco observes in *How to Read a*

Film, the dominant period of Hollywood cinema was precisely from the early thirties to the mid-forties, when its position in the world was virtually unchallenged. It was the period when a number of well-defined genres were elaborated in Hollywood (243–51). It is in this context that Hollywood adventure films such as *Tarzan and His Mate* (1934), *Gunga Din* (1939), and *King Solomon's Mines* (1950) emerged as a distinctive genre. *Temple* engages with this Hollywood genre of the thirties and forties, imitating these forebears with a self-conscious attention to detail. *Gunga Din* contributes many narrative elements to *Temple*; and Indiana Jones's suit and paraphernalia, for example, closely resemble those of the safari-going white hunters who appear in the other two movies cited above. Indiana Jones looks similar to Harry Holt and Martin Arlington, the white men in greedy pursuit of ivory in *Tarzan and His Mate*, even down to the whips they carry, although the whips of Holt and Arlington are always curled up with a modesty (or is it self-confidence?) of which Jones does not seem capable. The eagerness of Lucas and Spielberg to imitate these precursors leads also to the inclusion of such "stock" scenes in *Temple* as a performance of "native" dance and music and the depiction of white anxiety on confronting "native" food. In *Tarzan and His Mate*, an early scene shows at some length "natives" dancing and singing in the background as Holt and Arlington talk. In *King Solomon's Mines*, Elizabeth Curtis is disgusted at the food she is offered in an African village. Both these scenes have their counterparts in *Temple*.

Such imitation brings us back to the question with which we began: Is it irony that is on view in *Temple*? Is *Temple* a postmodern text in playful and ironic engagement with such modernist narratives as *Gunga Din*, *Tarzan and His Mate*, and *King Solomon's Mines*?[18] There is, indeed, a different mood in *Temple*, ascertainable in the self-consciousness with which these earlier scenes are reenacted in the movie. To make sense of this difference in mood—to consider whether *Temple* is simply historicist in its references or historical, whether *Temple* is postmodern or something else—requires us to explore the allusions to the past in *Temple* more closely.

"THUGGEE"

A reinvention of the cult of "thuggee," nearly a hundred years after its alleged "suppression" by William Henry Sleeman, is central to *Indiana*

Jones and the Temple of Doom. We cannot understand the allusions to the past in the film without first reviewing the chief features of this "thuggee," borrowed from *Gunga Din,* one of *Temple*'s cinematic forebears discussed in the previous section.

"Thuggee," defined by the British as ritual murder on behalf of Kali by certain robbers called "thugs," is part of a broad colonialist discursive agenda elaborated in the first few decades of the nineteenth century.[19] This discursive agenda aimed at sketching out the appropriate administrative shape of the growing British presence in India. By the third decade of the nineteenth century, as is well known, the British had completed the conquest of most of the territory that became a part of their Indian empire. It is in this context that the extensive discourse on "thuggee" was elaborated. The person who did the most for the elaboration of this discourse was William Henry Sleeman (1788–1856). Sleeman arrived in India as a cadet of the Bengal army in 1809 and went on to spend forty-seven years in various capacities. He is credited with having "suppressed" "thuggee" in the period between the mid-1820s and the early 1840s. Contemporary scholarship, however, is increasingly skeptical of "thuggee" as described by the British and questions whether such a phenomenon ever really existed. "Thuggee" is described by British writers of the early nineteenth century, such as Sleeman, Edward Thornton, and Philip Meadows Taylor, as an ancient and geographically extensive "fraternity" of evil devotees of the Hindu goddess Kali, who practiced robbery preceded by ritual murder. Sleeman gave decisive shape to this discourse on "thuggee" in his works, not only writing an account of it himself but also compiling and editing materials produced by other British officials.[20]

Indeed, Sleeman can be credited with not just "suppressing thuggee" but even "discovering" it. Richard Sherwood had produced an account of robbers who practiced ritual strangulation on behalf of Kali as early as 1816, but Sleeman must be credited with the "discovery" that "thuggee" was an evil, all-India, ancient and systematic conspiracy that constituted a fundamental challenge to good government. A careful examination of the discourse on "thuggee" suggests Stewart Gordon's claim that "thuggee" is virtually the invention of an ambitious colonial officer is not exaggerated (413). It seems probable, as Gordon persuasively argues, that Sleeman took the opportunity presented by the existence of certain robber gangs in certain districts of central India to "discover" a conspiracy of monstrous proportions.

It can be further argued that Sleeman's discursive invention of "thuggee" was taken up with such alacrity during the second and third decades of the nineteenth century because it meshed well with emerging ideas regarding the shape of the state in colonial India. What the "discovery" of "thuggee" permitted was the argument that this state should be a colonial law-and-order state, a state that saw its primary activity as that of restraining a criminal and violent population. Sleeman's writings on "thuggee," in which he repeatedly suggested that "thuggee" demonstrated the fundamental depravity as well as incompetence of Indians, helped perpetuate a view of India that made such a state possible.

The "thugs" that Sleeman wrote about, however, were most likely, as Gordon argues, ordinary robbers operating in gangs at a time of considerable social confusion in a particular area of central India. These gangs contained both Muslims and Hindus as well as individuals of all castes. British accounts reveal, despite themselves, the subalternity of the members of these gangs, not only as representatives of a colonized society but as criminals who are often described as following rules and conventions that prohibited attacks on women and certain members of the lower castes. What the British accounts of "thuggee" repeatedly do is appropriate the evidence for localized robber gangs expressing a horizontal solidarity with the subaltern segments of society to make instead an elaborate argument for a vast all-India criminal conspiracy whose *systemic* and *ancient* features are emphasized.

Such was the nineteenth-century "thuggee" that is reencountered a hundred years later by Indiana Jones in *Temple*. The chief "thug" in the movie is Mola Ram. The movie portrays Mola Ram, the evil priest of Kali, as working for the revivification of "thuggee" through his influence over Pankot palace. The maharajah of Pankot is a boy, Zalim Singh, under the spell of Mola Ram. When, at the end of the movie, he is touched by fire, apparently an antidote to Kali's power, he emerges from his mindless condition to aid Jones, Willie Scott and Short Round in their escape. The maharajah's "prime minister" is Chatter Lal (Roshan Seth, who also played Jawaharlal Nehru, nationalist leader and independent India's first prime minister, in Richard Attenborough's *Gandhi*). The westernized Chatter Lal (he speaks in English accents and has attended Oxford) is portrayed as a degenerate accomplice of Mola Ram.

Mola Ram is attempting to recover the sacred Shankara stones which were the source of the great power of the "thugs" before the

British destroyed their organization. Before the destruction of the "thugs" was accomplished, two of the five stones were hidden in the catacombs below Pankot palace which was, the all-knowing Indiana Jones notes at one point, the center of activity for "thuggee." With all five stones reassembled in his possession, Mola Ram will be able to reorganize the "thugs" and, he informs Jones, "The British in India will be slaughtered, then we'll overrun the Muslims, then the Hebrew God will fall, and then the Christian God will be cast down and forgotten. Soon Kali will rule the world."[21] It is for the furtherance of this grand plan that Mola Ram has stolen one of the five stones that was in the possession of the villagers and kidnapped the children of the village to dig in the catacombs below the palace for the two stones hidden there.

Whereas in nineteenth-century, British accounts of "thuggee" the "thugs" appeared as highly organized but mobile and secret gangs of highway robbers and murderers, in *Temple* they appear as subversives, still secret, but ensconced within the institutional structure of a palace and represented by such figures as Mola Ram and the prime minister Chatter Lal. The subaltern condition of "thugs," unacknowledged and uncomprehended in earlier accounts such as that of Sleeman, is here transformed into native elite status. This transformation may be regarded as the culminating point of that same logic that compelled the elaboration of "thuggee" during the nineteenth century as a system worthy of being combatted by an interventionist colonialism. The transformation hints at the West's contemporary perception of an elite "Third World" nationalism as its main opponent in the (neo)colonial contest.

Other differences between *Temple* and the texts which preceded it in the discourse on "thuggee" also provide clues to *Temple*'s historical conjuncture. The most obvious difference is the substitution of Indiana Jones for Sleeman (or for other British heroes who combat "thuggee," such as Savage in John Masters's "thuggee" novel *The Deceivers*).[22] The task of "suppressing thuggee" performed by Sleeman in the 1830s is performed a hundred years later by Indiana Jones. This substitution of Jones for Sleeman is matched by a substitution of the British Captain Blumburrt for "native Indian chiefs." Where Sleeman repeatedly cites corrupt or inefficient Indian rulers to explain the prevalence of "thuggee," *Temple* makes the British themselves responsible for the putative resurgence of "thuggee" a hundred years later.[23]

The British colonial authorities in India, signified by the figure of Captain Blumburrt, are portrayed as incompetent and ignorant of the "thuggee" cult right beneath their noses in Pankot palace. At one point during the conversation at dinner in Pankot palace (a thoroughly racist scene), Chatter Lal describes Blumburrt and the British as being obsessed with the long-gone "Revolt" of 1857.[24] Simultaneously, Blumburrt is shown to be oblivious of the sparring between Jones and Lal when the topic turns to "thuggee." Blumburrt's incompetence is especially reprehensible from a colonialist point of view since he is expressly present in Pankot for what is described as an "inspection tour." Reinforcing this pattern of incompetence, the army with Blumburrt at its head arrives at the end of the movie only after Jones has effectively done the job of saving the enslaved children and getting rid of Mola Ram. In *Temple*, it is Jones, and not Sleeman's British successor Blumburrt, who deserves the sobriquet "Thuggee" that had once been bestowed on Sleeman for his "eradication" of the alleged practice.[25]

Temple half-mocks the British, yet it repeats the colonialist attitude that is also at the heart of the earlier British accounts of "thuggee." In both *Temple* and these earlier accounts, Westerners intervene to save hapless "natives" who are being preyed on by other "natives." In both, there is an obsessive focus on Kali the evil goddess. As in other accounts of "thuggee," there is an anxiety in *Temple* regarding the possibility of Westerners being contaminated by Kali. The eating of the gur (the coarse brown sugar) of Kali that signified such contamination in earlier accounts (e.g., in the novel *The Deceivers* by John Masters) is transformed here into "the blood of Kali" that is forced into Jones's mouth to turn him into a zombie-like figure who is brought back only after being touched by fire. In details such as this, *Temple* continues a prior tradition of constructing "thuggee." At the same time, by portraying Indiana Jones, American hero, as the most effective intervening force in the proto–"Third World" scene of British India, *Temple* appropriates "India" on behalf of the United States.

Temple thus inhabits two sensibilities, colonialist and neocolonialist, at the same time—which is another way of explaining its geopolitics. A colonial situation is the setting for the narrative in *Temple*. Even as *Temple* validates this colonial setting, it implicitly displaces it by projecting to the neocolonial situation of the future, which is the moment of its production. Even as the British male colonizer shows himself weakening as a force of civilization, the American male neocolonizer steps gallantly into the breach to save the "natives" from themselves. Indiana Jones's figuration as the new and improved motive force of history is at the cost of Sleemans, Savages, and Blumburrts. Where the British William Savage at the end of the cinematic version of *The Deceivers*, produced around the same time as *Temple*, throws away the Christian cross he wears around his neck and thus reveals a moment of profound British self-doubt, the American Jones renews the battle against Kali on behalf of "the Christian god" Mola Ram would exile from India as a step toward world domination.[26]

POSTMODERNISM, OR THE CULTURAL LOGIC OF ADVANCED COLONIALISM

Critics such as Fredric Jameson who endorse a strong idea of post-modernity argue, as reviewed above, that a postmodern text neither respects the difference of the past nor practices a solidarity with it. *Temple*, in such a perspective, would seem to reveal its postmodernity in gestures of ahistorical—historicist—reappropriation. This is indeed how Kenneth Von Gunden reads *Temple* in his book. He borrows Jameson's notions of postmodernism to argue that Spielberg and the other four filmmakers he covers are "embodiments of their postmodern times" (1). How does this perspective fit with the "thuggee" antecedents alluded to in *Temple*? Does not the specific manner in which "thuggee" is alluded to, on the contrary, suggest that *Temple*, in its own way, does practice that "solidarity with the past" that Jameson insightfully suggests in *The Political Unconscious* is the hallmark of history, as opposed to historicism? *Temple* appears to be a text that both practices a solidarity with the past and does not respect its difference. The past it wants to practice a solidarity with is a colonialist one. Confronting the putative disappearance of certain reassuring metanarratives and genres, *Temple* aims at a properly nostalgic reconstruction of them.

Jameson's own critique of the postmodern misses this point because he focuses excessively on the pastiche mode of some "postmodern" texts. In naming the imitative mode of operation of these postmodern texts "pastiche" rather than "parody," Jameson does indeed recognize that postmodern texts do not set out to ironize modernist narratives in a self-conscious way (16–17). But this observation only leads him to define pastiche as "a neutral practice of . . . mimicry, without any of parody's ulterior motives, amputated of the satiric impulse, devoid of any laughter and of any conviction that alongside the abnormal tongue you have momentarily borrowed, some healthy linguistic normality still exists" (17), to advance ideas about the death of style in the postmodern age and to note that now "the past as 'referent' finds itself gradually bracketed, and then effaced altogether, leaving us with nothing but texts" (18). Even though Jameson is reluctant to be taken as suggesting that postmodern texts are therefore characterized by indifference or that their historicism is not "well-nigh libidinal," his argument does not lead him to recognize how a "postmodern" text like *Temple* also exhibits an active solidarity with the political sensibility of the modernist age that goes beyond historicism (18).

Temple does not simply approach the past as a series of spectacles, or texts, even if of well-nigh libidinal investment. On the contrary, *Temple* expresses a careful evaluation of both the past as a historical condition and the present as a real and putative continuation of that condition. Distinguishing her own attitude to postmodernism from that of Jameson, Linda Hutcheon writes in *A Poetics of Postmodernism,* another influential assessment, "What I want to call postmodernism is fundamentally contradictory, resolutely historical, and inescapably political" (4). Such a statement on postmodernism seems closer to that articulated here. However, Hutcheon's comments later in the book suggest there are differences. Expanding on the characteristics of postmodernism's resolutely historical nature, she writes, for example,

> [postmodernism's] aims are . . . : to make us look to the past from the acknowledged distance of the present, a distance which inevitably conditions our ability to know the past. The ironies produced by that distancing are what prevent the postmodern from being nostalgic: there is no desire to return to the past as a time of simpler or more worthy values. These ironies also prevent antiquarianism: there is no value to the past in and of itself. It is the conjunction of the present and the past that is intended to make us question—analyze, try to understand—both how we make and make sense of our culture. (230)

The argument in this book is that so-called postmodernism's solidarity with the past can indeed represent a desire to return to the past. During a *post*colonial period, which is also a *neo*colonial one, *Temple* explores quite *consciously* its historical link to a colonialist past.[27] The import of the argument, then, is that the term "postmodern" can be seen as expressing the cultural consequences of a tension between these two aspects of a global situation. The crisis of narratives that Lyotard identifies may not be the crisis of narratives as such but the crisis (not to be understood as the disappearance) of *Western* global narratives in the age of decolonization and after. Lyotard's lack of sensitivity to the postcolonial specificity of the narratives he is analyzing and his constant recourse to the discourse of developmentalism—"The object of this study is the condition of knowledge in the most highly developed societies," his book opens (xxiii)—allows him to analyze postmodernity in almost exclusively technological terms and disregard the possibility that postmodernism is the result of a Western ideological crisis forced by "Third World" acts of resistance.

Jameson's argument regarding postmodernism in this respect is more complex than that of Lyotard. For Jameson, "Postmodernism is what you have when the modernization process is complete and nature is gone for good. It is a more fully human world than the older one, but one in which 'culture' has become a veritable 'second nature'" (*Postmodernism* ix). Jameson pursues this theme consistently throughout his book, writing much later:

> One way of telling the story of the transition from the modern to the postmodern lies then in showing how at length modernization triumphs and wipes the old completely out: nature is abolished . . . ; even the surviving historical monuments, now all cleaned up, become glittering simulacra of the past, and not its survival. Now everything is new; but by the same token, the very category of the new then loses its meaning and becomes itself something of a modernist survival. (311)

Jameson repeats the gist of this argument in his more recent *The Geopolitical Aesthetic: Cinema and Space in the World System* (for example, 25–26 and 77). By this account, the past of nineteenth-century "thuggee," the past of thirties America (not discussed above but whose symbolism is surely as important in the movie) and the past of the Hollywood adventure films are mainly simulacra revived in a well-nigh libidinal, playful exercise of pastiche that is entirely comprehensible in the context of a fully modernized society unremittingly engaged in processes of commodification and of subjection to the power of the media. "In the postmodern, then," Jameson writes, "the past itself has disappeared (along with the well-known 'sense of the past' or historicity and collective memory)" (*Postmodernism* 309).

Captivated by the rhetoric of millenarianism hidden in the *post-modern*, commentary on it is continually compelled to portray the present historical conjuncture as one characterized by a radical, definitive novelty of epic dimensions. But a text such as *Temple*, produced within the so-called postmodern period, reiterates well-established strategies of colonialist discourse, suggesting a contravention of many of the central theses of the contemporary critical discourse on postmodernity. These borrowed discursive strategies work to contain potential disruption of what are modernist (colonialist) forms of expressing a global vision. If the terms "postmodernism" and "postmodernity" are to be methodologically useful at all, then, our declamations on them must be altogether more modest than they have generally been when the terms have been taken to indicate a broad historical condition. The critical discourse on such a "postmodernity" should be regarded as responding to both a Western crisis of cultural representation and a reactionary management of such a crisis (which is not to say, of course, that such a discourse is itself *necessarily* complicit with the reactionary management).

Crisis and management, neocolonialism and resistance—this is the context for postmodernism as, among other things, the cultural logic of advanced colonialism. In its specificities it does indicate a different cultural context. However, there remain numerous and powerful continuities with modernist narratives of cultural representation. As Kwame Anthony Appiah notes in *In My Father's House*, "What the postmodern reader seems to demand of its Africa is all too close to what modernism . . . demanded of it" (157). Making a similar point, R. Radhakrishnan writes, "If modernity functions as a structure-in-dominance that regulates and normativizes the relationship between the West and the Rest, postmodernism, despite the so-called break from modernity, sustains and prolongs this relationship" (307). And so it is appropriate to dissent when Perry Anderson writes in a recent survey of Jameson's comments on postmodernity that, "Jameson's theory of postmodernity has won a growing audience in countries once of the Third and Second World because it speaks of a cultural imaginary familiar to them, part of the web of their own experience" (75).

The continuities between the postmodern and the modern suggest a desire to redeploy strategies of containment on behalf of a West suffering from a crisis that is the result of a historical condition transformed by various movements of decolonization. In the final analysis, the deployment of such strategies is neither as unequivocally a result of narratival crisis as most commentators on postmodernism have suggested nor without moments of resistance to it. I began an earlier section by admitting the many different meanings associated with the various forms of the postmodern as a critical term. It is those usages that would interpret the postmodern in broadly historical terms—that would find a "postmodern" historical condition in the text of *Temple*—that are most contravened by the foregoing argument.

In *Temple*, the careful construction of the persona of Indiana Jones, sustained from movie to movie within the series, articulates so-called postmodern desire for the modern, represents a response to a Western ideological crisis resulting from decolonization and permits the subsequent neocolonial appropriation of India.[28] A discussion of the movie and its complicity with neocolonialism, then, cannot be complete without an analysis of the manner in which the identity of Indiana Jones is instrumental in the complicity.

INDIANA JONES IN INDIA

In his book, Kenneth Von Gunden offers the following comment on *Temple*:

> Spielberg and Lucas, resurrecting the old stereotypes along with the thrills and adventure, seem not to notice them or to believe that they're part and parcel of the package. And that is one of the problems postmodernist filmmakers face. In uncritically recycling the old films, they are often unaware of troubling political or sociological elements that may come with the old story lines; their inability to discriminate is directly related to the lions' [the five filmmakers'] ideological naivete. (126)

Later, he quotes Spielberg as apologetically declaring, "There is not an ounce of my personal feeling in *Temple of Doom*" (131). The issue however is not Spielberg's intention, but rather *Temple*'s textual economy. Even if Spielberg had been drawn to the narratival and stylistic elements of films such as *Gunga Din* out of naivete, *Temple*, as the students' comments noted at the beginning of the chapter indicate, performs a particular ideological function.

Perhaps a truer clue to *Temple* is to be found in an interview that Harrison Ford gave to the *New York Times*, where he noted: "This

[*Temple*] is a completely moral tale and in order to have a moral resolve, evil must be seen to inflict pain. The end of the movie is a proof of the viability of goodness" (quoted in Collins 21). It might be more appropriate, then, to call *Temple* a morality tale. Indeed, Patricia Zimmerman writing about *Temple*'s predecessor *Raiders of the Lost Ark* writes: "In the America of the early Eighties, *Raiders* and its publicity poses American muscle, machismo, technology and cunning as the solution to the complexities of the Third World, and refers back to a rewritten, bygone era that appears less complicated as an outline" (39). Arguably, the comment is even more relevant to *Temple* than to *Raiders*. In pointing to its moral-allegorical nature, Ford neglects to say that the movie associates white people with good and brown people with evil and/or passivity in a gesture typical of colonialist discourse. Indiana Jones—American, archaeologist, male—is the chief embodiment of good in the movie. He is also a traveler, and it is this aspect of his identity that brings the full force of his goodness to bear on India. By having Jones arrive in India during the 1930s so that he can be conveniently present to suppress an invented resurgence of "thuggee," *Temple* intervenes directly in the representation of colonial and neocolonial relationships. In doing so, it actively appropriates (as already discussed) a particular colonialist nineteenth-century conception of Indian criminality and the justification for a particular kind of British authority that accompanied it.

The identification of Indiana Jones as an archaeologist is telling here, for he is practicing a discipline closely allied to ethnography. He displays, indeed, a knowledge of Indian culture worthy of any Indophilic ethnographer. He shows an effortless mastery of languages, speaking Chinese (with what authenticity I cannot say) to the Chinese, some incoherent "Indian" language to the peasant villagers as well as to the evil priest of Kali (who clearly speaks Hindi), and deciphering an ancient manuscript that is in Sanskrit. He shows a complete command of Indian history both classical (he knows all about the ancient Shankara stones, which are the treasure at issue in this movie) and colonial (he discusses "the Revolt of 1857" with the British Captain Blumburtt and Pankot Prime Minister Chatter Lal, and shows knowledge of the "thuggee" cult). Perhaps most tellingly, he is completely comfortable among the "natives" without actually becoming one of them—a point repeatedly made in the movie by contrast with Willie Scott, who comes off as a racist—and shows an awareness of their customs that characterizes him more completely than anything else as an anthropologist.[29]

The very structure of address of the movie is significant, for it speaks not to the "natives" whom it presumes to represent but to a "First World" audience for whom Indiana Jones is a heroic, fictional (and comforting) ancestor from the thirties. *Temple* is a mass cultural expression of neocolonialist vision centered on the figure of an archaeologist/anthropologist, who provides the movie with its point of view. In this characteristic, *Temple* continues a long and powerful tradition within the history of Western cinema. "[T]he beginning of cinema," as Robert Stam and Louise Spence have pointed out, "coincided with the height of European imperialism" (6). Since the days when the novelty of cinema as a visual medium was exploited for the depiction of "exotic" non-Western cultures, Ella Shohat notes in this context, Western cinema has existed in an intimate relationship with colonialist forms of knowledge ("Imaging Terra Incognita" 41).[30]

The archaeologist/anthropologist identity of Jones in *Temple* is important to its structure as a neocolonialist travel narrative. This dimension of his identity provides the immediate impetus for Jones's leap across the geographical interval between the land of the traveler and the land of the "native." It allows him to begin that journey whose narrativization will discover goodness in his person and, by association, transfer the ideological value of this goodness back to the West whence he came. The narratival establishment of the geographic interval over which Jones the traveler journeys appears in *Temple* in the isolated location of Pankot palace and the village of peasants neighboring it. The remoteness of the palace and the village is emphasized both at the beginning (when Jones and his party arrive through a fall from the sky into a wilderness) and at the end (when references are made to the great distance at which Delhi lies). In this fashion, the narrative strives to invest the goodness that Jones comes to embody with even greater weight, for it is earned (discovered) only after a dangerous expedition into the wilderness. The goodness finally transferred to the West, whose representative Jones after all is, is also accordingly weighty.

A conjunction may be noted here between cinema and many travel narratives produced in a colonial context. The cross-cultural assumptions that underlie the portrayal of a Western traveler as the very embodiment of good also underlie the typical Hollywood film about non-Western societies. "Cinema . . . has operated," Ella Shohat observes, "as an epistemological mediator between the two spaces—

that of the Western spectator and that of the culture represented on the
screen—linking two distinct loci and figurally separate temporalities in
one moment of exposure" ("Imaging Terra Incognita" 42). Is not the
traveler also a mediator? *Temple* exploits this homology between a
filmic code of epistemological mediation and a narrative code of travel
by adopting for the most part the scopic perspective of Indiana Jones in
its point of view editing. It is his "disciplinary gaze of empire" (to echo
one part of the full title of Shohat's essay) that surveys the landscape of
colonial India and makes sense of it for an audience whose representative figure he is meant to be.

One prominent way in which *Temple* attempts to compel an identification between spectators and Indiana Jones is through the relationship between Jones and the Chinese boy, Short Round. The film
continually emphasizes Jones's status as a mentor in this relationship.
Short Round is portrayed as hero-worshiping Jones and following him
around with, to put the matter in what may be regarded as the ideological idiom of the movie itself, "a touching loyalty." As Short Round tells
Jones after a near-fatal mishap in a secret tunnel below Pankot palace:
"I step where you step." The scene becomes a summary representation
of the relationship between them. The semantics of this relationship are
formally underscored by such manipulations of mise en scène as the
inclusion of Short Round's imitative actions in the background as Jones
fights with these most recent versions of "thugs" in the final scenes of
the movie.[31] In general, it is the non-Indian characters—Jones, Short
Round, Willie Scott—who are allowed the privilege of being individualized through close-up shots (unless it is to capture the despair or the
"evil" on a particular "native" face, such as Mola Ram's). Short
Round's membership in this group should be understood in the context
of his status as a mentee and a child. Of the three in the group, however,
Jones benefits from the privilege of being individualized more than any
other character, thus positioning the spectator in a colonialist relationship to the India that is represented on the screen. Cinematic mediation
parallels narratival mediation. The camera reinforces the gaze of the
colonialist traveler.[32] In *Temple*, the metropolis (the US) is elaborately
produced as the location of a copious goodness: as the site of a concentrated moral, cultural, and historical value continually replenished by
travelers like Jones. And in recognizing the production of this value
within *Temple* we are led, of course, to contemplate its status as a textual economy.

The Textual Economy of *Temple*

As already seen, the idea of a "textual economy" indicates a dynamic system that distributes "value" in a particular way among the different elements that go to make up the system. Other ways to put this, we have already seen, would be to say that a textual economy concentrates value at particular sites within the text, or that a textual economy transfers value in a particular direction within the text. We have seen—for example, in the discussion of the postcard above—how this aspect of a textual economy may be described as an ensemble of evaluative structures. But a textual *economy* is more than simply an ensemble of evaluative structures. The term suggests the production of "value," rather than simply a distribution of it. The production of this value is not some intrinsic feature of the text but arises out of the (human) praxis that finds expression in the text and that the text itself, taking up its assigned position in a chain of events, makes possible.

While some hypotheses on the economy of the text have been ventured above, it should be noted that a (general) textual economy is an abstraction from concrete examples. The understanding of a textual economy advanced here arises not simply out of reading Marx on capitalism but out of the analysis of *Temple* (and, indeed, of the other travel narratives in subsequent chapters). The textual economy of *Temple* may not map *exactly* on the political economy of capitalism and no purpose is served in trying to force it to do so. The commodity's journey—described above—from the realm of (potential) use-value through the realm of exchange to the realm of use-value, transfers value to the capitalist and does not correspond in this respect to Indiana Jones's journey which, as we have seen, transfers value ultimately to the United States. However, what both examples (capitalism and *Temple*) amply reveal is that value is produced and then appropriated, to be concentrated at a specific site, by the displacement of an "object" through a system. The trafficking in and appropriation of a "surplus" value whether by a capitalist or by Jones/United States/metropolis requires such a displacement. The aspect of the textual economy brought into view here in this manner—the appropriation and concentration of value at a particular site within the text—is what has been described as taking place within a structure of evaluation or, in brief, an "evaluative structure." The discussion above of the ways in which value is distributed and appropriated in *Temple* suggests that more than one evaluative structure is a part of the textual economy of *Temple*. Two—that of the travel narrative and of the cinematic text—have been identified. A third—Spivak's comments cited early in the chapter have already alerted us to its existence—is the evaluative structure of patriarchy.

In "Gender and Culture of Empire: Toward a Feminist Ethnography of the Cinema," Ella Shohat notes,

> The intersection of colonial and gender discourse involves a shifting, contradictory subject positioning, whereby Western woman can simultaneously constitute 'center' and 'periphery,' identity and alterity. A Western woman, in these [cinematic] narratives, exists in a relation of subordination to Western man and in a relation of domination to 'non-Western' men and women. (63)

Certainly, the operation of the gender code of patriarchy is obscured in certain places within a cinematic narrative such as *Temple*. Ambiguity in the expression of a patriarchal gender code allows Willie Scott to be sometimes portrayed as an autonomous agent invested with the camera's privileged perspective, even as she is more often subjected to the disciplinary authority of Indiana Jones because of her aberrant behavior. She challenges Jones, complains often about him and shows her disgust, despite Jones's disapproval, at the meagre food that the villagers offer her. Of course, such a portrayal of Scott as apparently willful and independent only allows Jones to be alternatively depicted as a sensitive individual at home in this "premodern" culture. And so, in the scene in which Scott expresses her disgust for the food she is offered, Jones is able to insist in the soft voice of the benevolent but stern patriarch that she eat because "this is more than these people eat in a week."

At the same time, Willie Scott is portrayed in *Temple* as a weak woman who must be protected by Jones. Scott is compelled by accident to accompany Jones during his flight from Shanghai and is not with him by choice. In the early part of the movie, she repeatedly indicates her distaste for Jones. However, by the middle of the movie, after he has had occasion to save her from danger a number of times, she is telling the temporarily unforthcoming Jones, "I could have been your greatest adventure," revealing the overlap in Western discourse between ethnic and gender codes, between alterity as ethnicity and alterity as gender. The homology between the gender code of patriarchy and the generic code of the neocolonialist travel narrative is illustrated in this detail. Willie Scott's portrayal as morally inferior and (finally) passive in relationship to Indiana Jones parallels the depiction of Indians as morally inferior and/or passive in the movie, even as she herself gives expression to the idea that the "natives" are inferior. Passive and racist, incompetent and insensitive, Willie Scott's "contradictory subject positioning" in *Temple* allows the double articulation of Indiana Jones as liberal and benevolent colonizer and strong and protective male.

The homology between "woman" and "colonized" in their relationship to Jones is revealingly represented in the final scene of the movie when Jones, having completed his task of releasing the enslaved children and returning the sacred stone to the villagers, snakes out his trusty whip to pull Willie Scott into his arms. This is the same whip that has been so useful to Jones in his battle with evil "natives" in the previous scenes of the movie. As Indy Jones and Willie Scott kiss surrounded by the festive villagers, we are led to understand the overdetermined nature of the power that is made celluloid flesh in the figure of Harrison Ford as Indiana Jones. The whip is also a gendered extension of the master. The phallus is also the weapon through which the benevolent colonizer exercises his discipline.

At the beginning of the movie, both gendered space and colonized space are in disorder, threatening to exceed the disciplinary rule of the master. Upstart natives are threatening to overthrow the master's rule by a revival of a vicious cult. Similarly, Willie Scott, in her willful (if childish) refusal to place herself in the care of the man, is threatening Indiana Jones the patriarch. At the end of the movie, both aberrations have been removed because of the comprehensiveness of Jones's male and colonial power. Such is the complex summation of identifications and subject positions beneath both the apparent innocuousness of the name "Indiana Jones" and of the familiarity (bred of the star system) of the image of Harrison Ford on the screen.

At the same time that the evaluative structure of the travel narrative transfers value back to the West through the vehicle of the Western Indiana Jones, then, a patriarchal evaluative structure transfers value to masculinity and withholds it from femininity. Through numerous scenes in which Jones and Scott are compared to each other, the movie establishes the superior ability as well as understanding of Jones unequivocally and shows Scott's dependence on him. When Jones snakes out his trusty whip to coil it around a Willie Scott still pretending to be reluctant and draws her to himself, the viewer is presented with a dramatic visual representation of the functioning of this patriarchal evaluative structure. What is encoded in this scene, we might say, is the transference of a certain "value" to masculinity, as represented by Jones, through the mediation of the phallus, as represented by the whip.

Both these evaluative structures—of the neocolonialist travel narrative and of patriarchy—find their expression, as already seen, beside a filmic evaluative structure governed by the formal conventions of the Hollywood adventure movie. Through the instrument of a camera that reproduces a neocolonialist and patriarchal aesthetic, the movie locates its putative audience (male and Western) in a voyeuristic relationship to both the female and the neocolonial objects of its gaze.[33] The filmic evaluative structure established by the camera produces and distributes value in a selective fashion between the audience and the objects presented for its gaze. The filmic syntax and point of view continually invite the audience to appropriate to itself a status that is shown to be "valuable" in contrast to some of the objects of its gaze presented on the screen, and to identify itself with other of such objects (most important, Jones himself).

There are, then, at least three different evaluative structures within the textual economy of *Indiana Jones and the Temple of Doom*. In all three of these mutually reinforcing structures, value is transferred in a particular direction through the mediation of the traveler, the whip-phallus and the camera respectively. The "meaning" of the text, as it emerges in the text, is a product of the interplay between these (and perhaps other) evaluative structures. To describe *Temple* as a textual economy is to recognize in it an ensemble of evaluative structures. *Temple* (and indeed any textual economy, as we have seen), we might say, contains a collection of "evaluative structures." *Temple*, like any other text, we might say, is an ensemble of structural elements that distribute value within the text.

Thus, an attention to "economy" and "value" leads us to a recognition of the complexity of the textual processes in *Temple*. Steven Spielberg's mass cultural extravaganza is a patriarchal cinematic travel narrative that sets out to recolonize the "Third World." Through the narration of the journey performed by Jones, cultural value is continually assimilated to the person of Jones and withheld from the India to which he journeys. Finally, as Jones travels back to the metropolis (the United States), whence he came and whose representative he is, he delivers this value to the metropolis itself.

The textual economic analysis of *Temple* has led us, then, to discern the colonialist and patriarchal values encoded within it. It has led us to refigure its so-called postmodernity as postcolonial crisis and neocolonial management in the West. It leads us now to recognize that crisis and management, colonialism and patriarchy, are all terms eminently expressive of praxis. We are compelled to note by our attention to the economy of the text how *Temple* is a particular expression of human praxis and recognize that the consideration of the postmodernity of *Temple* above is concerned both with the praxis expressed there and with the adequacy of certain analyses in capturing such praxis. We begin to see how *Temple* is not separate from history which is, in Georg Lukacs's words, "on the one hand, the product (albeit the unconscious one) of man's [sic] own activity, on the other hand, it is the succession of those processes in which the forms taken by this activity and the relations of man to himself (to nature, to other men) are overthrown" ("Reification and the Consciousness of the Proletariat" 185–86).

Temple, which represents one of the forms taken by human history-making activity, then, was challenged, if not overthrown, soon after its phenomenally successful release. In 1986, the Cinema Certification Board of India, a regulatory body appointed by the federal government and entrusted with the responsibility of deciding which films may be appropriate for public consumption, banned the film. Postmodern irony, if indeed present in *Temple*, clearly escaped the notice of the members of the Certification Board. Instead, they evaluated the praxis given form in *Temple* as neocolonial and responded with their own (nationalist) praxis of censorship. The reason given for the ban was that the film "projected Indians in an unfavorable light."[34] It is worth asking whether (nationalist) censorship was an adequate response to the neocolonialist praxis given form in *Temple*. But a textual economics takes us inexorably from narrow questions regarding the evaluative structures of the text and reminds us of these other issues.

Similarly, textual economics reminds us that the impetus for the discussion of *Temple* here also lies in a scene, albeit small, of human praxis. In a classroom devoted to very different questions and texts, a series of exchanges amongst teacher and students quickly, unexpectedly, erupts into a discussion of *Temple*. The scene attests to the power of the praxis given form in *Temple*. Textual economics asks us to reflect on the ideological work done in the text. It also asks us to reflect on the pedagogical practice within which the text of *Temple* is engaged in the classroom. In retrospect, the classroom scene is a reminder that *Temple* has never been, is not now and will never be separate from the fraught world of human praxis.

PROLOGUE TO AN ARGUMENT

Temple begs the question—is it a postmodern text? In work such as Kenneth Von Gunden's as well as in responses to presentations of the material that appears in this chapter—at conferences, in reading groups, at more informal gatherings—this question has been posed in different forms. At the same time, it has been well-recognized that *Temple* is a deeply problematic text in its neocolonialist depiction of Indians. The preceding sections of the chapter have explored the significance of this conjunction of so-called postmodernity and neocolonialism. In the process, they have raised questions of critical methodology and ventured answers in the form of a "textual economics." Even as this chapter has been led to reevaluate influential formulations of the postmodern, it has observed the limitations of a "postmodern" cultural politics of representation and been led to explore alternatives. A cultural politics of praxis has been advanced in contradistinction to the ubiquitous cultural politics of representation. Thus, the critique of the idea of postmodernity as well as a cultural politics broadly commensurate with such an idea proceed hand in hand. The notion of a textual economics—already set out in detail here—is refined through further instances in subsequent chapters. The questions regarding neocolonialism and postmodernity broached here are explored by reference to colonial and modern antecedents in Part II.

The argument of the book is enabled by an exploration of the genre of the travel narrative produced in the colonial and post-/neo-colonial contexts. *Temple* is one such narrative. It has led to the others examined in the remaining chapters, chosen for the ways in which they allow the argument to advance. Narratives of travel written in such contexts, as many scholars have argued, mediate between representations of the colonizer and the colonized through different strategies. The generic colonialist narrative of travel effectively encodes the colonial relationship as a confrontation between the colonizer (as traveler), on the one hand, and the colonized (as "native"), on the other. However, the protocols of such a narrative are also transformed and subverted in various alternate deployments. One of the objectives of the book is to scrutinize the strategies of such deployments and redeployments.

And so the next chapter takes up in detail the structure of the travel narrative produced in a colonial context. The historical period under review in this book is that from the high colonialism of the late nineteenth century to the neocolonialism of the contemporary moment. I turn to Jonathan Swift's *Gulliver's Travels*, then, primarily for its self-reflexive comment on the colonialist travel narrative, for its instructive mapping of the genre that enables the argument in this book. Nevertheless, the discussion in the next chapter also permits us to raise certain questions regarding modernity's relationship to colonialism. This and the succeeding chapter, then, appear as prologue to the argument of the book.

CHAPTER TWO

TRAVEL NARRATIVES AND
GULLIVER'S TRAVELS

Centuries of criticism on an Irish text, Jonathan Swift's *Gulliver's Travels* (1726; henceforth *GT*, when abbreviated), considered it a work of eighteenth-century "British literature." Only in the last two and a half decades is sustained attention being paid to the theme, so much a part of the text, of colonialism. An examination of *Twentieth Century Interpretations of Gulliver's Travels*, edited by Frank Brady and published in 1968, shows where the emphasis of criticism has lain until the seventies. The two great themes of the volume are political satire, understood in a narrowly English context, and the metaphysics of human nature. A review of Rodino's bibliography of Swift studies from 1965–1980 reveals a similar emphasis; and Milton Voigt's survey of nineteenth-century views of Swift in *Swift and the Twentieth Century* suggests how that great age of European imperialism systematically ignored the issue of colonialism in *GT*. Of course, Swift's activities on behalf of colonized Ireland have long been acknowledged, but a more ambitious argument can be made on behalf of Swift's anticolonialism. A number of works have begun to do this only in the last two and a half decades.[1]

These moments in centuries-long criticism are worth reviewing because it is possible to argue that the recent transformations in the reception of *GT* are illustrative of a postcolonial politics of culture, of a change in the conditions of reading from "colonial" to "postcolonial." As David Lloyd has noted in *Anomalous States*, "canonization is itself a process of appropriation, abstracting works from their dialogical relation to traditions which the canon cannot accommodate" (8). It is as a consequence of dramatic moments of decolonization in "distant lands" such as Algeria, Ghana, and India (to name only three), as well as Ireland, that the assimilation of a pivotal text into the canon of British literature is being challenged and rewritten within the history of the colonized. In the process, Irish Studies is also being decolonized. Scholars whose readings are mediated by the postcolonial context of their work have begun to reveal what was always present within the textual economy of GT—a pungent critique of the ideology of European colonization.[2]

Thus, the critical practice of reading responds to the currents of history. A changed practical context leads to the recognition that GT is the formal expression of an anticolonial praxis, to the expectation that it will contain commensurate evaluative structures. The relevance of the two themes that the scholars of *Twentieth Century Interpretations* find within GT is not to be denied. The textual economy of GT is a complex ensemble of evaluative structures. However, attention has generally been deflected from its anticolonial values. Now, it is possible to insist that eighteenth-century England itself may not be spoken of, without significant political oversights, outside the history of the English global expansion then beginning to unfold. Critical practice, then, must necessarily attempt to link the practical context provided by this expansion to the textual fabric of GT.

The textual fabric of GT (its anticolonial evaluative structures) is woven out of Swift's appropriation, transformation, and critique of the generic conventions of the colonialist travel narrative. GT provides a critical analysis of the colonialist travel narrative, understood as a narrative of travel, fictional or nonfictional, written by a colonialist traveler to non-European countries (whether these countries were currently under occupation or not) during the period of modern colonialism. Standing at the very beginning of the modern colonialism whose later manifestations are a subject of this book, GT offers an instructive "theoretical" mapping of the (neo)colonialist travel narrative as a genre.[3] Hence, the generic focus of the book is explored in detail in this chapter through recourse to GT, as well as the work of such contemporary scholars as Michel de Certeau and Mary Louise Pratt.

Ethnographic Vision and Travel Writing

"Ethno-graphy" (as Michel de Certeau writes it) may be seen as an allegory for the epistemological correlates of the colonial encounter between cultures.[4] The *graphing* of *ethnos* is the "writing" up of "people," a deceptively innocent label for an ambitious project of codifying the folkways of non-European cultures as well as those of hegemonized European and North American subcultures.[5] The substitution here of "non-European" and "subculture" for "people" recognizes the long-unacknowledged colonialist bias within ethnography that goes back all the way to its origins as a subdisciplinary formation of the Western academy. Again, only in the last two and a half decades has anthropology, ethnography's master discipline, begun in a self-critical moment to explore seriously the underlying assumptions of its practice. Just as much as in the recent critical reception of *GT*, the mediating pressure of the postcolonial context is to be noted here; for what is an unreconstructed anthropologist to do if the erstwhile objects of his analysis will no longer offer themselves up with the disciplined obedience of colonial subjects? In the early seventies, toward the end of a period of decolonization across the world, Dell Hymes in his introduction to an important volume of essays entitled *Reinventing Anthropology* was responding to this question when he noted, "People everywhere today, especially (and rightly) third world peoples, increasingly resist being subjects of inquiry, especially for purposes not their own . . ." (5). In more recent years, James Clifford's work has also repeatedly explored the implications of this question. Surveying the condition of ethnography in the postcolonial era, he has referred to the "pervasive postcolonial crisis of ethnographic authority" (*Predicament of Culture* 8). Elaborating on this later, Clifford adds, "The present predicament [of ethnography] is linked to the breakup and redistribution of colonial power in the decades after 1950" (22).[6] Expressing this predicament, Johannes Fabian in his critical examination of anthropology entitled *Time and the Other* declared:

> Formulated as a question, the topic of these essays was: How has anthropology been defining or constructing its object—the Other? Search for an answer has been guided by a thesis: Anthropology emerged and established itself as an allochronic discourse; it is a science of other men in another Time. It is a discourse whose referent has been removed from the present of the speaking/writing subject. This "petrified relation" is a scandal. (143)

"Anthropo-logy" or the science of the human is to be historicized, as Trinh T. Minh-ha does, by christening it "A Western Science of Man" (55). "Anthropology as a human science," she notes, "is nowadays the foundation of every single discourse pronounced above the native's head. . . . What has been written never addresses the Yellow, the Black, or the Red. The anthropologist's pen smudges are by-products of a science of man in which the non-civilized man—the very element that permitted its founding—is excluded" (57–58). Minh-ha's point is that anthropology in its origins has not been a conversation among cultures, as anthropology often likes to characterize itself, but a conversation among Western codifiers of non-Western cultures. Thus, in Claude Lévi-Strauss's *Triste Tropiques*, for example, the anthropologist journeys to Brazil not to "converse" with the Caduveo or the Tupi Indians (despite all his sympathy for them) but to "converse" with Rousseau about the "noble savage." How can anthropologists converse with someone who is not able to talk back except as an interrogatee? The postulation of this particular question has dramatized for anthropology its "present predicament" of authority. Anthropology is not alone in its postcolonial predicament. Other academic disciplines (such as "literary criticism") also have been compelled to reevaluate the premises of their practice. The writing of this book, then, can be said to have been undertaken in the midst of a "predicament" of literary criticism, forcefully articulated by Gayatri Chakravorty Spivak in *In Other Worlds* and *A Critique of Postcolonial Reason* and by Edward Said in *Orientalism* and *Culture and Imperialism*.

Traditional ethnography, a subdiscipline of anthropology, is a discursive practice that foregrounds the epistemological concerns of colonial contact between cultures through the unequal relationship that is repeatedly made evident within it. Its practitioners textualize and categorize the subject positions that they confront through what may be called the *ethnographic vision* of their discipline without their own subject positions being reciprocally textualized and categorized. There is a circular relationship between colonialism and such ethnographic vision, making it impossible to say whether the expansion of European colonial interests many centuries ago brought a peculiar worldview (ethnographic vision) into existence or the ethnographic vision—as a specific form of relating to and constructing the racially or ethnically alien—made colonialism possible. It is, however, clear that ethnographic vision and colonialism bear a close relationship to each other.

Mary Louise Pratt has summarized some of the traits of this specific form of relating to the alien that is ethnographic vision as:

a very familiar, widespread, and stable form of "othering." The people to be othered are homogenized into a collective "they," which is distilled even further into an iconic "he" (the standardized adult male specimen). This abstracted "he"/"they" is the subject of verbs in a timeless present tense, which characterizes anything "he" is or does not as a particular historical event but as an instance of a pre-given custom or trait. (In contexts of conquest, descriptions are likely to focus on the Other's amenability to domination and potential as a labor pool.) Through this discourse, encounters with an Other can be textualized or processed as enumerations of such traits. ("Scratches on the Face of the Country" 120)

Pratt points in this fashion to ethnography's postulation of what can be called "the objectifiability of the Other"—the reification of an Other perceived through the normative lenses of "race" and "cultural difference."[7] It is more as a signifier for this problematic postulation, rather than as a specific disciplinary practice, that the term *ethnographic vision* will be understood and used throughout this book, preferred to (at the same time that it draws on) such an awkward term as *othering* for the greater suggestion it carries of an ideology, a complex world*view*. The elaboration of such an ethnicized and racialized ideology of alterity in a colonial context is neither restricted narrowly to the disciplinary boundaries of ethnography nor uncriticized within those boundaries.

The ideological possibility of constructing the alien as an object to be studied is at the heart of the (neo)colonialist travel narrative as a genre. However, many other travel narratives written in colonial and post-/neocolonial contexts do challenge or problematize this ideology in practice. Hence, one of the aims of this book is to explore the many ways in which the generic traits of the (neo)colonialist travel narrative are reiterated as well as transformed in the colonial and the postcolonial periods in "real" travel narratives (narratives by writers who were actually travelers and produced narratives of their travels, for example Zora Neale Hurston or Richard Wright or V. S. Naipaul) as well as fictional travel narratives (narratives by writers or filmmakers who, whether they actually traveled or not, invented travel accounts, e.g. Jonathan Swift or Joseph Conrad or George Lucas/Steven Spielberg). The ethnographic vision that is at the heart of the (neo)colonialist travel narrative should not surprise us since to travel, especially in a colonial or post-/neocolonial context, is most often to find oneself among Others who are already codified as different. Thus, (neo)colonial travelers often find themselves compelled to systematize and

explain the racial and cultural difference that confronts them at every turn
and often reify the objects of their gaze as ethnographic curiosities, becoming thereby (neo)colonialist travelers. Such a succumbing to ethnographic
vision is most common when the bias of an unequal relationship is in favor
of the traveler, the case in most situations of colonial encounter where the
traveler is a member of a "civilizing race."

Pratt has examined a number of travel narratives produced by such
travelers in her book *Imperial Eyes* and her two essays "Fieldwork in
Common Places" and "Scratches on the Face of the Country; or, What
Mr. Barrow Saw in the Land of the Bushmen." "Scratches on the Face of
the Country" and, especially, *Imperial Eyes* are extended examinations of
such travel writing.[8] Pratt categorizes the travel writing she examines
under two headings—narratives written by explorer writers engaged in
information gathering and narratives written by travelers who dramatized
their own subjective experiences. If the first kind of narrative aspires to
scientific status, the second is sentimentalist in tenor ("Scratches" 131). In
many narratives, perhaps most, these two "modes" of travel writing co-
exist. But both modes are marked by an unacknowledged complicity with
the project of colonialism in the manner in which they attempt to render
their own interventionist presence in the alien scene passive, and thus
reveal themselves to be colonia*list* travel writing. In *Imperial Eyes*, Pratt
expands on this theme further. "The two [scientific and sentimental modes
of writing] could not be more different," she writes,

> because they are so much defined in terms of each other; they are
> complementary and in their complementarity they stake out the
> parameters of emergent bourgeois hegemony. On the imperial fron-
> tier, the sentimental subject shares certain crucial characteristics
> with his scientific counterpart: Europeanness, maleness, and middle
> classness, of course, but also innocence and passivity. (78)

Imperial Eyes is in many ways an exemplary book, both for its wealth of
detail and its sensitivity to the historical and cultural record that forms
the context to the narratives that are examined in it. But the two categories of narratives that Pratt sets out by no means exhaust the possibilities of the colonialist travel narrative. Nor is the colonialist traveler's
complicity with colonialism always mystified in the travel narrative. At
some points in her work, Pratt thinks of the travel narrative in ways that
admit such qualifications:

> What I hope to underscore in these writings [the travel accounts] is
> not their tendency towards single, fixed subject positions or single,
> fixed systems of difference. Rather, I wish to emphasize the multi-
> plicity of ways of codifying the (seemingly) given sets of differences
> that they posit. European penetration and appropriation is seman-
> ticized in numerous ways that can be quite distinct, even mutually
> contradictory. ("Scratches" 122)

And later in the same essay she suggests that "travel writing is one of the
most polyphonous of genres. . . . [The readers of the travel narratives]
were presented with multiple sets of differences, multiple fixed subject
positions, multiple ways of legitimizing and familiarizing the process of
European expansion" ("Scratches" 141). Ethnographic vision as well as
challenges to such vision are complex discursive operations. The
approach in this book is not to specify one or two (or more) modes of
travel writing in colonial and post-/neocolonial periods based on the
manner in which an ethnographic vision is put forward. Rather than
exemplifying a discourse analysis that attempts an exhaustive catalog of
discursive conventions, the argument here finds a more productive terrain in pursuing a variety of evaluative structures to their appropriate
practical contexts. The attention is on the textual economy of the travel
narrative written in a (neo)colonial context.

Clues to the evaluative structures of colonialist travel narratives
are to be found in two essays by Michel de Certeau. In "Montaigne's 'Of
Cannibals': The Savage 'I'" and "Ethno-graphy—Speech, or the Space
of the Other: Jean de Léry," Michel de Certeau explores the colonialist
travel narrative in a manner that uncovers its formal structure. The first
work is a close reading of Montaigne's well-known essay "Of Cannibals." De Certeau's piece makes an exegesis of Montaigne the occasion
for some comments on the structure of the colonialist travel narrative.
The second work is a close reading of Jean de Léry's account of his voyage to Brazil in 1578; in this essay de Certeau shows the profound association that Léry's text makes between the speech of the "savage" and
the culture of the "savage." In exploring this theme, de Certeau also
demonstrates how the structure of the travel account operates as "a
hermeneutics of the other" (218). De Certeau's comments sketch in a
preliminary manner a structure of the "typical" colonialist travel narrative whose evaluative significance and practical context can then be further explored in a reading of *GT*.

In "Ethno-graphy," de Certeau shows how the mechanism of the travel narrative works to return Jean de Léry to his selfhood, from which he has been temporarily alienated. "To be sure," de Certeau writes,

> the literary *operation* that brings back to the producer the results of signs that were sent far away has a condition of possibility in a *structural* difference between an area "over here" and another "over there." The narrative plays on the relation between the structure which establishes the separation and the operation which overcomes it, creating effects of meaning in this fashion. The break is what is taken for granted everywhere by the text, itself a labor of suturing. (218, italics in original)

"The break" is the separation between the "over here" and the "over there" which allows the operation of a *travel* narrative, an account of spatial displacement that also allows the text to enact what de Certeau calls "The Work of Returning" (219). "[T]he narrative," de Certeau writes, "as a whole belabors the division that is located everywhere in order to show that the *other returns to the same*" (219, italics in original). The purpose of this work in Jean de Léry's text, as de Certeau presents it, is to reconstitute for Jean de Léry his own "humanity."

De Certeau wants to illustrate here how a certain process of codification of the culture of the Other is carried out so as to subsume (finally) the difference of the "savage" under the sign of the universal sameness of "man." "Finally, nature is what is other," de Certeau writes, "while man stays the same" (220). Elsewhere, de Certeau calls this Jean de Léry's "return to himself through the mediation of the other" (213). At issue here is a universal humanity and the interpretation of the "savage" as belonging to that humanity so that Jean de Léry can return to the selfhood with which he set out from Geneva and which he finds challenged by the existence of these Others. Jean de Léry's "Self-hood" is reconstituted by the assimilation of the Other under its (Self's) own signs. Under the pressure of the colonial context, such assimilation ventures beyond the legitimate claims of humanism and foregoes a careful and critical working through of it.

Instead, de Certeau shows, the colonialist travel narrative reconstitutes and consolidates a transcendent European subjectivity. At the same time, this subjectivity is invested with historical agency (this will become clearer below) in a manner which is, perhaps, finally contradictory. Such contradiction should not surprise us. Colonialist ideology, as

Albert Memmi has noted, is notoriously inconsistent. "[I]t is useless," he writes, "to seek this consistency [in trying to understand the colonial relationship and colonialist ideology] anywhere except in the colonizer himself. . . . In the last analysis, these traits are all advantageous to the colonizer, even those which at first sight seem damaging to him" (83). De Certeau's essay examines the role of the travel narrative in making an apparently contradictory "hermeneutics of the other" possible through a certain idea of travel. The idea of travel foregrounded by de Certeau is one already encountered in the neocolonialist travel narrative *Indiana Jones and the Temple of Doom*. Its trajectory is circular. There is a journey out and a return to a point of origin.[9]

In his other essay "Montaigne's 'Of Cannibals,'" de Certeau sets out in greater detail the circularity of the colonialist travel narrative (69). He notes that the travel account has three stages: First is "the outbound journey," a journey of search for the strange, which is presumed to be so because of "the place assigned it in the beginning by the discourse of culture" (69). This assumption of difference "results in a rhetoric of distance in travel accounts," which is "illustrated by a series of surprises and intervals (monsters, storms, lapses of time, etc.) which at the same time substantiate the alterity of the savage, and empower the text to speak from elsewhere and command belief" (69). De Certeau's phrase "rhetoric of distance" conveys well what in the essay "Ethno-graphy" he has called "the break." It captures the manner in which the postulate of geographical or spatial discontinuity both produces the difference of the "savage" and empowers the traveler who has traversed the geographical or spatial discontinuity to speak with authority—"the discourse that sets off in search of the other with the impossible task of saying the truth returns from afar with the authority to speak in the name of the other and command belief" (69). "Next," de Certeau writes, "comes a depiction of savage society, as seen by a 'true witness.' . . . [T]his 'ethnological' depiction lies at the center, between accounts of the outward journey and of the return. An ahistorical image . . . is framed by two histories (the departure and the return) that have the status of meta-discourses, since the narration speaks of itself in them" (69).

The "ethnological depiction" that de Certeau notes lies at the heart of the travel narrative is a reminder of what Pratt has called the abstracted "'he'/'they' [which] is the subject of verbs in a timeless present" in ethnographical depictions ("Scratches on the Face of the Country" 120). This abstraction of "savage" (non-European) society from history is tantamount to the denial of equivalent status to such a society, to the Other.[10] What the Other is seen to lack is historical agency. The traveling European, however, narrates her own historical agency in the account of the journey to and from the scene of the Other.

These comments of de Certeau on the travel narrative provide a useful preliminary summary of what may be called the "typical" structure of colonialist travel narratives. Such a narrative is an abstraction. While its "typical" structures always direct value away from the "native" or "colonized" or "alien," they find practical expression, as this book will demonstrate, in a variety of ways, in a variety of textual economies.

WHERE (OR TO WHAT) DOES GULLIVER TRAVEL?

By the eighteenth century, travel for trade had become well-established. It was more than two hundred years since Columbus and Vasco da Gama had visited America and India respectively. It was more than a hundred years since the establishment of the East India Company for trade with India. The East India Company's rule over large portions of India had not yet been instituted but was only half a century away. Already, British presence in India was considerable. *Gulliver's Travels* itself testifies to this presence by its references to Surat and Fort St. George (present-day Chennai or Madras) as the trading destinations of the voyages which open Parts II and III respectively (67 and 138). England's colonies in America were approaching political crisis, and independence from England was only a few decades in the future. West European mercantile capitalism was past the nascent stage and, indeed, the foundation of the monopoly capitalism of empires was being laid.

In the wake of this global expansion of English capitalism and colonialism came a flood of travel narratives. Percy Adams in *Travel Literature and the Evolution of the Novel* surveys extensively the literature of travel produced during the seventeenth and eighteenth centuries. The quantity of this literature is indicated by a statistic that he cites: "Edward Heawood's volume (1912), still the most helpful for the seventeenth and eighteenth centuries, refers to more than 125 different travel books by explorers themselves, only a small percentage of the total" (60–61). "[O]ne German of the time insisted," Adams notes further on, "[that] travel was so popular it was an 'epidemic' that spread its germs by means of countless books" (70). Much of this body of work, enormous both in quantity and diversity, related directly to the phenomenon of colonialism. Some of these travel narratives, in all their diversity, are the objects of analysis in the first part of Mary Louise Pratt's book *Imperial Eyes.*[11]

Swift's public in *GT* is also the audience for this flood of travel narratives. It would therefore have possessed considerable familiarity with the discursive protocols of travel narratives as a genre. That Swift was conscious of this familiarity is evident in *GT*. When Gulliver is advised by the captain who rescues him at the end of Part II to recount his experiences in Brobdingnag in the form of a book, he writes: "My answer was that I thought we were already overstocked with books of travels; that nothing could now pass that was not extraordinary" (*GT* 131). The interest and familiarity of his audience is something that Swift skillfully exploits right from the outset in the indignant "letter" prefacing *GT* written by Gulliver to his "cousin Sympson" in which he refers to "my cousin Dampier" and "his book called, *A Voyage round the World*" (*GT* xxxiii). These allusions quite explicitly identify the genre of the travel narrative as the stage on which the drama of Gulliver's narrative is presented. By such identification, Swift's text is referring to its own practical context. The twin processes of colonialism and capitalism were making available to the English public of Swift's time an unprecedented volume of travel narratives. This popular genre then becomes, quite self-consciously the allusions reveal, the context for Swift's literary practice.

As Fredric Jameson remarks in *The Political Unconscious,* "Genres are essentially literary *institutions,* or social contracts between a writer and a specific public, whose function is to specify the proper use of a particular cultural artifact" (106, italics in original). *GT* practices a careful mimicry of the "real" travel narrative in order to place the social contract represented by the colonialist travel narrative under a rigorous critique.[12] This mimicry has not always been recognized sufficiently. In an essay considering the different "literary allegiances" of *GT*, Frederik Smith writes, "Travel literature is only nominally Swift's genre (just as nominally his narrator is a retired sea captain). . . . [H]e attempts neither a travel book nor an antitravel book but rather explores . . . a range of literary allegiances inside the superstructure of his chosen genre" (247). On the contrary, it is being argued here, travel literature (and, more specifically, colonialist travel literature) is much more than the nominal genre of *GT*. Indeed, it is attention to *GT*'s mode of engagement with the generic protocols of the travel narrative that leads us to understand its anticolonial textual economy. Such attention uncovers the arrogance of the typical assumptions that underlie what de Certeau calls "the hermeneutics of the other," the violent project of appropriating the Other by the Self (the narrating Subject). It discloses the manner in which *GT* dislocates the textual economy of the colonialist travel narrative by mimicking it. The consequence of this act of sabotage is nothing less than a profound challenge to the ideology of colonialism itself.

Every "Part" of *GT* has recourse to what de Certeau calls "the rhetoric of distance." Gulliver's voyages to Lilliput, Brobdingnag, Laputa, and Houyhnhnmland all involve locations (albeit only in the crazy geography of *GT*) either in the southern hemisphere or the Pacific.[13] Gulliver's voyages involve, in other words, displacements to extremities away from England along both axes of the globe. The voyages are also always by ship across an ocean that constitutes "the break" from what is England. There also appear "monsters, storms, lapses of time" in Gulliver's narrative of his many journeys to the distant parts of the world. One example here is the huge bird (a great eagle) that carries Gulliver off Brobdingnag and returns him to the society of Europeans at the end of the second part (124–25). At the end of this part of the text, as indeed at the beginnings and the ends of all the parts, Gulliver finds himself at "my own House" with wife and family (133), suggesting that rather than distinguishing simply between an "over here" and an "over there," a travel narrative visualizes the two spaces separated by a break as a difference between a Home, with all its associations of intimacy and ownership, and an Out There, a contrast to Home.

The "Home" that is contrasted to an "Out There" is a space of great importance in the travel narrative. In *Home and Harem*, Inderpal Grewal has discussed many of the nuances of "home" within what she calls the "cultures of travel" in the context of colonialism.[14] Beyond making possible that very "rhetoric of distance" that underlies an ethnographic vision, home suggests to us the different ways in which the (neo)colonialist travel narrative draws on a patriarchal ideology. Alison Blunt, in her analysis of Mary Kingsley's travel writings, shows how "home" was configured differently in Kingsley's case than it was in the case of male travel writers. She writes:

> "Home" is constructed in an arbitrary, retrospective way while the traveler is away, and, by necessity, "home" changes on the traveler's

return. It can be argued that travels themselves exist only when bounded by departure and return and are thus similarly retrospective. The significance of such a dialectical relationship between "home" and away for imperial women travel writers lay in their own perceptions of "home" and how they were perceived by others on their return. . . . [W]omen travel writers . . . were constructed primarily in terms of gender difference, and . . . this paralleled but differed from such constructions prior to departure. (114)

Gulliver's masculinity obviates for Swift the necessity of marking his gender as extraordinary (as Blunt argues that Kingsley's gender was). The generic protocols of the colonialist travel narrative in fact presume a masculine traveler. Swift subjects to critique the colonialist bias of the travel narratives he takes as the generic context for his text, but is not similarly attentive to the gender bias inherent in these narratives. The discussion of *Indiana Jones and the Temple of Doom* in the previous chapter has already explored the ways in which one (neo)colonialist travel narrative devalues femininity and concentrates value in masculinity.

Gulliver's rhetoric of distance, then, depicts the displacement of a male protagonist from a Home to an Out There and back. What it attempts to hide, quite unsuccessfully because Swift has deliberately let us into the know by the exorbitant excess of his satiric imagination, is the fact that Gulliver has not left Home at all—has not left England at all—that Lilliput, Brobdingnag, Laputa, and Houyhnhnmland are but so many critical reformulations of English or European assumptions. The Lilliput section is a satire on the political practices of early eighteenth-century England; the Brobdingnag section of Renaissance political ideology and Eurocentrism; the Laputa section caricatures eighteenth-century (bourgeois) science and economics; and the section on Houyhnhnmland turns its attention to the rationalistic humanism of eighteenth-century metaphysics. The gesture of critical reformulation functions through a subtle parody of that mechanism of casting the Other in terms of the Self that de Certeau observes in the travel narrative. Instead, Swift's text casts the Self in the terms of a series of fictitious Others. The effect of this is to displace the Self, the European Subject, from its position of privilege. Shown to be susceptible to the same mechanism of ideological appropriation it has thus far deployed against its Others, the European Subject is rendered quite as contingent. It is in such details that *GT* attains an anticolonialist posture. It can be seen now that the centuries-long criticism of

GT reviewed at the outset of this chapter isolates certain subsidiary themes and ignores the larger anticolonialist framework within which these themes exist and to which these themes contribute. Such criticism abstracts *GT* from its full practical context. The moment we return *GT* to such a context the anticolonial structures of evaluation within which the other themes exist begin to heave back into view.

The project of recasting the Self in terms of a series of Others through certain anticolonialist evaluative structures is initiated by Swift from the very first section but comes to its fullest expression in the fourth section (the voyage to Houyhnhnmland) and in the prefatory letter that Gulliver writes, which shares with other *fore*words the irony, as Jacques Derrida points out in "Outwork," of being really an *after*word. "The preface would announce," Derrida notes, ". . . the conceptual content of significance . . . of what will *already* have been *written*. And thus sufficiently *read* to be gathered up in its semantic tenor and proposed in advance. From the view-point of the fore-word the text exists as something written—a past . . . [presented] . . . to the reader as his future" (7, italics in original). *Gulliver's* past, his alienation from his European consciousness, is presented by Gulliver as the reader's future.[15] This accounts for the evangelizing tone of the prefatory letter. Swift, however, has a different future in store for the reader. What Swift has already written and proposed in advance is the toppling of the Self, the European Subject, from a place of privilege into the abyss of contingency, rather than an alienation from European consciousness or assertion of Houyhnhnm superiority.[16] In other words, what Swift proposes is the dislocation of the evaluative structures, such as those already encountered in *Temple* in the previous chapter, of the (neo)colonialist travel narrative.

It is with the foreshadowing of a promised yet still unclear future, with a foreknowledge, that the reader reads the sections dealing with the first three voyages in which the project of making the European Subject contingent is begun, though it will not be completed until Gulliver's journey to Houyhnhnmland. During his sojourn in Houyhnhnmland, Gulliver is fully alienated from his European consciousness. He returns, is compelled to return by his master (*GT* 263–65), to England as a spokesman for what he considers Houyhnhnm superiority. He returns, in fact, the proselytizing Gulliver of the prefatory letter. His narration of his experiences in Houyhnhnmland then is a narration from/of the position of a Houyhnhnm subjectivity. We for our part are faced with the promised demonstration of the contingency of the European Subject. Instead of the displaced Other ("savage") being assimilated to the Self (the transcendental European Subject, Jean de Léry), in Swift's text the displaced Self (Gulliver) returns to the Other (now England) in a startling reversal of the mechanism of the travel narrative—England is recovered as the monstrous Other for an Other that *should* have been monstrous.

Such an articulation of monstrosity becomes most evident in Gulliver's attitude to the body of the Yahoos, whose ancestors, Gulliver notes, "for anything I know, may have been English, which indeed I was apt to suspect from the lineaments of their posterity's countenances" (*GT* 306), and apprehension of whose "teeth" and "claws" Gulliver yet possesses at the end of his long narration (*GT* 280).[17] He always describes the body of the Yahoo as that of a monstrous animal. When Gulliver's Houyhnhnm master, on the other hand, asserts that the Houyhnhnm body is the more natural and efficient, he finds this perfectly reasonable (*GT* 226–27). The body, whether Houyhnhnm or Yahoo, becomes the site for the articulation of difference and monstrosity. And it is to live among monstrous Yahoos that Gulliver, himself a Yahoo, returns.

To propose that *GT* renders a privileged European Subject contingent by reformulating it in terms of and contrasting it to a series of fictional invented Others is not in fact to argue that either Gulliver or Swift manages to present a complete, "real" alterity for a European subjectivity. Gulliver and Swift would have to be able to step outside of their own ideology and history to be able to do that. The various invented Others are but versions of the Self cast in new forms; they are aspects of the European Subject seen from displaced perspectives. The casting in new forms, the displacement, is achieved by an inversion of the mechanism of the colonialist travel narrative so that the Self is faced with the paradox of a version of itself that claims to be an Other *and* superior. This "inversion" does not affect the nominal narratival structure of the travel narrative, which, as we have seen, is carefully, repeatedly, mimicked by *GT* in the travel from a Home to an Out There and back. What does such an inversion involve then? We must answer that it involves the appropriation and assignation of cultural value to a new site through the mechanism of the colonialist travel narrative. It involves the disruption of the given evaluative structures of the colonialist travel narrative even as the structures nominally remain the same.

If Gulliver is the instrument of the disruption, Swift is the agent. An important theme in the history of criticism on *GT*—whether Gulliver can be given the status of a full character or not—is signaled by this formulation.[18] This theme has centered on a discussion of the psychological consistency of Gulliver as a character and of the credibility of his transformation in the course of the book. There is sufficient evidence in the book to indicate that Gulliver is not a full psychological character. The most telling bit of evidence is the discrepancy between the Gulliver of the preface and "Part IV," on the one hand, and the Gulliver of the first three parts, on the other. The first and third parts of the book display a Gulliver who shows few signs of the alienation from a European subjectivity that is achieved in the fourth part of the book. The second part, the voyage to Brobdingnag, ends with Gulliver beginning to display some of the signs of alienation that he displays more fully in the fourth part and the preface.

How are we to make sense of this? Clearly a contradiction is revealed if we postulate a single period of composition for the entire book (for Gulliver as author, not Swift). Gulliver should then show the same alienation from European subjectivity throughout the book; he should display the same perspective in portraying and interpreting all his adventures. After all, the entire text is being composed in the present, *after* Gulliver's return from the land of the horses. But he does not show the same perspective. It is clear we are confronted with what seems to be a conundrum only because we are investing Gulliver with a status that he perhaps never achieved in Swift's own mind—that of a full character. If we regard Gulliver instead as simply a narrative device for the critiquing of a particular European subjectivity, in the manner set out above, we are no longer confronted with this conundrum.

Swift in fact composed and inserted Part III of *GT* last, even though he had conceived of it at the outset of the project (Harold Williams xvii and xxi). Without Part III, *GT* reveals a purposeful design—the expression of a largely unchallenged European subjectivity in Part I, the relativization and partial dismantling of this subjectivity in Part II, and the final historicization of this subjectivity in Part IV, which is promised as Gulliver's past and the reader's future in the preface. It can be suggested, then, that we revise the allusion to Gulliver's alienation from an European subjectivity that I have allowed myself to make for convenience in the earlier pages of the chapter. If Gulliver is not a full character (i.e., a fiction understood to function according to *conven-*

tional ideas of subjectivity), it is meaningless to speak of his "alienation" from a European subjectivity. Furthermore, reference to Gulliver's alienation tends to make Gulliver himself the focus of *GT*, whereas Swift's ambitions are much greater—they are, we have seen, the subversion of the very premise of a transcendent European subjectivity.

The typical uninverted colonialist travel narrative is what Abdul JanMohamed calls an "imaginary" colonialist text—one that observes the Other at an emotive level, seeing it as completely evil; against this "imaginary" text JanMohamed postulates the "symbolic" colonialist text, more aware of cultural differences, and of two kinds—one that attempts futilely "to find syncretic solution to the Manichaean opposition of the colonizer and the colonized," and another that "realizes that syncretism is impossible . . . [and becomes] . . . reflexive about its context, by confining itself to a rigorous examination of the 'imaginary' mechanism of colonialist mentality" (84–85). The second type of symbolic text refuses to speak of the Other (100). *GT*, it seems to me, is a reflexive symbolic text that in its insistence that it is an imaginary text places the mechanism of the imaginary text under scrutiny. Thus, if in Jean de Léry's travel account, as de Certeau notes, from the moment of Jean de Léry's "departure from Geneva a language sets out to find a world," then, we might say, in *GT* Swift's reflexive symbolic text sets out to lose a world (224).

In this attempt to lose a world, *GT* clearly maps the terrain of the colonialist travel narrative and identifies it as an imaginary text. Through its acute metacommentary on the colonialist travel narrative, *GT* declares its resistance to the dominant (colonialist) praxis of its times and declares itself to be the formal expression of an anticolonialist praxis. The inversion in *GT* of the evaluative structures of the typical colonialist travel narrative (an inversion that withholds value from England or the metropolis) is now seen to be the embodiment of a particular anticolonialist content, which is itself the embodiment of a particular praxis. Contrary to the formalist doctrine of the New Critics, form is not clarified but obscured by its isolation from its practical context.[19] A careful attention to evaluative structures permits us to see how form is really expressive of a certain kind of intention, comprehensible now not according to the tenets of an individualist psychology, but those of a (historical) praxis—that is, of a purposeful, social and human mode of being in the world that finds collective expression. Is it not a recognition of intention that continues to lie hidden in common literary critical

usage that often refers to the "actions" of a text (e.g., *GT*), as opposed
to an author (e.g., Swift)? In this manner, usage retains a sense of intention while disowning explanations based on an inaccessible psychology
of the individual. A textual economics suggests that intention should
really be understood as emerging from and contributing to historical
praxis rather than as the self-generated effect of autonomous literary
forms or of linguistic rules. In the evaluative structures of a text, such
intention finds accessible expression. In the critique advanced "by" *GT*,
the evaluative structures of colonialist travel narratives stand revealed.

SWIFT AND THE CRITIQUE OF MODERNITY

The textual economy of the colonialist travel narrative is complicitous
with a colonialist *political* economy. Colonialist travel narratives construct a view of the non-European (discussed thus far only through the
abstract and abstracting, though useful, terminology of Other-ness) that
is of service to the project of colonialism. In the early stages of colonialism, they made practical information about far-off lands available to the
colonizing metropolis. "Travel narratives prefigure the data of the
Atlas," José Rabassa notes (5), going on to remark that "the signalling
power of the *Atlas* reopens territories to domination and appropriation
within a historical dimension" (6). The colonialist travel narrative is of
utility to colonialism in more than one way. Such utility is fundamentally guaranteed by the colonialist travel narrative's appeal to the "real"
no matter how fantastic the "real" may be. The travel narrative presumes to present to its European reader a "real" picture of an alien culture, of which it is uniquely equipped to speak because it is also an
account of a journey to this alien place and back.

By its very existence, *GT* disrupts this protocol of authenticity
which underwrites the colonialist travel narrative's praxis. As a fictional
travel narrative that pretends to be "real," it adds nothing to the signalling power of the *Atlas*, but instead introduces the contamination of
disinformation to trouble the functioning of this mechanism of colonialism. As an ironic commentary on travel narratives, *GT* is a metadiscourse pretending to be a discourse, a distorting mimicry that refuses to
confess its own derivative status, to confess that it *"say[s] the thing that
was not"* (i.e., that it is fictitious) except by accident (*GT* xxxiii, italics
in original). Such an insistence on the veracity of what is written is

repeated numerous times in the book. The ironic intransigence of the text of *GT* deflects scrutiny to the praxis of "real" travel narratives whose difference Swift's text has seemingly refused to acknowledge. The "truth" status of these other narratives, which also insist on their veracity and the ethical legitimacy of their praxis, is placed under question with an immediacy that we can no longer feel at our removed historical moment. The refusal of *GT* to make a distinction between its own status as a metadiscourse and the status of the "real" travel narrative—a refusal achieved by an ironic mimicry of the protocols of the "real" travel narrative—is a profoundly subversive move. However, it can not be assumed that *GT's* subversive practice necessarily succeeds. Even as *GT* attempts a subversion, literary criticism (of the kind reviewed at the beginning of this chapter) works to neutralize its praxis by a praxis of its own. It confers on *GT* the status of satire, understood in a narrowly English sense, or regards the text as an autonomous form divorced from its practical context, or turns to Swift's own life to cite his "misanthropy" or "insanity." Thus, such literary criticism aspires to deflect attention from *GT's* praxis.

In its turn, textual economics as a form of critical practice aims to counter these other critical practices. It aims to redirect attention to the point in the narrative of *GT* (and this is a point for which the text has long been preparing) where the problematization of legitimacy occurs most disruptively. It is in a passage near the end that Gulliver begins by confessing "it was whispered to me that I was bound in duty as a Subject of *England* to have given in a memorial to a Secretary of State at my first coming over; because whatever lands are discovered by a Subject belong to the Crown" (277, italics in original). Gulliver goes on to give reasons why this would be impractical—the Lilliputians are not worth it, attempting either the Brobdingnagians or the Flying Island would not be safe, and the Houyhnhnms may seem easier to conquer but this may not prove so in practice and he would not betray them anyhow (277). The most telling stroke, however, comes in the justly famous passage where Gulliver describes modern colonialism:

> But I had another Reason which made me less forward to enlarge his Majesty's Dominions by my Discoveries: To say the Truth, I had conceived a few Scruples with relation to the distributive Justice of Princes upon these Occasions. For Instance, a Crew of Pyrates are

driven by a Storm they know not whither; at length a Boy discovers
Land from the Top-Mast; they go on Shore to rob and plunder; they
see an harmless People, are entertained with Kindness, they give the
Country a new Name, they take formal Possession of it for the King,
they set up a rotten Plank or a Stone for a Memorial, they murder
two or three Dozen of the Natives, bring away a couple more by
Force for a Sample, return home, and get their Pardon. Here com-
mences a new Dominion acquired with a Title by *Divine Right*.
Ships are sent with the first Opportunity; the Natives driven out are
destroyed, their Princes tortured to discover their Gold; a free
Licence given to all Acts of Inhumanity and Lust; the Earth reeking
with the Blood of its Inhabitants: And this execrable Crew of Butch-
ers employed in so pious an Expedition, is a *modern Colony* sent to
convert and civilize an idolatrous and barbarous people. (278, italics in original)

With these words, Gulliver's text explosively declares its difference-in-
sameness from the innumerable other "real" colonialist travel narratives
it has been mimicking. Gulliver's text refuses to do what most other
colonialist travel narratives readily do, participate in the economy of
colonialism. Yet it refuses at the same time to accept that it "*say*[s] *the
thing that was not*" (*GT* xxxiii). In the irony of this dislocation of the
colonialist travel narrative, which typically participates in the economy
of colonialism *and* insists on its legitimacy, the violence of the colonialist traveler and travel narrative in particular and colonialism in general
stands revealed. This violence includes within its pale British colonialism
despite Gulliver's disingenuous disclaimers (278), for it is in the name of
"divine right" and "modernity" that Britain as much as any other European nation carried on its colonial project.

Gulliver calls his refusal to fulfill the imperial responsibility of the
traveler to his "Sovereign's name," "the *only* Objection that can ever be
raised against me as a Traveller" (279, italics in original). Nothing illustrates the sharpness of Swift's irony (that the italicization insists on) as
this; for it is precisely virtually everything else in *GT* that the exorbitant
excess of Swift's satire has ensured that we recognize as not literally true.
With the formal inexorability of a mathematical proof we are led to
invert Gulliver's words and acknowledge that it is *only* Gulliver's refusal
to fulfill his imperial responsibility that we can accept. We are, despite
Gulliver (and here we should remember to regard "Gulliver" as a device
rather than a "character" of which we may demand some consistency),

to object to a literal acceptance of the tiny Lilliputians, the gigantic Brobdingnagians, the Flying Island, and the rational horses, but not to the critique of colonialism. There is of course nothing inherently disruptive about *GT*'s mimicking of colonialist travel narratives. We may take note, for example, of such a text from the same period as Daniel Defoe's *Robinson Crusoe*, which also imitates a colonialist travel narrative, not to disrupt it but to reinforce it by its careful practice of verisimilitude. We see that it is *GT*'s ludicrous refusal to accept its difference from other "real" colonialist travel narratives while making no attempt to hide its exorbitant difference that allows it to go beyond a critique of the colonialist travel narrative and become a critique of the ideology of colonialism itself.

Even as the narratival form—of a journey from Home to Out There and back—of *GT* seems to remain unchanged, the injection of a corrosive irony corrupts the significance of Home and glorifies the Out There. The irony transforms subtly the colonialist travel narrative's evaluative structures. Instead of investing value in a transcendent European Subject, we might say (returning to terminology used in earlier pages), it is invested in its Other. The transformation finds its culmination in the indictment of colonial practices in general in the passage cited above. This indictment is commensurate with Swift's own activities against the English colonization of Ireland. "'Be independent' is the text," Temple Scott notes, "of all [Swift's] writings to the people of Ireland" (xvii). With this exhortation to independence must be reconciled a conservatism Edward Said describes as follows:

> [A]ll of Swift's work does in fact support a fairly strict, not to say uninteresting, conservative philosophy. Man is either unimprovable or predisposed to nastiness, corruption, or pettiness; the body is naturally disgusting; enthusiasm, like schemes of conquest or of pseudo-scientific projection is dangerous and threatens the polity; the Church of England, the classics, and the monarchy (those three institutions Swift believed were fully comprised in the right-minded sentiments of a Church of England man) together formed the pillars and the legacy of moral and physical health—this is not an unfair summary of Swift's doctrine. (*The World, the Text, and the Critic* 74)

Much of what Said sets out as Swift's "strict, not to say uninteresting, conservative philosophy" is to be found in *GT* (in, e.g., his attack on the

Whigs and defence of the Tories in Part I, or his ridiculing of experimenters in Part III). What allows *GT*, then, to participate in an anticolonialist praxis in the manner that it does?

The answer lies in that Swift's conservatism was a conservatism in exile—both literally and figuratively. Swift wrote with the indignation of a Tory supporter watching an ascendant bourgeoisie consolidating its hold on power. That he had to do this from a literal exile in Dublin did not help. All around him he was forced to observe what Carole Fabricant calls the "excremental reality" of Dublin (35). With considerable clarity, Swift diagnosed the source of this Irish misery as an English economic subjugation of Ireland. In pieces like "A Modest Proposal," "A Short View of the State of Ireland," "The Story of the Injured Lady," and "A Proposal for the universal Use of *Irish* Manufacture," he sets out at some length the details and history of this subjugation.[20]

Swift's position was not, J. C. Beckett tells us in *A Short History of Ireland* (124) and *Literature and Society in the Ireland of Swift and Grattan* (4), untypical of an Irish Protestant nationalism in the eighteenth century. It is this nationalist praxis that enables Swift's own acute critique of English society in the form of a travel narrative. The anticolonialist literary practice of *GT* arises both from a conservative's dislike of the ascendant (Whig) bourgeoisie and the vehemence of Swift's indignation, as Warren Montag holds in *The Unthinkable Swift*, on behalf of Anglo-Ireland. Montag explores in his book on Swift what he calls "The Spontaneous Philosophy of a Church of England Man" (the subtitle to the book).[21] He argues that throughout his career Swift attempted to defend the increasingly indefensible philosophy of the Anglican church. His writings were largely an attempt to set out the social and historical vision of the Church of England and to counter the competing and increasingly ascendant ideology of bourgeois liberalism. In his comments on *GT*, Montag leaves largely unexamined the book's intimate engagement with the enterprise of modern colonialism. However, he does note at one point:

> Whatever his intentions and despite his own participation in an institution of a colonial outpost, Swift, insofar as he rejects the juridical ideology of early modern Europe, is led to (state) a rejection of the colonial enterprise in even its most modern form. The supreme irony is that Swift's arguments (both rational and rhetori-

cal) for the independence of the colony from the metropole would, by the end of the eighteenth century, be appropriated by the Catholic masses in their struggle to free themselves from protestant domination, an important component of which remained the Anglican church. (135)

Thus, the full complexity of the practical context out of which *GT* emerges is revealed. A conservative polemic against an emerging bourgeois modernity, *GT* is an early travel into the contradictions and ideological inconsistencies of this modernity, which now declares its mission to be humane and civilizing and now reveals itself to be dominating and disciplining. Simultaneously, *GT* foregrounds the centrality of colonialism for the project of modernity, for, inevitably, Swift in his polemical engagement with this modernity is led to an engagement with colonialism.

This intimacy of connection—between colonialism and a (capitalist) modernity—revealed in Swift's conservative critique has been famously explored in a key passage in Karl Marx's *Capital*. Now, it is possible to regard Marx himself as a *modern* figure, a practical intellectual who explores themes we have come to recognize as modern (civil society, revolution, the political economy of social justice, industrial society, etc.) in highly representative ways. It cannot be denied in this context that there are portions of Marx's voluminous writings that reproduce the colonialistic bias at the heart of modern thought. The most well-known recent indictment of Marx in this regard is surely that advanced by Edward Said in *Orientalism* (see pages 153–56). It is not necessary to deny the justice of Said's complaint regarding the distressing orientalism of Marx to acknowledge Marx's expression of anticolonial sentiments elsewhere. It is not necessary to deny the modernity of Marx to recognize in his work a thoroughgoing critique of this modernity, including its roots in colonialism; for modernity is, as discussion in Part II will make clear, susceptible to internal critique. Marshall Berman is only following many before him when he writes in *All That Is Solid Melts Into Air*: "[The voice of Marx, amongst other nineteenth century figures] is ironic and contradictory, polyphonic and dialectical, denouncing modern life in the name of values that modernity itself has created" (23). Thus, despite his orientalism, Marx is able to write in the first volume of *Capital*:

> The discovery of gold and silver in America, the extirpation, enslavement and entombment in mines of the indigenous population of that continent, the beginnings of the conquest and plunder of India, and the conversion of Africa into a preserve for the commercial hunting of blackskins, are all things which characterize the dawn of the era of capitalist production. These idyllic proceedings are the chief moments of primitive accumulation. (915)

All the varied activities of colonialism are thus linked to capitalism by Marx. He uncovers the violence of colonialism at that very originary instant of capitalism—primitive accumulation. How fundamental a role is being ascribed by Marx to colonialism here will become clear if we remind ourselves that for Marx primitive accumulation is essential in making the very genesis of capitalism comprehensible: "The whole movement [of the extraction of capital from surplus value and surplus value from capital], therefore, seems to turn around in a never-ending circle, which we can only get out of by assuming a primitive accumulation . . . which precedes capitalist accumulation; an accumulation which is not the result of the capitalist mode of production but its point of departure" (*Capital*, vol. 1, 873).

In contrast to a common way of characterizing the origins of colonialism as capitalist, the origins of capitalism are seen here to lie in colonialism. Instead of reading colonialism as an effect of the history of capitalism, capitalism can be read as the effect of the history of colonialism. Further, if the emergence of what is conventionally referred to as modernity is taken to be coeval with the emergence of capitalism (as it is, e.g., by Marshall Berman in the above-mentioned *All That Is Solid Melts Into Air*, a text that is taken up in greater detail in the fifth chapter), then we may read both as the effects of a history of colonialism. It may seem then that there are these two contrasting ways of formulating—either as capitalist or as colonial—the origins of what is, ultimately, *modern* history. However, it serves no purpose to pose an artificial choice between these contrasting formulations. Marxism has generally associated modernity primarily with the emergence and development of capitalist society. But the passages from Marx cited above suggest how colonialism is itself integral to the emergence of capitalism. Modern society, then, may be best understood as being coeval with the emergence of West European colonialism and capitalism. This hypothesis, hinted at in Swift's own travels into modernity, is explored in Part II of this book through a series of texts chosen because they take us from high colonialism at the end of the nineteenth century through anticolonial resistance in the middle of the twentieth to the contemporary postcolonial situation, which is also the situation in which the "postmodern" *Indiana Jones and the Temple of Doom* finds itself.

PART TWO

COLONIALISM AND MODERNITY

———————— ~

CHAPTER THREE

INTO DARKNESS AND OUT OF IT

Aside from sketching the thematic concerns of this book, Part I has concerned itself with methodology and genre. In it, we have seen how travel narratives constitute a form of textual economy centered on an "ethnographic vision." We have noted how Jonathan Swift in *Gulliver's Travels* subjects this textual economy of the colonialist travel narrative to a profound critique, revealing how such an economy both presumes a "valued" transcendental subject position for the European traveler and works to r*eproduce* it. In the process, we have also come to recognize in a preliminary way the co-implication from the outset of "colonialism" and "modernity" as historical categories. A detailed examination of the co-implication of these two categories begun in this chapter by a turn to Joseph Conrad and Zora Neale Hurston is the chief subject of Part II.

Joseph Conrad's *Heart of Darkness* (first published in 1899) and Zora Neale Hurston's *Mules and Men* (first published in 1935) come from very different authors with very different preoccupations. On the one hand, Conrad, a Polish immigrant to England at the height of its imperial power, wrote *Heart of Darkness* out of his varied experiences as a seaman. His novella, in recent years, has become a site of contestation within ongoing debates about the literary consequences of the colonial project. Set in an unnamed African locale (clearly identifiable as the Belgian Congo from evidence within the text and from what we know of Conrad's travels in the Belgian Congo a few years earlier), it deals in a prose of great coyness with the legitimacy of the colonial enterprise.[1]

Mules and Men, Hurston's account of her journey into the African American community in the South, on the other hand, does not deal with what is generally called colonialism. Yet, the segregated South, and indeed U.S. society of that time more generally, depended for its functioning on institutions very similar to those of colonialism. "Although the race/class dialectic of the [contemporary] United States cannot be adequately or accurately described as neocolonial," Manning Marable writes in *How Capitalism Underdeveloped Black America*, "it is undeniable that the process that gave birth to a Black elite here is virtually identical to that of modern Africa" (135). He thus recognizes a similarity between Africa and Afro-America that the title (which alludes to Walter Rodney's seminal work on African history) also recognizes. Indeed, this recognition is no recent matter. More than seventy years ago, Scott Nearing in *Black America* compared the colonial empires of the British, the Dutch, the French, the Japanese, the Belgian and the Italian to "[t]he American empire [which], in addition to its subject races in the Philippines and in the Caribbean, has within its own national boundaries a subject race of more than twelve million American Negroes" (5). Finally, Hurston's very identity of an anthropologist is evidence for the approximate homology between the condition of African Americans then and the colonial world. At a time when anthropologists turned their attention exclusively "outward," outside their metropolitan location and to the colonial world, Hurston's intellectual enterprise is legitimized under the rubric of anthropology, indicating the external location of the black South as well. The homology between the black South and the colonial world is only approximate, but to therefore overlook similarities is to be insufficiently attentive to the lessons of history.

Following these leads, this chapter will both assume and demonstrate the validity of the claim that the condition of the African American population within the United States is analogous (but not therefore identical) to a (neo)colonial situation by showing how *Mules and Men* as a travel narrative engages antagonistically with the colonialist travel narrative. It is this analogy that is identified in my staging of a contestatory relationship between two otherwise widely separated texts. Although *Heart of Darkness* was written at the turn of the century and *Mules and Men* well into it, the two are related to each other generically by their shared reference to the textual economy of the colonialist travel narrative, which one reproduces and the other contests. In other words, they are linked by their references to the same (global) practical context of colonialism (which includes slavery and the slave trade) and separated by the differences in their respective textual practices. This detailed examination of *Mules and Men* and *Heart of Darkness* as travel narratives prepares the ground for the discussion regarding colonialism and modernity taken up in earnest at the end of the chapter.

LESSONS IN CRITICAL PRACTICE

Critical opinion on both Joseph Conrad's *Heart of Darkness* and Zora Neale Hurston's *Mules and Men* has been transformed within the last twenty-five years by polemical essays written by two black writers of considerable renown. Chinua Achebe has helped chart a new trajectory of criticism on *Heart of Darkness* through his essay "An Image of Africa: Racism in Conrad's *Heart of Darkness*," while Alice Walker has helped retrieve Zora Neale Hurston's reputation from obscurity through a celebratory (and symbolic) description of her search for Zora Neale Hurston's grave in "Looking for Zora" (originally published as "In Search of Zora Neale Hurston").

The year in which these essays by Achebe and Walker appeared is significant. Chinua Achebe's essay was first delivered in the form of a lecture at the University of Massachusetts, Amherst, in 1975 and Alice Walker's article describing her discovery of Zora Neale Hurston's work and her subsequent search for Hurston's unmarked grave also appeared the same year in *Ms.* magazine. The appearance of two contentious essays in 1975 seems accidental only if we forget that the seventies was a decade when the process of decolonization set in motion earlier, though beginning to ebb, still had considerable force across the world. Decolonization, always a contested historical process, had still not entered the era of reactionary revanchism that was the eighties. Chinua Achebe, one of black Africa's most well-known authors, and Alice Walker, one of literary Afro-America's premier figures, in producing their essays in 1975, engage in a cultural politics. They are intent on reclaiming cultural territory on the strength of Nigeria's independence in 1960, on the one hand, and the Civil Rights movement of the sixties in the United States, on the other.

In "An Image of Africa," Chinua Achebe argues that *Heart of Darkness* is a profoundly racist text for its dehumanization of Africa. In setting his examination of the moral decay of a European mind (Kurtz's) in Africa, Achebe contends, Conrad reduces an entire continent to the status of props for what seems an exclusively European drama. This move cannot be innocent for Achebe—he points out that Africa emerges in Conrad's narrative as an appropriate locale for this drama because it signifies "'the other world,' the antithesis of Europe and therefore of civilization" (252). Achebe makes these remarks not in ignorance of Conrad's vehement critique of imperialism in Central Africa in *Heart of Darkness* but despite it. He suggests that the liberalism implied by this critique of imperialism is still incapable of granting equality between white and black (256). He concludes his essay by noting, "Conrad saw and condemned the evil of imperial exploitation but was strangely unaware of the racism on which it sharpened its iron tooth" (262). Achebe finds Conrad finally to be on the side of racism, the ideological underpinning of colonialism.

Robert Kimbrough, in the introduction to the third Norton Critical Edition of *Heart of Darkness*, identifies "the public remarks of Chinua Achebe on Conrad's racism" as one of the "three most important events in *Heart of Darkness* criticism since the second edition of this book" (xv).[2] He proceeds in the "Criticism" section of the edition to give a sense of this debate by bringing together four essays—Achebe's, Wilson Harris's "The Frontier on Which *Heart of Darkness* Stands," Frances B. Singh's "The Colonialistic Bias of *Heart of Darkness*," and C. P. Sarvan's "Racism and the *Heart of Darkness*." To these essays may be added the following to get a representative sense of what the debate has been like—Ian Watt's "Conrad's *Heart of Darkness* and the Critics," Patrick Brantlinger's "Heart of Darkness: Anti-Imperialism, Racism, or Impressionism?" Cedric Watts's "'A Bloody Racist': About Achebe's View of Conrad," Peter Nazareth's "Out of Darkness: Conrad and Other Third World Writers," Edward Said's comments on Conrad in *Culture and Imperialism* and Hunt Hawkins's "Conrad's Critique of Imperialism in *Heart of Darkness*."[3]

Of these critics, Cedric Watts, Ian Watt, C. P. Sarvan, Wilson Harris, Hunt Hawkins, and Peter Nazareth are the most vehement defenders of Conrad. Most of these critics are careful to acknowledge that a charge of racism may be brought against some of Conrad's remarks, both in *Heart of Darkness* and elsewhere, but insist that the final effect of *Heart of Darkness* is to critique both colonialism and racism. The fact that some of these critics are themselves from the "Third World" has helped to complicate the debate initiated by Achebe, by not allowing it to be reread in a simplistic fashion as a conflict between critics from the "First World" and from the "Third World." In contrast, Achebe's remarks on *Heart of Darkness* are echoed by Frances Singh. Singh is not as direct as Achebe in charging racism in *Heart of Darkness*, but the effect is a similar indictment of Conrad's narrative. Patrick Brantlinger's stimulating piece, unlike the other essays, looks at the debate surrounding the charge of racism that Achebe makes and finds *Heart of Darkness* a deeply ambivalent narrative that both articulates an anti-imperialism and undercuts it by its racism and impressionism. Similarly, Said finds *Heart of Darkness* ambivalent—simultaneously critical of imperialism and unable to visualize its end.

On the whole, Achebe has been in the minority in the discussion caused by his polemical comments on *Heart of Darkness*. Many critics have rushed to defend Conrad against Achebe by pointing to the numerous scathing comments about colonialism that Conrad has his narrator make in *Heart of Darkness*. Ian Watt's concluding judgment may be taken to be representative of many such defences of Conrad—"[Conrad's] skeptical balance, of course, does not clear Conrad completely from the charge of being a colonialist; but it comes close to doing so. . . . On the general charge of Conrad's supporting colonialism, however, we must acquit him. This is largely on the basis of his [critical] treatment of whites" (13). Chinua Achebe, however, has continued to make his assertions about *Heart of Darkness*. He has repeated his charges in a "Viewpoint" article published in the *Times Literary Supplement* in 1980 and in an interview granted to Bill Moyers in 1988. His essay "An Image of Africa" was also included (with minor changes) in the third Norton Critical Edition of *Heart of Darkness* when it was published in 1988. There is a moment in "An Image of Africa" when Achebe, in considerable exasperation, poses the central question of his essay. "Can nobody see," Achebe exclaims, "the preposterous and perverse arrogance in thus reducing Africa to the role of props for the break-up of one petty European mind?" (257). Achebe's question requires that the issue of how to read *Heart of Darkness* be posed not simply at the level of an indictment of Marlow or Kurtz or Conrad, but at the level of ideology. Why, Achebe is asking in his question, is Africa often so conveniently the site within a colonialist textual economy for (devalued) symbolic representations of bestiality, irrationality, inhumanity, and moral decay? Achebe's complaint recognizes that references to Africa in the textual economy of *Heart of Darkness* are aimed at a concentration of value in Europe and a corresponding draining of it from Africa.

Such a textual economy, we know by now, is not unique to *Heart of Darkness*. Achebe himself refers in his essay to two anecdotes and a

news story from *The Christian Science Monitor* that demonstrate eth-
nocentric Western attitudes with regard to Africa. Arguments about
Conrad's statements for or against colonialism are relevant to literary
critical practice that is biographical in its main thrust, but more important to a textual economics is the colonialist textual economy that is
given expression by Conrad in *Heart of Darkness*. Such a textual economy is primarily a clue not to Conrad's individual idiosyncrasies but to
a broader historical praxis.

A different kind of critical drama surrounds the literary reputation
of Zora Neale Hurston. In the last twenty-five years, the work of the
African American anthropologist and novelist has moved from being
relatively neglected to being the object of extensive and varied research.[4]
Henry Louis Gates, one of the key figures in the rehabilitation of
Hurston, noted in 1990, "More people have read Hurston's work since
1975 than did between that date and the publication of her first novel,
in 1934" ("Afterword—Zora Neale Hurston" 292). This transformation in the reputation of Hurston has been the result of the collective
effort of a younger generation of African American scholars, many of
whom are female. It is partly as the object of a feminist scholarship that
Zora Neale Hurston's reputation has undergone a significant revival.

Of central importance to this revival of interest in Zora Neale
Hurston has been the influence of Alice Walker. Through her zealous
personal and professional allegiance to the memory of Zora Neale
Hurston, Walker has been instrumental in both making Hurston's work
more readily available and in fostering scholarship on Hurston. The centrality of Walker's influence is acknowledged quite explicitly in the
chronology of Zora Neale Hurston's life provided in recent editions of
her work.[5] The two final dates in the chronology appended to the edition of *Mules and Men*, for example, are August 1973, when Alice
Walker discovered and marked Hurston's grave, and March 1975, when
she published "In Search of Zora Neale Hurston" in *Ms.*, "launching a
Hurston revival" (*Mules and Men* 309).

In "Looking for Zora" (the title under which "In Search of Zora
Neale Hurston" was published in *In Search of Our Mother's Gardens*),
Walker describes her trip to Eatonville, Hurston's birthplace and the
scene of so many memorable incidents in Hurston's works. In the company of a white female acquaintance, Alice Walker goes there to gather
information about Hurston and possibly discover her grave and place a
marker on it. Walker's essay ends with her account of how she discov-

ered what she presumes to be Hurston's grave in the "Garden of Heavenly Rest" and arranges for a marker with the following legend to be placed on it:

ZORA NEALE HURSTON
'A GENIUS OF THE SOUTH'
NOVELIST FOLKLORIST
ANTHROPOLOGIST
1901   1960

As the legend on the marker amply demonstrates, Alice Walker's journey to Eatonville and her discovery of Hurston's grave are also symbolic of her quest for an African American Southern intellectual and literary tradition.[6]

Zora Neale Hurston's reputation has not always been held in such high regard as it is now. Robert Hemenway in his literary biography of Hurston notes the criticism that Hurston encountered during the thirties when she chose in books like *Mules and Men* to ignore the impact that the Depression was beginning to have on black townships. He also notes her almost complete neglect during the latter part of her life when she became increasingly conservative. In an African American literary scene in which Richard Wright's combative writings were increasingly respected, Hurston's celebrations of Southern black life, which emphasized the autonomy of some black communities, seemed to many particularly compromised by their failure to indict white America for its many violences. Even sympathizers of Hurston have agreed with this criticism. Alice Walker, in her foreword to Hemenway's work, notes:

> During the early and middle years of her career Zora was a cultural revolutionary simply because she was always herself. . . . During her later years, for reasons revealed for the first time in this monumental work (as so much is!), she became frightened of the life she had always dared bravely before. Her work, too, became reactionary, static, shockingly misguided and timid. (xvi)

What is interesting about the contemporary rehabilitation of Hurston's reputation is that it does not necessarily depend on new revelations regarding Hurston's politics. Hurston's indisputable conservatism is as freely acknowledged now by African American scholars like Walker and Hemenway as it ever was before. But these same scholars, writing with an urgency imposed on them by the neocolonial context of their own critical practice, have found in Hurston a unique record of a

rapidly disappearing African American world. The differences between
two Eatonvilles—the Eatonville of Zora Neale Hurston's works and the
Eatonville of Alice Walker's essay "Looking for Zora"—accurately capture the historical transformation referred to here. This historical transformation, Susan Willis argues, is the central experience of African
American female writers—"I know of no other body of writing [than
that of such writers] that so intimately partakes of the transformation
from rural to urban society or so cogently articulates the change in its
content as well as its form" (4).

The pastoral scenery of Hurston's Eatonville is replaced in Alice
Walker's Eatonville by the steel, macadam, and Afro hairdos of the black
U.S. in the seventies. For her unapologetic and assertive record of an
African American folk culture now in the process of being erased, some
contemporary scholars have been prepared to forgive Hurston her own
erasure of the many violences of economic deprivation, Jim Crow laws
and lynching that were one part of the reality behind the pastoral world
of her works. The horrifying dimensions of this part of the reality have
been amply demonstrated by such writers as Manning Marable (in *How
Capitalism Underdeveloped Black America*), Robin Kelley (in *Hammer
and Hoe*) and Scott Nearing (in *Black America*). In such alternate valu-
ations of one and the same reality are captured the complexity of the
politics of remembering, the politics of the historical record.

At issue in the contrast between Hurston and these other writers is
a particular evaluation of black historical praxis. In the African American context, as Henry Louis Gates suggests in trying to explain the ups
and downs of Hurston's reputation, this is also a matter of contending
"'racial ideologies'" ("Afterword—Zora Neale Hurston" 291). One
racial ideology argued that "racism had reduced black people to mere
ciphers" (291). Hurston, Gates continues, "thought this idea degrading . . . and railed against it" (291). For Gates, it might be said,
Hurston's work is a reminder that racism can never erase the praxis of
black people. Yet, while observing the renewed appreciation of
Hurston's work by influential African American literary critics and writers such as Alice Walker and Henry Louis Gates, dissenting voices
should also be noted. In *Reconstructing Womanhood*, Hazel Carby
remembers a different history. She writes:

a pattern has been established from Alice Walker back through
Zora Neale Hurston which represents the rural folk as bearers of

Afro-American culture. This construction of a tradition of black women writing has effectively marginalized the fictional urban confrontation of race, class, and sexuality that was to follow [Nella Larsen's] *Quicksand*. (175)

Carby's attempt in *Reconstructing Womanhood* is to retrieve an urban tradition of African American women's writing from the kind of literary tradition represented by Hurston's turn to the African American "folk" in her writing.

The critical moments focused on above—Achebe's criticism of *Heart of Darkness* and Alice Walker's celebration of Zora Neale Hurston—are emblematic of two dimensions of the cultural politics of the literary canon. The two moments are similar to the extent that they both offer a challenge to the given constitution of the canon. But they are different in the manner in which the challenges are offered—whereas Alice Walker's project is the transformation of the canon by the forced inclusion of the work of Hurston within it, Chinua Achebe's project is a similar transformation of the canon but by the forced exclusion of *Heart of Darkness* from it. This is not to imply that Achebe is demanding that we stop reading *Heart of Darkness* altogether. A canon is more than simply a collection of representations; it is also a collection of reading practices. Indeed, representations are intimately linked to reading practices in the way of knowing texts we call literary criticism. Achebe's suggestion that we read *Heart of Darkness* in a different way is as much a challenge to the canon as his suggestion, if he can be said to have made one at all, that we stop reading Conrad's novella altogether.

It is instructive in this context that Alice Walker's project of inclusion has met with a success that Achebe's project of exclusion has not. Zora Neale Hurston's position as one of the major literary figures of twentieth-century U.S. literature is secure for the moment. *Heart of Darkness* shows no signs of being demoted from its status as one of the "great classics" of British literature, of being incapacitated as a vital muscle in the heart of the canon. The reasons for the mixed result that has greeted Achebe's project are not immediately clear. It may be argued that the critics who disagree with Achebe simply believe that Achebe is wrong in his characterization of *Heart of Darkness*. But it may also be speculated that the contrast offered by the two attempts to revise the canon also tells us something about the institutional practice of contemporary literary criticism in the North American academy. The ideology of such a literary criticism is a liberal pluralism that is able "to make a place" for alternative perspectives but is at the same time less able "to take a stand" (except, perhaps contradictorily, about the values of liberal pluralism itself) in proscribing attitudes. The opportunities made available and limitations imposed by such a pluralism are the practical context for literary criticism in North America today and the fraught terrain that any cultural politics of praxis must negotiate.

Journeys into Darkness or Dark Journeys?

Criticism on *Heart of Darkness* has commonly alluded to Marlow's status as a traveler; but renewed scrutiny, focusing on the specific evaluative structures through which Marlow's journey is narrativized, will clarify some of the issues in the contentious debate reviewed in the previous section.

Over the years, much criticism on *Heart of Darkness* has emphasized the symbolic nature of the journeys performed by Marlow and Kurtz. Marlow and Kurtz in their journeys up the unnamed African river have often been seen as journeying into interior recesses of the Self. The drama of Kurtz's "going native" is then interpreted as the dangers of succumbing to atavistic forces deep within the mind. In such criticism, words like "evil" appear with frequency.[7] *Heart of Darkness* permits such a reading by its deliberate lack of historical specificity, by the predictable facility (Chinua Achebe would say) with which it turns Africa into a site for symbolic renderings.

While such symbolic deployments of the journey are not necessarily problematic, the question of the historical ground on which such deployments are made remains important. What kind of impact does the journey as symbol have on history as a record of human praxis? For *Heart of Darkness*, Walter Rodney's treatment of the history of Africa in *How Europe Underdeveloped Africa* allows us to get at an answer. In his book, Walter Rodney refers to the Belgian Congo and its ivory trade during the period that Conrad traveled there and underwent the experiences that led to *Heart of Darkness*. Ivory trade, let us remind ourselves, is the activity in which the company that Marlow and Kurtz belong to is involved. Rodney writes:

> [T]he most decisive limitation of ivory trade was the fact that it did not grow logically from local needs and local production. . . . [A]ny

African society which took ivory exports seriously . . . had to restructure its economy so as to make ivory trade successful. That in turn led to excessive and undesirable dependence on the overseas market and an external economy. . . . [A]t all times one must keep in mind the dialectical opposite of the trade in Africa: namely, production in Europe or in America under European control. . . . In that way, the gap between Africa and Europe was constantly widening; and it is on the basis of that gap that we arrive at development and underdevelopment. (112–13)

This historical record of violent underdevelopment, which is in fact the main subject of Rodney's book, is completely missing in Conrad's *Heart of Darkness*. Instead, Conrad's text stages a colonialist narrative of travel that empties the Congo of its history to such an extent that it is not even named. Such emptying is perfectly consistent with Conrad's desire, well-recognized by conventional literary criticism, to produce an allegory of the dissolution of a mind.

The colonialist travel narrative, it has already been seen, projects the journey as circular. The traveler departing from Europe in quest of a difference which is presumed by the "rhetoric of distance" is expected to bear witness to what he (or, more rarely, she) finds there. It is the possibility of return and testimony that justifies the presumption of the journey outward across what de Certeau calls "The Break." There are two travelers in *Heart of Darkness* who depart from Europe across the Break, Marlow and Kurtz. There are two journeys performed, Marlow's and Kurtz's. Both journeys begin with the presumption of return; only Marlow's fulfills it and, thus, the structural requirements of the travel narrative. Kurtz's journey back to Europe is interrupted permanently by his death and burial in Africa.

Kurtz, however, does conform to the stereotypical identity of the colonialist traveler, at least in the beginning when he leaves Europe. Kurtz has that ethnographic vision of the world referred to in the previous chapter. Like many an other colonialist traveler, part of his purpose in journeying to Africa is to codify the difference he expects to find there. Thus, Marlow tells his audience, Kurtz had been entrusted with a brief to write a report for the "International Society for the Suppression of Savage Customs" (50). In keeping with this brief and his own inclination, Kurtz has made himself an "expert" on Africa during his residence there. This expertise of Kurtz is a point that the narrative repeatedly makes by contrasting Kurtz's knowledge of the ways and dialect of the African tribe to the ignorance of the other European travelers in the river boat. When finally the moment of Kurtz's departure from the Inner Station arrives and is greeted by shouted words from the African woman who is apparently his consort, it is only Kurtz who can understand the words. "Do you understand this?" Marlow asks him: "Do I not?" Kurtz responds, without elaboration (66). Kurtz's response to Marlow in an earlier draft of *Heart of Darkness* was less evasive. He had simply replied, "I will return" (66, footnote). By replacing the initial statement of conviction with a rhetorical question aimed at Marlow, Conrad redirects attention to the difference in knowledge between the two characters. The question, whose answer Marlow does not *definitively* know ever, only underscores Marlow's ignorance at this point in comparison to Kurtz, who implies that he does indeed understand.

Marlow's lack of knowledge of the language means that we too remain ignorant of what exactly has been said, but Kurtz's status as an "expert" is established in the text. Part of the value of Kurtz and the documents he has left behind, as the company official who visits Marlow on his return to Europe clearly recognizes, is his "knowledge of unexplored regions" (70). Kurtz's status as expert is useful for the testimony he can give of "savage" society. The "expert" status Kurtz enjoys is closely linked to the "witnessing" function of the ethnographer. What is at issue here is not so much what Kurtz "really" knows, but rather the kind of discourse that Kurtz will elaborate with his authority as a witness. The extent to which the contours of this discourse have already been defined is indicated by the name of the society—"International Society for the Suppression of Savage Customs"—on whose behalf Kurtz is to write his brief.

Kurtz himself, however, does not return to Europe to bear such witness, only some of his documents do. In this he fails to fulfill one part of that larger unspoken brief that comes with being a colonialist traveler. It is death that finally prevents Kurtz from fulfilling his unspoken brief; but consideration of Kurtz's departure from the Inner Station suggests that the import of this failure reaches much further than may be apparent at first.

The most significant detail regarding Kurtz's departure is that Kurtz does not want to leave. Thus, on the night before the steamer is to sail down the river, he attempts to crawl back to the camp of the Africans and has to be brought back by Marlow (64–66). "Do you know what you are doing?" Marlow asks him. "Perfectly," Kurtz replies. It is never made clear by Marlow, Conrad's narrator, what brings Kurtz back to the steamer, but a combination of three elements are suggested—Marlow's warning to him that he would be "lost" completely if he went back to the Africans, Marlow's threat to attack him physically, and Marlow's promise to him that his fame in Europe is assured. Earlier versions of *Heart of Darkness* emphasized Kurtz's reluctance to leave even more. In these versions, as I have noted above, Kurtz says "I will return" instead of "Do I not?" when Marlow asks him if he knows what his African consort shouts out as the steamer is leaving the Inner Station. Nevertheless, Kurtz's desire to stay at the Inner Station is not without ambivalence. While his reluctance to return to the ship on the night he attempts to escape, Marlow's narrative suggests, is only because he has succumbed to "forgotten and brutal instincts, by the memory of gratified and monstrous passions," another part of Kurtz draws him back to Europe, making it possible for Marlow to convince him with arguments of fame on his return (65). Marlow's depiction of Kurtz in this matter is that of a figure pulled in two directions at the same time, until the finality of a grave in Africa resolves the ambivalence forever.

The colonialist travel narrative presumes a journey to *other* regions but in its structuring of the journey as circular assumes the unshakeable nature of the transcendental subjectivity of the European (or metropolitan) traveler. The traveling subject in such a narrative is positioned above and outside the colonial scene being observed. For the traveler to return to Europe (or the metropolis) and bear testimony as a "true" witness, she must maintain the inviolability of the subjectivity she left with. Failure to do so, Swift's critique of the colonialist travel narrative in *Gulliver's Travels* reveals, is to be labeled insane, as Gulliver implicitly is, on his final return to England. "Insanity" is a convenient reinterpretation of something far more dangerous—admission of the historical contingency of the traveler's European subjectivity. The far greater danger of a collective failure of colonialist praxis is narratively contained by its reinterpretation as the private failure of an individual.

Viewed in this light, Kurtz's death and burial in Africa begin to have more than a nominal significance. Marlow's elaborate account of Kurtz on the steamer before his death encodes his condition as insanity. "The wastes of [Kurtz's] weary brain were haunted by shadowy images now" and "Sometimes [Kurtz] was contemptibly childish" are some of Marlow's descriptions of Kurtz (*Heart of Darkness* 67). Through numerous references to Kurtz's lack of restraint, Marlow's narrative implies that Kurtz's insanity is the consequence of having gone "too far" in the gratification of his baser instincts. But this insanity, we have already noted, can be seen as a code-word for a much more profound failure—the dangerous failure of Kurtz to maintain his transcendent position as an European subject, to maintain the historical record of colonialist praxis in Africa. It is this failure that is reflected in Kurtz's aborted journey to the heart of darkness, a journey that violates the circular structure of the travel account by his failure to return to Europe. Since he is a failed colonialist traveler, Kurtz is consigned by Conrad's fictional narrative to an appropriate grave in Africa. Simultaneously, there is a treatment of Kurtz as heroic and larger than life that only serves to reinforce the sense of Kurtz's failure by the time we come to the end of the text. Swift's Gulliver, who is his own narrator, returns to England to become the instrument by which both the colonialist travel narrative and European subjectivity are to be critiqued. Though Swift's text too hints at the possibility of Gulliver's condition being considered insanity, the text offers an alternative interpretation in the critique of colonialism and of European assumptions of ahistorical transcendence through the satire of Swift and the self-representing words of Gulliver. Conrad's text, by contrast, fails to present such an alternative to the reader and conveniently buries Kurtz in Africa. Unlike Swift's text, therefore, Conrad's text fails to break through the constraining structures of a colonialist textual economy.

Furthermore, there is, in *Heart of Darkness*, a traveler who successfully passes through the circular structure of travel required by the colonialist travel account. Marlow returns to Europe to bear witness— not about some alien society as one would expect, but about the alien society's effect on a European traveler. The issue of Marlow's bearing witness to the effect that the alien society has on Kurtz comes up twice, once in his meeting with Kurtz's fiancée, the Intended, and the second time on the *Nellie* when he tells his story to the unnamed narrator who passes it on to us. In the case of the Intended, the issue turns upon the question of Marlow's lie to the Intended some time after his return to Europe. When the Intended asks him what Kurtz's last words were, Marlow does not confess they were "The horror, the horror" and instead tells her Kurtz had called out her name (75). This deception is the concluding incident of the narrative that Marlow tells his audience on the *Nellie*. Much has been made of this lie, acting as it does retrospectively on the narrative that Marlow has just presented to us.[8] Why, many readers have asked, does Marlow tell the lie? Marlow himself suggests that it is his attempt to protect the Intended because to tell the truth "would have been too dark—too dark altogether . . ." (76).

It should now be possible to understand, in the light of the above discussion of *Heart of Darkness* as a travel narrative, the darkness that is implied here. The darkness that the Intended must be protected from is that of Kurtz's failed behavior as a traveler in Africa. When Marlow arrives at the Intended's front door, it is with the scene of Kurtz's failure in his mind. In a panoramic sweep, Marlow describes the vision that enters the house with him—"the stretcher, the phantom-bearers, the wild crowd of obedient worshippers. . . . It was a moment of triumph for the wilderness, an invading and vengeful rush which it seemed to me I would have to keep back alone for the salvation of another soul" (72). The irony with which Marlow's narrative treats the Intended's contrasting deification of Kurtz's memory at the interview that follows, one of the important scenes of the narrative, is a clue to Conrad's purposeful foregrounding of this theme of failure in the text. The irony, it should be noted, is directed not as much at the ideals that the Intended voices so zealously but at her inaccurate assessment of Kurtz's character.

In *Sexual Anarchy*, Elaine Showalter notes that at the end of the nineteenth century male novelists threatened by the popularity of female novelists revived the genre of the "masculine quest romance" (83). In these romances, Showalter suggests, "themes of the male muse, male bonding, and the exclusion of women came together in a complicated response to female literary dominance, as well as to British imperialism and fears of manly decline in the face of female power" (83). *Heart of Darkness* is one of the texts that Showalter examines as a masculine quest romance. Showalter's comments are instructive in illustrating the extent to which the colonialist travel narrative is part of a masculine tradition of writing. In this context, the colonialist travel narrative may be termed a male-gendered genre. Revealing itself to be true to such evaluative structures of the male quest romance as already encountered in *Temple*, *Heart of Darkness* ironizes the Intended's status in its narrative and consigns her to the margins.

The other testimonial that Marlow gives of Kurtz's behavior, the truth as he understands it, is to his audience on the *Nellie*. In the nautical space of that cruising yawl—a space that, unlike the Intended's drawing room, echoes the space of the steamer in the Congo—Marlow tells his audience what he has not told the Intended. His entire narrative, which is about the failure of Kurtz, has been withheld from the Intended. He now presents it to his other (male) audience in minute detail. The complementarity of the situations suggests a question supplementary to the one posed earlier. Why does Marlow tell "the truth" to the audience in the *Nellie*?

The party on the cruising yawl consists of a Director of Companies (who is appropriately "our Captain and our host"), a Lawyer, an Accountant, Marlow and the narrator (7). "Between us there was," the narrator tells us, ". . . the bond of the sea" (7). This listing of the audience in what is the prologue to Marlow's narrative is a rather obvious positioning of the recipients of the narrative (and Marlow) as energetic, professional men. Presented as anonymous social identities rather than individualized names, Conrad's interest in these men is as key functionaries of bourgeois society, the managers of its global interests. They may be regarded in this light as the custodians of the imperialist project. For such an audience, it is vital that Marlow bear proper witness to what "really" happened out there in the heart of darkness, so that they may all learn from it. One of the functions of the lie to the Intended, then, is to emphasize that Marlow is now speaking the truth to his male colleagues. Perhaps this didactic purpose in telling what "really" happened is being alluded to when the narrator tells us, in a much-discussed passage, that, for Marlow, "the meaning of an episode was not inside like a kernel but outside, enveloping the tale which brought it out only as a glow brings out a haze" (9). The purpose of Marlow's tale is not so much Kurtz's moral decay as it is the lessons that his privileged audience is to draw from it for the appropriate conduct of the affairs of the mighty British empire, which must be different from the conduct of the Belgians in the Congo. To bolster this point the text has already established a profound difference between British and other imperialisms in the earlier listing of heroic British explorers by the narrator (8).

The two different audiences for Marlow's witnessing—Kurtz's Intended and the men on the cruising yawl—constitute two different engagements with the colonialist project. Both audiences represent immense ideological and material investment in colonialism. The involvement of the audience represented by the Intended is only indirect, but this audience is the keeper of the idealistic fervor that fuels colonialism. The audience on the *Nellie* represents men concerned not only with ideals but with the pragmatic details of conducting the affairs of colonies. For idealistic fire and missionary zeal to continue unabated,

Conrad's narrative suggests, the myth of European superiority (transcendent subjectivity) must not be destroyed. Despite Marlow's masculine distaste for the Intended's deification of Kurtz and his criticism of the corruption of idealistic purpose by many colonialists (e.g., the Eldorado Exploring Expedition),[9] he realizes the necessity of keeping idealism safe. Marlow's purpose is not to question such idealism in itself but rather a corrupt expression of it and he finally lies to keep such idealism alive. For pragmatic conduct of the everyday affairs of colonialism, on the other hand, veiled warnings in cryptic language must reveal the dangers of allowing the myth of European superiority to be destroyed. Therefore, Marlow lies to one audience and tells "the truth" to the other about Kurtz's improper behavior in the heart of darkness. Through this strategy, Conrad both devalues European women (by excluding them from the masculine business of managing empires) and produces them as naively idealistic creatures to be indulged. Simultaneously, the value of both pragmatism and a more robust idealism are attested to to a male audience.

What Conrad's text reveals further, in its concern for the proper behavior of the colonial traveler, is its fear of cultural miscegenation. Kurtz, by his inappropriate behavior, had messed things up, had blurred boundaries, had allowed things to move from their appropriate places. Such a concern with things moving from their places recurs throughout *Heart of Darkness*. Achebe notes of Conrad's parodic treatment of the steamer's African fireman in European clothing, "For Conrad things being in their place is of utmost importance" (254). Perhaps the most explicit expression of anxiety at the possibility of miscegenation is the portrayal of the African woman who is possibly Kurtz's consort. The dramatic contrast between the Intended and the African woman underscores the suggestion that Kurtz had crossed taboo boundaries.

This theme of things and people being in their places, within their boundaries, emerges directly out of the textual economy of the colonialist travel narrative; for, as has been noted earlier, in order to transfer value to the metropolis the typical colonialist travel narrative presumes a (temporary) spatial displacement at the same time that it demands a traveler who remains ideologically undisplaced, secure in his place. Colonial travel and the textual economy of its narrativization thus make special demands on the colonialist traveler. Human frailty and the heroic discipline required for the satisfaction of these demands is a recurrent theme in Conrad's work in general. As a protagonist who fails under what the narrative describes as extraordinary circumstances, Kurtz echoes the protagonist of *Lord Jim*. Conrad knew well that the project of colonialism depended for its success on the proper behavior of such travelers in the societies of the colonized.

Hunt Hawkins's essay "Conrad's Critique of Imperialism" argues a position opposite both to Achebe's in "An Image of Africa" and to what has been detailed above by suggesting that Conrad critiques colonialism's interventionist disruption of non-European cultures by his ironic treatment of two values that were used, in a complex way, to underpin colonialism at the end of the nineteenth century—"efficiency" and "the idea." Summarizing his position, he writes, "I do not find any positive 'colonists' in these works [of Conrad]. Rather I find paternalists who are condoned relative to monsters like Kurtz but who are still condemned absolutely for their dominative intervention" (298). Both Achebe and Hawkins look at the "fireman in breeches" passage alluded to above and find the portrayal of the fireman dehumanizing, but for radically different reasons.[10] The difference may be formulated as follows—for Hawkins, responsibility for the dehumanization lies with the process of colonialism, which is represented and critiqued by Conrad within the anticolonialist textual economy of *Heart of Darkness*; for Achebe, responsibility for the dehumanization lies with Conrad's own colonialist textual economy, which is presented to us in the form of the narrative of *Heart of Darkness*.

It is the assumption of many critics that these two positions are mutually exclusive that has led to much misunderstanding about the kind of text that *Heart of Darkness* is. The contention here is that in *Heart of Darkness* Conrad is both critical of interventionist colonialism (intervention being understood as something excessive and unrestrained by definition) and problematic in his portrayal of Africans as "savage" and "primitive." Thus, he is critical both of Kurtz's rapacious lust for ivory *and* of his succumbing to the demonic rites of "savages." While there is genuine horror at the violence that some kinds of colonialism do to Africans, Conrad's greater concern with interventionist colonialism is always the danger of cultural miscegenation that it brings with it. It seems to me that Hawkins has overstated the argument by declaring that any colonialist is "still condemned absolutely for [a] dominative intervention" in Conrad's works. As the implicit juxtaposing of British colonialism against Belgian in *Heart of Darkness* indicates, there are alternatives in Conrad's work to "dominative, interventionist" colonialisms.

The most important individual example of an alternative to interventionist colonialism is Marlow himself. As in many Conradian stories, Marlow's function is to offer a counterpoint to the deeply flawed protagonist whose story he recounts. Marlow too, we should remember, is a colonial traveler, who quietly contributes his mite to the colonial project and inevitably returns to tell the story of heroic but flawed protagonists. In this, Marlow (and his audience on the *Nellie* in *Heart of Darkness*, we may add) offers an alternative frame of reference for colonialist praxis. Marlow as traveler, despite the ambivalence of his character, is Conrad's prototype of a good colonizer. By repeatedly fulfilling the circular structure demanded by the travel narrative and returning to affirm the transcendence of European subjectivity (i.e., its ability to remain above and untouched by the colonial society it manages and travels to), Marlow sets at nought the interventionist excess of the Kurtzes and shows that it is possible to travel out to the colonies and perform colonial duties with pragmatism as well as idealism, as long as one has restraint.

Thus, Marlow's journey successfully transfers that value to England or the metropolis that Kurtz's journey promises but finally fails to deliver. Despite all the superficial indications, Marlow is the hero of *Heart of Darkness*. His individual actions are faithful to that colonialist praxis whose aim, indeed, is the transfer of value to the metropolis. By its endorsement of Marlow's journey rather than Kurtz's, *Heart of Darkness* reveals itself to be the formal expression of such colonialist praxis.

SIS CAT TAKES A TRIP

Zora Neale Hurston wrote two travel narratives in addition to her novels and other occasional writings. In *Mules and Men* and *Tell My Horse* (1938), Hurston drew on her training as an anthropologist to produce accounts of her travels through the southern states of the United States and through Jamaica and Haiti respectively. *Mules and Men* is structured much more explicitly as a travel narrative than *Tell My Horse*. Both these books are occasioned by travel for ethnographic research; but in *Mules and Men* Zora Neale Hurston also dramatizes her journey first to Florida and then to New Orleans as a personal journey into her culture. Many critics have noted this prominent aspect of *Mules and Men*.

In *Mules and Men*, Arnold Rampersad writes in his introduction to the book, Hurston "found at last the proper form for depicting herself in relationship to the broad range of forces within the African American culture that had produced her, as well as for portraying the people of which she was but one member" (xvi). Echoing this sentiment in "Mules and Men and Women: Zora Neale Hurston's Strategies of Narration and Visions of Female Empowerment," Cheryl Wall makes a convincing case that Hurston in *Mules and Men* journeys back into her selfhood and her African American culture to discover her identity as a woman. This discovery of female selfhood is figured, Wall suggests, by the growing empowerment of the narrator "Zora," who is transformed positively by her successive associations with Big Sweet and Marie Leveau, two powerful female personalities.

To these observations, it may be added that in *Mules and Men* Zora Neale Hurston also proposes a novel relationship between traveler and object of narration. This is achieved through the formal transposition of the colonialist travel narrative and the rearticulation of its textual economy. It is this that makes it possible for Hurston to narrate her positive engagement with African American culture and that empowerment of the self that it leads to. In "Thresholds of Difference: Structures of Address in Zora Neale Hurston," Barbara Johnson suggests that Hurston in her works deconstructs "structures of address" to reveal that her identity is differently constructed in different situations. By "structure of address" Johnson means "the interlocutionary strategy of [the text's] formulation," that is, the way the text relates to its audience (323). "If I initially approached Hurston out of a desire to re-referentialize difference," Johnson concludes, "what Hurston gives me back seems to be difference as a suspension of reference. Yet the terms 'black' and 'white,' 'inside' and 'outside,' continue to matter. Hurston suspends the certainty of reference not by erasing these differences but by foregrounding the complex dynamism of their interaction" (328). It will be argued in this chapter that Hurston's "deconstruction" of structures of address in *Mules and Men* is accomplished through a particular understanding and contestation of the textual economy of the colonialist travel narrative.

Mules and Men begins with an "Introduction" that is the narrative frame for what Zora Neale Hurston—or, more appropriately, the narrator "Zora" who appears as "I" in the text—describes as an "expedition" to gather folklore (4).[11] "I was glad," *Mules and Men* begins, "when somebody told me, 'You may go and collect Negro folklore'" (1). So Zora climbs into her "little Chevrolet" and "kick[s] [it] right along to Eatonville" (3). Eatonville is her hometown, where she, Zora, is well known as "Lucy Hurston's daughter" (2). Zora's choice of Eatonville to begin her collecting is deliberate—"I knew that even *I* was going to have some hindrance [in collecting folklore] among strangers. But here in Eatonville I knew everybody was going to help me" (3, italics in original).

Already, in this brief introductory chapter of a few paragraphs, Hurston's *re*deployment of the narrative of travel, counter to the typical evaluative structures of the colonialist travel narrative, becomes clear. A journey into the unexplored that seems to be expressed by the conventional anthropological terminology of "expedition" and "collecting folklore" is shown to be actually a return. The difference between traveler and place traveled to implied by such a word as "expedition" (invoking memories of Mungo Park and David Livingstone) is undone by the solidarity and shared experience implied by a homecoming. "Home" is not the space in which ethnographic research was conventionally done, but it is this same space in which Zora proposes to do it. Hurston effectively subverts conventional understanding of "ethnographic distance" even as she declares that "the spy-glass of Anthropology" had provided her with new ways of looking at "negroism" (1). Unlike the Kurtzes of male quest narratives, Zora does not set off into the "jungle" for her adventure. At the end of the introductory chapter, Zora appears as a very different kind of traveler engaged in a very different kind of travel. We should, then, expect *Mules and Men* to be a very different kind of travel narrative. Hurston's text does not disappoint us.

Chapter 1 of *Mules and Men* builds on this alternative deployment of the travel narrative as Zora drives, literally as well as symbolically, physically as well as psychologically, into her hometown in her Chevrolet. The chapter begins, "As I crossed the Maitland-Eatonville township line I could see a group on the store porch" (7). We know from other texts of Hurston (e.g., her autobiography *Dust Tracks on a Road*) that Maitland is the white town adjacent to Eatonville.[12] With this significant crossing of the line between white town and black town, Zora completes the journey out from New York, where she is a graduate of Barnard College and a student of eminent anthropologist Franz Boas, to the familiar community of her childhood. The introduction of the store porch at the end of the sentence indicates clearly a cultural matrix very far removed

indeed from the New York of Franz Boas and Barnard, and even of the
Harlem Renaissance.[13] The porch, a recurring locale of immense importance in Hurston's work, is a communal arena expressive of that black,
rural, Southern culture that Zora has arrived in Eatonville to record in
her capacity as an anthropologist.[14]

Although *Mules and Men* gathers together the results of years of
research in the South, the narrative of the book is a deliberate and artificial construction and does not correspond to the real history of
Hurston's trips to the South from New York. Some of the research for
the book had been done as many as six years before the publication of
the book in 1935. In the meantime, Hurston had become a novelist and
a dramatist. Her publisher encouraged her to revise the manuscript in
such a manner that it would be accessible to a general public.[15] *Mules
and Men* reflects the practical context of publishing pressures and literary ambitions that Hurston found herself in. "Hurston condenses,"
Hemenway observes, "a two-and-a-half-year expedition into one year
and nine months, with a one-year segment (Florida) and a nine-month
segment (New Orleans). Her two return trips to Eatonville in 1927 and
1928 are telescoped into a single dramatic homecoming" (165). There is
no doubt that some of Hurston's revisions of the conventions of the
colonialist travel narrative have their origins in the revisionism of
Boasian anthropology. It is equally certain, however, that some of them
arose from her growing literary ambitions. *Mules and Men* is a text com-
pounded of these related but distinct sources.

Hurston's literary ambition finally found formal expression in
Mules and Men in a transposition of the travel narrative so that it organizes the scattered folktales and accounts of hoodoo rites she had gathered into a coherent dramatization of an individual's relationship to her
community. The purpose of the traveler in a typical colonialist travel
narrative, as we have seen, is the depiction of an *other* culture for a metropolitan audience. Hurston's metropolitan audience is in New York.
Apparently faithfully performing one of the duties of the traveler, she
packages for that audience the cultural artifacts of the black South in the
narrative of *Mules and Men*. Yet, the typical evaluative structures of the
colonialist travel narrative do not find expression in the text she produces. As much as a quest for an authentic selfhood, then, *Mules and
Men* also becomes a negotiation of a practical cultural politics.

Setting up a narrative that reads "Out There-Home-Out There"
rather than "Home-Out There-Home," *Mules and Men* turns the colo-

nialist travel narrative inside out. The appropriate point of entry for Zora into the "home" of Southern African American culture is her own hometown. In Eatonville, she begins the process of collecting folktales (or "lies," as they are called within the community) from her relations and friends. The work progresses well for many weeks, but there comes a point when she is told, "Course, Zora, you ain't at de right place to git de bes' lies. Why don't you go down 'round Bartow and Lakeland and 'round in dere—Polk County? Dat's where they really lies up a mess and dats where dey makes up all de songs and things like dat" (*Mules* 55). So Zora bids, "[a] hasty good-bye to Eatonville's oaks and oleanders and the wheels of the Chevvie split Orlando wide open—headed southwest for corn (likker) and song" (*Mules* 57).

In this passage further south, there is once again a significant passing of a line—"Twelve miles below Kissimmee I passed under an arch that marked the Polk County line. I was in the famed Polk County" (*Mules* 59). The violence and exuberance of Polk County soon identifies it as a space even more radically removed from New York than Eatonville was. In Polk County, Zora is befriended by the authoritative and self-possessed Big Sweet, "woofed" at by the men, and almost knifed to death by Lucy. "Paynights used to mean two or three killings" Hurston tells her readers to evoke the social environment of the lumber camp of Loughman, Polk County, where she takes up residence (*Mules and Men* 144). Hurston's characterization of the saw-mill camp as "sordid" at one point in the narrative of *Mules and Men* has been regarded as problematic by Cheryl Wall.[16] Wall argues that it makes Hurston seem patronizing and plays into her audience's expectations and values regarding such places (670). For the reasons indicated by Wall, "sordid" is indeed a problematic word-choice for a description of the saw-mill camp.

However, the more important problems with Hurston's treatment of the saw-mill camp of Loughman lie elsewhere. Sterling Brown, in a mixed review of *Mules and Men*, when it first appeared, faulted the text for its incomplete portrait of the South and its lack of social consciousness. "*Mules and Men*," he asserted, "should be more bitter; it would be nearer the total truth."[17] It seems Brown finds Hurston's depiction of the camp problematic for its lack of historical contextualization, for its blindness to one dimension of the world it sets out to represent. Only a few years before *Mules and Men*, Scott Nearing in *Black America* had explored in great detail this other dimension. And in *How Capitalism*

Underdeveloped Black America, Manning Marable has more recently offered statistics that suggest the practical context of the world Hurston depicts in *Mules and Men.* During the first half of this century (the period of most of Hurston's life), employment potential in the North as well as economic hardship in the South and "the omnipresent fear of white lynch mobs were powerful factors pushing Blacks out of Dixie," Marable notes (34). "The number of Black people who left the South rose," he continues, "from 454,000 from 1910–1920, 749,000 from 1920–1930, to 1, 599,000 from 1940–1950" (34). Zora Neale Hurston, who was for some time a part of this massive migration that was changing the nature of the African American community, leaves both the migration and the conditions that produced it out of her account of the black South in *Mules and Men* even as she declares the saw-mill camp sordid.[18]

In another passage that helps us understand Hurston's narration of violence and rebellious behavior in Polk County in a different light, Marable writes:

> Outside of imprisonment for debts owed to planters, or the 'recruit-ment' of blacks to replenish the numbers of convicts leased by coun-ties or states, the frequency of arrests and imprisonment of Blacks was relatively low during the period of Jim Crow laws from 1890 to the 1930s. The reasons for this are rooted in the profoundly racist world-view most whites of all classes had adopted by this time. Writing in 1941, sociologists Allison Davis, Burleigh and Mary Gardner noted in *Deep South* that "the police, like the whites in general, believe that fighting, drinking and gambling among Negroes are not crimes so long as they are strictly limited to the Negro group and are kept somewhat under cover . . ." (113)

The knives and jook joints of Loughman, it now appears, are of a piece with segregationist laws and racist attitudes. The belated entry of the white Quarters Boss into the scene of confrontation between Ella Wall and Big Sweet, where the two women almost come to knives in a jook joint over Joe Willard, becomes comprehensible as a calculated policing of the segregated space of the saw-mill camp by white authority (148–53). But Hurston does not draw any of these conclusions in *Mules and Men.* We must turn to writers like Manning Marable to provide that practical context for the social condition of the deep south that is left out by Hurston. Hurston and writers such as Marable narrativize different versions of the same history—as do Rodney and Conrad with regard to the Belgian Congo.

Hurston's literary practice in *Mules and Men*, then, can be perceived as being compromised by errors of omission. This is what Sterling Brown is bemoaning in his review of *Mules and Men*. Yet, the same scene that I have described above ends with a defiant challenge thrown out by Big Sweet to the white Quarters Boss. When the Quarters Boss attempts to confiscate the knife with which Big Sweet had confronted Ella Wall, she responds, "Naw suh! Nobody gits *mah* knife. . . . Don't you touch me, white folks!" (152, italics in original). The Quarters Boss backs down and the scene ends with the departure of Ella Wall and the exultant celebration of Big Sweet by her companions for making "dat cracker stand off a *you*" as Joe Willard tells her (152, italics in original). The scene is a good illustration of the political complexities of Hurston's work. It is illustrative both of the limitations of Hurston's understanding of the practical context to African American oppression and the radical possibilities inherent in her insistence on the autonomy of African American praxis and her racial self-pride. In the exemplary ambiguities of this scene, we can find some of the reasons for the varied responses to Hurston's literary reputation over time.

After Loughman, Zora travels farther into the South to investigate the occult hoodoo practices of New Orleans. This move from Loughman to New Orleans represents an even deeper journey into the recesses of African American culture. Hoodoo, with its associations of mystery and magic, exists as a well-guarded and underground religion. "Hoodoo, or Voodoo, as pronounced by the whites, is burning with a flame in America, with all the intensity of a suppressed religion" Hurston writes as we move to the New Orleans section of the book (183). To gain entrance into the world of hoodoo, Zora must gain the trust of one of the great practitioners and become an initiate herself. Beginning with Luke Turner, Hurston narrates Zora's experiences with a number of "two-headed doctors" (191). This section on hoodoo and the earlier section on folktales is linked by Hurston's manner of narration and her general thematic preoccupation. In the New Orleans section, too, Zora appears in the role of an anthropologist traveling to gather cultural artifacts to display to a metropolitan audience and, at the same time, as the protagonist of a dramatic personal journey of discovery. Here, as much as in the earlier sections of the book, Hurston's conception of the relationship between anthropologist and the object anthropologized distinguishes itself from an "ethnographic vision." If the narrativization of the personal journey may be said to have its source in Hurston's literary ambitions, then her refusal to succumb to an ethnographic vision certainly owes a great deal to the brave revisionism of Boasian anthropology. George Stocking, in an essay in *Race, Culture and Evolution*, has argued that Boas is a transitional figure in whose work "a number of central elements in the modern anthropological culture concept—historicity, plurality, behavioral determinism, integration, and relativism—can be . . . seen emerging from older evolutionist or humanist usages" ("Franz Boas and the Culture Concept" 230).[19] All of the characteristics picked out by Stocking may not be relevant to a discussion of Hurston's work. However, a cultural relativism certainly plays a key role in the challenge that Hurston offers to ethnographic vision in *Mules and Men*.

"Relativism, in the sense of the withholding of judgment by any external or a priori standard," Stocking writes, ". . . came in Boas' work to be a fundamental premise of anthropological method, a necessary basis for accurate observation and sound interpretation" ("Franz Boas and the Culture Concept" 230). The trouble that Zora goes to to be initiated into the rites of hoodoo and her language in describing the rites to her metropolitan audience illustrate not so much her subscription to this tenet of Boas but, indeed, a radical interpretation of it which arguably goes beyond Boas. The initiation rite that Zora undergoes to become Luke Turner's assistant includes a ceremonial meal, an animal sacrifice in the dark of the night and lying naked, without food, for three days on a snake skin that once belonged to the great hoodoo practitioner Marie Leveau (198–202). Following this elaborate initiation ceremony, she begins to assist Luke Turner in his ministering to the people who come to him for help. "I studied under Turner and learnt all of the Leveau routines," Hurston writes in the persona of Zora, offering in her portrayal of Zora as an initiate a contrast to Conrad's portrayal of Kurtz as an expert (202).

What follows in the rest of the book is a matter-of-fact and remarkably unanalytical description of the occult practices of Turner (and later others). Despite her use of the word "routine" (suggestive of a staged performance, rather than a religious ritual) to describe these occult practices, Hurston's explicit opinion on hoodoo remains unrevealed to her audience to the end. Hurston in fact does enough in the book to suggest to the reader a belief in the actual powers of hoodoo doctors. When Hurston is working under Anatol Pierre, a client comes to Pierre to have another man (a rival for the affection of a woman) killed. Pierre agrees to do so and with Zora's assistance an elaborate ritual is performed. Hurston concludes, "Every night for ninety days Pierre slept in his holy place in a black draped coffin. And the man died" (211). This simple statement is not qualified or framed in any fashion in the book.[20] Nowhere is Hurston's sympathetic treatment of hoodoo and its practitioners and her special personal involvement with them revealed better than in the passage in which she describes her leave-taking from Luke Turner. With great poignance Hurston writes, "One day Turner told me that he had taught me all that he could and he was quite satisfied with me. He wanted me to stay and work with him as a partner. . . . He wanted me to stay with him to the end. It has been a great sorrow to me that I could not say yes" (205).

Hurston's presentation of both the folktales and the hoodoo rituals are marked by the sympathy with which she treats the cultural processes that produce them. Adopting the perspective of one within the cultural process rather than that of an "objective" spectator on the outside, she manages to reproduce the folktales and hoodoo rituals without reducing them to the status of "objects of inquiry." Many commentators have noted the liberty that Hurston takes in gathering her material together in *Mules and Men*. John Roberts, for example, notes that many professional folklorists would be dismayed by the lack of any description, in *Mules and Men*, of how she recorded the folktales and considers it likely that Hurston was less than faithful in her rendering of the texts of the folktales (464). On the other hand, "[t]he reason there is no clear line," Hemenway notes,

> between Zora Hurston's mind and her material [when there are uncanny parallels between folk-tales and short stories] is that she operated from within a different aesthetic, one which made no distinctions between the lore inherited by successive generations of folk and the imagination with which each generation adapted the tradition and made the lore its own. (80)

Hurston's "different aesthetic" revises the ethnographic vision of the codifiability of *other* cultures by adopting a perspective that is, in a deeply ambivalent way, both within and outside the *other* culture at the same time. This revision is surely made possible mainly by Hurston's assumed solidarity with the African American culture into which Zora journeys. In contrast, even as Kurtz is shown attempting a similar revision of the ethnographic vision, Marlow's narrative consigns him to the realms of the insane. Certainly, a cultural relativism learned from Boas is an instrument in Hurston's challenge to ethnographic vision; but it is worth asking whether she remains an anthropological relativist. Can she not be seen as passing on to a profoundly nonrelativistic affirmation of southern African American culture? An affirmative answer to this question would be more consistent with the racial self-pride that so many readers of Hurston have recognized in her.

As argued earlier, Hurston's critique of the ethnographic vision in *Mules and Men* initially takes the form of a travel narrative that is turned inside out, a transposition of the Home-Out There-Home narrative of the colonialist travel narrative to an Out There-Home-Out There narrative. In the light of this subversive transformation of the colonialist travel narrative, it is perhaps appropriate that Hurston does not narrate an explicit return journey in her text. But the vantage point implied by Hurston's "Introduction" at the beginning of *Mules and Men* is indeed that of one who has performed the return leg of the journey—someone who has decided to "go back there" and return (2), even though the text of *Mules and Men* does not end with a narration of Zora "kicking" her "Chevvie" back to New York. Is New York "Home" or Eatonville "Home"? *Mules and Men* ends without opting for one or the other. The text instead suggests that both are "Home" in different ways for Zora. This, as we will see in the next chapter, offers an interesting contrast to Wright in *Black Power*.

Instead of a narration of a return to New York, Hurston places a sly tale of Sis Cat and Rat at the end of her text which captures well her critique of ethnographic vision in *Mules and Men* (245–46). Presented to the reader without any introduction, the tale frames by its positioning Hurston's entire performance in *Mules and Men*. Once Sis Cat, the folktale goes, caught herself a rat and sat down to eat him. She was about to begin when Rat suggested she should first wash herself before beginning her meal. To do anything else would be bad manners. Sis Cat, who hated to be thought she had bad manners, went off to have her wash. When she came back, Rat was gone. The next time Sis Cat caught a rat, Rat again reminded her of the good etiquette of washing, but Sis Cat had grown wiser. Her reply was that she had "plenty manners" and ate and washed, rather than washing and eating. She went ahead and made a meal of the rat. In the last sentence of the book, Hurston makes this folk tale a comment on the book as a whole. She writes, "I'm sitting here like Sis Cat, washing my face and usin' my manners" (246).

This semantically rich passage is a subversion of many different cultural codes. In its gendering of the cat as female and the rat as male, it poses a feminist challenge to a society ordered around males. But the folktale is also a subtle reminder of the very existence of different codes. Not content with simply subverting or challenging prevalent codes, the tale tells readers that there are completely different codes, completely different ways of looking at the world. Just as there are different codes of etiquette, Hurston implies to her reader, there are different codes of aesthetics, different codes of social behavior, different codes through which to signify (the word is used here in all its African American richness) reality. This is what Hurston's sympathetic account of the people who produce the folktales and practice the hoodoo rites, in *Mules and Men*, has been attempting to show. While codifying African American culture, Hurston has also been proposing a different way of understanding both what she is codifying and what it means to codify.

Mules and Men, a text that proposes a counteraesthetic and a counterreality, may be called, like *Gulliver's Travels*, an anticolonialist travel narrative. In it, Hurston illustrates how her literary practice must transform the colonialist travel narrative to produce evaluative structures appropriate for the purposes of her own travel. Through the elaboration of alternative evaluative structures, her textual economy disturbs the seamless production of Home as a valued site that is contrasted to a devalued Out There in a colonialist travel narrative. Just as was the case with Joseph Conrad's literary practice in *Heart of Darkness*, Zora Neale Hurston's example is less interesting as the practice of an individual than as a point of access through which we can pass to questions of (historical) praxis and textual economy. It is time to make the passage in a more deliberate manner.

A Tale of Three Travels

Heart of Darkness, it has been noted, reiterates the textual economy of the colonialist travel narrative. The very ambivalence of Conrad's text lies in the thoroughness with which it sets out to accomplish this reiteration. Through the aborted journey of Kurtz, who fails to return to Europe, the text raises the possibility of alternative textual economies; it

approaches the limits of a colonialist textual economy. But the possibility of disrupting this textual economy is recontained as soon as it is considered. Marlow's presence in *Heart of Darkness* occasions a framing
evaluative structure: Kurtz's putative passage beyond the protocols of
the colonialist travel narrative is quickly rearticulated as insanity and
aberrant behavior. The drama of recontainment is heightened by the
heroic portrait of Kurtz. By investing Kurtz with a nearly superhuman
status, Conrad's text emphasizes the necessity of vigilance on the part of
everyone of "us," as signified by Marlow's representative male audience
on board the *Nellie*. *Heart of Darkness* teaches this lesson in proper
colonial behavior in a deeply cryptic language because, as a text that for-
wards a colonialist textual economy, it cannot question the legitimacy of
the colonialist travel narrative in any meaningful way. It cannot recognize even a putative dislocation of the protocols of the colonialist travel
narrative as anything other than insanity. To regard the behavior of
Kurtz as at all rational would be to approach dangerously the limits of
colonialist ideology.

Much critical discussion of *Heart of Darkness* turns on those
last words that Kurtz speaks in the hearing of Marlow—"The Horror! The Horror!" (68). On the one hand, those critics who read
Heart of Darkness as an anticolonialist text interpret "the horror" to
refer to the colonialist excesses in the heart of Africa. If, on the other
hand, "the horror" were to be interpreted as referring to the
"unspeakable rites" of "savages," *Heart of Darkness* may be read as
a racist and colonialist text. The argument here tends in the direction
of the latter reading, despite the book's vehement opposition to the
excesses of certain kinds of colonialism. Besides the fact that a
patronizing liberalism can also be racist, Marlow/Conrad's opposition to particular versions of colonialism is fueled very much by what
is seen as their dangerous habit of indiscriminately untidying things.
The consequence of such a miscegenation, such a disruption of the
neat separation of black and white, is illustrated in Conrad's text by
what happens to Kurtz.

Kurtz's exclamation "The Horror! The Horror!" it may be suggested, is a retrospective comment on his own failure to respect the
prevalent divisions of the colonial world. Besides referring to colonialist excesses as well as "savage" rites, then, "the horror" refers to the
personal failure of Kurtz—more significantly, his failure to participate
in a colonialist praxis. At the moment of his death, Kurtz finally

acknowledges in this manner his failure to fulfill the obligations of a metropolitan traveler in the colonies. Thinking back on what he has become by crossing over the line separating black and white, Kurtz breathes out a repentant confession before a representative of his own kind, Marlow. Marlow, who is both a sympathizer of Kurtz and a quietly conventional counterpoint to him, snuffs out the candle on his death and consigns him to the darkness whose depths he has plumbed. In the coda to Kurtz's story, then, Marlow proceeds to do what Kurtz has not been able to—perform the return leg of the circular journey and come "home" to Europe.

In *Mules and Men* too, just as in *Heart of Darkness*, there are many crossings of lines into territory that is alien to a metropolitan audience. In the New Orleans section of Hurston's text, Zora engages in many occult religious practices similar, in a superficial reading, to those Kurtz apparently engaged in. Hurston's narration of these hoodoo rites, however, is dramatically different from that of Marlow/Conrad in *Heart of Darkness*. Whereas we are told that Kurtz is worshiped as a god by the Africans in *Heart of Darkness* (58), Zora appears in the altogether more modest guise of an initiate and a disciple. Instead of unspeakable savagery, Zora finds in hoodoo simply an alternative version of reality. The differing perspectives that *Heart of Darkness* and *Mules and Men* offer on the world that lies on the other side from the metropolitan audience to which they both speak becomes clear if we juxtapose a passage from *Mules and Men* with the above passage in which Kurtz confesses his horror to Marlow.

During the time that Zora is an initiate of the Reverend Father Joe Watson (also known as the Frizzly Rooster), she undergoes a ceremony meant to allow her "to walk invisible" (220–21). The ceremony involves throwing a live, unfortunate black cat that has been caught by Zora with her own hands into a pot in which specially collected rainwater is boiling. The ceremony takes place in a prepared place in the woods. Hurston's description of the climactic moments of the ceremony bears repeating at length, especially as it can be read as a counterpoint to the passage describing Kurtz's last words before his death in *Heart of Darkness*:

> When he [the black cat] screamed, I was told to curse him. He screamed three times, the last time weak and resigned. The lid was clamped down, the fire kept vigorously alive. At midnight the lid

was lifted. Here was the moment! The bones of the cat must be
passed through my mouth until one tasted bitter. Suddenly, the
Rooster and Mary [his wife and assistant] rushed in to close the pot
and he cried, "Look out! This is liable to kill you. Hold your
nerve!" They both looked fearfully around the circle. They com-
municated some unearthly terror to me. Maybe I went off in a
trance. Great beast-like creatures thundered up to the circle from
all sides. Indescribable noises, sights, feelings. Death was at hand!
Seemed unavoidable! I don't know. Many times I have thought and
felt, but I always have to say the same thing. I don't know. I don't
know. Before day I was home, with a small white bone for me to
carry. (221)

In this passage, Hurston refuses to judge the ceremonies and rites she is
describing. The closest she comes to an evaluation is to suggest that perhaps she had gone "off in a trance." However, the very next sentence,
by its matter of fact statement, undoes the implied rationalization. Her
final pronouncement on the matter is an admission of ignorance—"I
don't know."

Clearly, there is an easy resolution to the ignorance. Did Zora ever
"walk invisible?" An answer to that question might help resolve the vexatious issue of whether Zora really felt the presence of supernatural
beings or was simply in a trance. But Zora never tells us the resolution
to the ceremony. We never know whether it is successful. Why does
Hurston withhold this information? The answer lies in Hurston's purpose in *Mules and Men* which, as has been argued, includes a critique of
the premise of ethnographic vision. For Hurston's purpose in this context, whether she walked invisible is irrelevant. What is relevant is the
refusal to bear witness according to conventional ideas of a certain kind
of anthropology. "Witnessing" is neither "objective" nor "innocent,"
but the fulfillment of a specific method of rendering an *other* culture. By
refusing to codify African American culture from the perspective of an
already prescribed role of the anthropological witness, Hurston critiques
ethnographic vision.

In all this, *Mules and Men* offers itself as a textual economy
counter to *Heart of Darkness*. Where Kurtz bearing witness to his fellow white man in the heart of Africa at the climactic moment in the text
confesses the horror of both his submission to savage rites and the rites
themselves, Hurston at a similar moment in *Mules and Men* confesses
only her ignorance and her inability to bear witness. *Mules and Men*

suggests the fallacies of that textual economy that *Heart of Darkness* is at pains to reestablish. It, despite Hurston's problematic conservative politics, manages to visualize a textual economy at the center of which lies a different anticolonialist (magical) praxis and offers itself as an alternative to the textual economy of *Heart of Darkness*, at the center of which lies a colonialist (rationalistic) praxis.

Thus, the same set of issues emerges as did in a preliminary way at the end of the second chapter. There we saw that the success of Swift's endeavor in subverting a colonialist textual economy was notable in the effectiveness with which he turns the commensurate evaluative structures on England itself. The subversion is achieved by a mimicking of the narratival structure (of the colonialist travel account) through a savage and exorbitant satire that exposes its allegiances. *Gulliver's Travels* imagines a possibility other than that offered by a colonialist textual economy, but it cannot imagine the content of this possibility. It cannot move beyond a formally reactive gesture. *GT*'s ironic rhetoric keeps a colonialist textual economy at the center; it sees its task as the systematic inversion of the assumptions of the colonialist travel narrative. In this, it bears an uncanny resemblance to Richard Terdiman's characterization of Stéphane Mallarmé's aesthetic, in *Discourse/Counter-Discourse*, as an "inversion machine" whose "function is to say the contrary" (332). The anticolonialist textual economy of *GT* remains, like that of Mallarmé's aesthetic, figural. A movement beyond the figural would have to go beyond a simple offering of the *possibility* of a different social order. It would have to sketch out the content of a social vision. This *GT* does not quite manage to do, perhaps because of the very excess of its satiric imagination; its sketch of a different social order is the impossible land of the horses. Its anticolonialist praxis remains parasitic, neither pointing to an achieved desirable condition nor sketching the future contours of such a condition.

An analysis of *Gulliver's Travels*, *Heart of Darkness*, and *Mules and Men* offers three different perspectives on the textual economy of the colonialist travel narrative, permitting us to distinguish between three different modes of praxis. While *Heart of Darkness* reasserts the colonialist textual economy (after hinting at an alternative in the aborted journey of Kurtz), both *Gulliver's Travels* and *Mules and Men* challenge such an economy's validity in very different ways at very different historical moments. In contrast to *Gulliver's Travels*, *Mules and Men* aspires to escape the colonialist textual economy altogether. *Mules and Men* clearly does not succeed because it repeatedly falls back on convenient stereotypes of "the folk" which have their origins, in fact, in a racist and segregationist ideology. It remains implicated with a colonialist textual economy by its errors of omission.

All three texts set up a contrast between a Home and an Out There through the narrative structure of the journeys that they articulate. "Home" is that to which the traveler owes allegiance. The relationship between "Home" and "Out There" is typically hierarchical. In traveling out from a "Home" and returning to it in a circular journey the traveler committed to a colonialist ideology produces "Home" as more valuable in contrast to "Out There." At the end of *Heart of Darkness*, London (Marlow's Home) appears as a "civilized" contrast to Africa. Where Africa is the very heart of darkness, London has only the barest vestiges of such darkness. Criticism sympathetic to Conrad has made much of his description of the sky over London as dark (*Heart of Darkness* 9) but, viewed in the context of a discourse of evolutionary developmentalism, London is well "advanced" on the ladder of civilization compared to Africa. If, on the one hand, *Heart of Darkness* produces the metropolitan space (of London) as the site of value, *Mules and Men* suggests the possibility of inverting the relationship to produce the actually existing Home of southern Afro America as more "valuable" than the metropolitan space (of New York). *Gulliver's Travels*, on the other hand, by inverting the relationship between England and an exorbitantly fictitious Out There, brings ironic scrutiny to the valued space of Home (England) itself without advancing an alternative content of value that is anything other than figural.

MODERNITY, THE PREMODERN AND MODERNISM

Colonialist and anticolonialist. Civilized and primitive. Such terms come to us still reeking of the world, still smelling of the praxis that is associated with them. The ideological intent captured by the suffixes of the former pair may convey this sense of praxis more readily than is the case with the latter. But it is not difficult to see that civilized and primitive do mark differing levels of praxis in such a text as *Heart of Darkness*.

In a famous passage in *Heart of Darkness*, Conrad's narrator Marlow is confronted by a sense of the incomprehensibility of Africa and Africans. Describing the jungles that face him as he is sailing up the river toward Kurtz, Marlow tells his audience: "The steamer toiled along slowly on the edge of a black and incomprehensible frenzy. The prehistoric man was cursing us, praying to us, welcoming us—who could tell?" (37). This is only the most explicit expression of that practical difference between himself and the Africans that Marlow discovers at every turn in "the dark continent." What is revealed in the process is a well-rehearsed method of managing alterity in colonialist textual economies. The radical disjuncture of alterity poses an epistemological problem for Marlow; it presents him with an entity apparently completely beyond the appropriative structure of his consciousness. The particular narrative of history that Marlow invokes in the same sentence, however, reassigns that constitutive difference-beyond-comprehension that confronts him to a position outside the margins of history. The African is "prehistoric man." What Marlow is telling us in his description of the African scene before him is that the scene is incomprehensible *because* it is prehistoric. History is the knowable, the recognizable, for Marlow; therefore, in that Western European linear conception of history that begins to acquire especial currency in the nineteenth century, Africa which proves itself unknowable must be outside of history. Marlow believes that the Africans are unknowable because they are prehistoric; I want to venture, however, that it is because Marlow finds them unknowable that he consigns them to a prehistory.

Furthermore, for Marlow, the difference between the prehistoric and the historic is a difference in degrees of praxis. Elsewhere in his narrative, Marlow is explicit about what is at issue. Referring to the cannibals he had engaged to work on the steamer, he declares, "I don't think a single one of them had any clear idea of time as we at the end of countless ages have. They still belonged to the beginnings of time—had no inherited experience to teach them" (42). At the end of *Heart of Darkness*, as noted above, London as civilization is contrasted to Africa. When viewed in the context of a Eurocentric view of history—as a particular kind of progressive development, as a particular kind of evolution of human praxis—Conrad's description of the sky over London as dark loses its significance as that much vaunted European self-criticism beloved of Conrad's defenders.

Walter Rodney in *How Europe Underdeveloped Africa* offers a pathbreaking critique of this Eurocentric view of history. First, in his book, he contests the view that precolonial Africa was "primitive" and stagnant. With painstaking care, he surveys the history of Africa to show that different parts of Africa had achieved significantly high levels of social, political, and economic organization and that many African societies had entered decisively on the stage of feudalism before the blighting impact of the slave trade and colonialism was laid on them. In this fashion, he counters the idea that historical agency was the preserve of European peoples. Development, he writes, is "an overall social process which is dependent upon the outcome of man's [sic] efforts to deal with his natural environment" (6). His careful survey of African history is meant to demonstrate that Africans have been no less resourceful in dealing with their natural environments than the Europeans. He is thus interested in restoring to Africans the status of historical agents, the kind of status often denied by colonialist ideology. He is interested in recovering for Africans the legacy of praxis ("inherited experience," if you will) denied them by Eurocentric historians.

Second, Rodney presents a carefully argued thesis that development is a dialectical phenomenon; societies do not develop in isolation but in relationship with one another. Development is expressive of not only the internal relations of a society but also its external relations. Since development is a universal but uneven phenomenon (that is, all human societies undergo development, but in different ways and at different paces), societies come in contact with one another when they are in different conditions of development. One society then enters into an exploitative relationship with the other and achieves its own development at the cost of the other. Rodney's term for the historical experience of the subjugated society is underdevelopment. He thus argues that contemporary Africa's "underdevelopment" is not the result of the inferior practical capabilities of Africans, genetic or otherwise, but rather the deviant historical path into which Africa as a continent was forced due to the accident of having come into contact with Europe when the two continents were in different conditions of development.

Where Conrad in *Heart of Darkness* sees the sources of African underdevelopment summarized within the reified if unclearly delineated figure of the "prehistoric man" (is he biologically prehistoric or culturally prehistoric?), Rodney locates the sources of this underdevelopment within the historical relationship between Europe and Africa. Implied in his thesis is the idea that if Europe had not intervened so disastrously in Africa, Africa would have progressed on an appropriate path of development on its own. Thus, for example, in a passage cited earlier in this chapter, Rodney argues that the Belgian Congo's entire economy is transformed by the peculiar and ultimately destructive demands made on the region by the ivory trade. Conrad, on the other hand, not only empties the history of the Congo of this specific detail, he also empties it of any larger acknowledgment of "how Europe [as a whole and not just Belgium] underdeveloped Africa."

In this fashion, Walter Rodney's attention to history as a record of human praxis contests an entire way of seeing Africa as backward, underdeveloped, in a word, premodern, that Conrad's *Heart of Darkness*, in however complicated a fashion, reproduces. Rodney's historiography does this by redefining the meaning of the word "underdeveloped." Rodney is troubled by the view of Africa implied in the discourse of developmentalism; but it must be acknowledged that he cannot see his way out of this discourse. For all his criticism of the particular way in which such a discourse is applied to Africa, he consents to a developmentalist view of history. He only wants to set right racist versions of the African record in such a history and to offer certain theoretical corrections that can still be contained within the general rubric of a developmentalist view of history.

Three decades after Rodney a considerable critique of the discourse of development is now in existence—carried out mostly from a perspective different from that of Rodney and situated completely outside the discourse itself. Ashis Nandy, Vandana Shiva, and Claude Alvares in India, for example, have offered profound and polemical denunciations of developmentalism, and modernity as its prescribed telos, that draw, in a variety of more or less sophisticated ways, on traditions that may be considered indigenous.[21] In a broadly similar spirit, Arturo Escobar has set out a self-confessedly Foucauldian critique of developmentalism in his recent book *Encountering Development*. Because of the greater determination with which these scholars move beyond developmentalism, their works can certainly be read as departures from the more limited critique of developmentalism on the part of Rodney. However, as Escobar admits in the conclusion to his book, alternatives to development remain hard to imagine. Rodney and these other scholars offer critiques, radical in different ways, of developmentalism. Whether Rodney is misguided in not wanting to discard a developmentalist view of history, aiming only to reimagine it in a more authentic way, remains to be seen. Possibly, the present historical conjuncture will not allow a conclusive answer to this question.

From the passage from *Heart of Darkness* quoted above, it also appears that the modernity of Marlow and London becomes recognizable only because of its difference from the premodernity of the Africans and the Congo. If, as suggested above, it is because Marlow finds the Africans unknowable that he consigns them to a prehistory, it would appear that the separation of the modern from the premodern is fundamentally constituted across a racial and ethnic divide. It is in this sense that it might be accurate to call this modernity a colonial modernity, since the content of it issues out of an experience of the opaqueness of racial and ethnic difference in a colonial context. Modernity or civilized society (to use Conrad's term) or developed society (to use Rodney's term) is also a sign here, as Rodney so clearly realizes, of the degree to which societies as a whole can transform or have transformed the environments in which they live. Rodney postulates this as the measure of development; Conrad assumes something similar as the measure of civilization when he has Marlow declare that the cannibals "still belonged to the beginnings of time—had no inherited experience to teach them" and thus had no record of doing to draw on. Modernity (or either one of its approximate synonyms) is here the cryptic sign of superior historical agency, of superior (human) praxis. It might be asserted, then, that Rodney's anticolonialist historiography, basing itself on different criteria, assesses the praxis of Africans differently, while Conrad's colonialist travel narrative is willfully skeptical of a rich notion of African praxis. The corollary of this assertion might also be pointed out: in the ways in which Rodney and Conrad thematize the praxis of Africans and Europeans within their texts is to be found an index to the praxis of which their texts are expressive.

A review of Manning Marable's *How Capitalism Underdeveloped Black America* offers a similar contrast to *Mules and Men*. In his book, Marable adapts Rodney's thesis to the specific case of the history of African Americans, suggesting that the development of capitalism within the United States required the concomitant underdevelopment of the African American community: "Blacks have never been equal partners in the American social contract, because the system exists not to develop, but to *underdevelop Black people*" (2, italics in text). American underdevelopment of the African American community produced a schism between a Black working-class and underclass majority and a Black elite minority, distinguished by color and caste (24). The Black majority provided labor to be used within the capitalist economy of the United States. For most of this history of Black underdevelopment, such labor was used in a rural economy in the South, policed first by slavery and then by a Jim Crow law.

It is this social milieu in the early twentieth century that provides Hurston with her setting in most of her works. Hurston's account of life in this milieu in *Mules and Men* is, as noted above, in contrast to the historiography of Marable. Hurston does not so much hide the violence and poverty of life in the segregationist South as present that life, encapsulated in the "lies" that she collects, as the authentic expression of, in Hazel Carby's words, "a metaphysical 'folk'" (164–65). Carby feels that the construction of such a "folk" allows Hurston in her works to elide many questions relating to the class confrontation between a Black elite and a Black majority that followed the great migration to the North. Hurston, it would seem then, evacuates what Marable has called the history of African American underdevelopment to replace it with a utopic construction called the "folk."

It is true that Hurston abjures (at least in *Mules and Men*) the kind of developmentalist view of history that Marable endorses. Although Hurston is not very consistent on this point, her refusal on many occasions to offer a "rationalist" assessment of the hoodoo rites that she describes can be seen as an attempt to counter a rationalist, "modern" view of "superstition." Hurston's Zora, writing from within that opaqueness that so baffles Conrad's Marlow, for the most part successfully refuses the seductions of colonial modernity. This successful stratagem, however, is achieved at the cost of a virtual abstraction of the black "folk" from history, from any meaningful practical context. If there are ruptures in the abstracted utopic picture that Hurston wishes to create, it is because the hard materiality of this practical history, visible for example in the very clothes worn by Hurston's interlocutors in Polk county, is too enormous to be dissolved by such a stratagem.[22] In Conrad's novella the visible signs of a similar history (the clothes of the fireman) are efficiently placed in the service, through parody, of the construction of the "premodern." If a reading of Conrad's novella reveals the colonial dimensions of modernity, a reading of *Mules and Men* suggests the dangers of a facile rejection of the very idea of modernity. To reject uncritically the idea of modernity might be to reject history itself, with its concomitant associations of progress, with its promise of liberation. Such a rejection might quickly become a full-fledged flight from history as a record of praxis into the kind of myth that Roland Barthes analyzes in *Mythologies*.[23]

Between the prehistoric of *Heart of Darkness* and the folk of *Mules and Men*, then, lies colonial modernity. Conrad's fictional travel narrative fully embraces such a modernity, raising questions, because of his vaunted expression of an emerging modernism, regarding modernism itself.[24] Modernism has commonly been seen as a reaction against modernity. "Modernist innovation," Randall Stevenson suggests, "results at least as much from an urge to resist as to reflect changes in contemporary life. . . . [F]rom a need to compensate for—rather than just represent—new conditions in modern experience" (14–15). In addition to resistance and reflection, compensation and representation, modernism was often, a reading of *Heart of Darkness* suggests, an active endorsement of a (colonial) modernity. Modernism was indeed a complex response to "new conditions in modern experience," but it endorsed some besides reflecting some others and rejecting still others.

Georg Lukacs, much more than Randall Stevenson, arrives at a negative assessment of modernism. For him, modernism is the evocation of "a primitive awe in the presence of an utterly strange and hostile reality," that is, modernity ("The Ideology of Modernism" 36). A reading of *Heart of Darkness*, and indeed Conrad's works in general, suggests that modernism often worked to exorcize this awe by uncovering an even more strange and hostile reality in colonized realms such as Africa. Though "Man [*sic*] [conceived as] . . . an ahistorical being" is a central tenet of modernism in his view, Georg Lukacs admits "[a] gifted writer, however extreme his theoretical modernism, will in practice have to compromise with the demands of historicity and social environment" ("The Ideology of Modernism" 21). In such a text as *Heart of Darkness*, modernism's flight from history finds itself severely compromised. Conrad's elliptical style, his focus on an internal, psychological drama, his recourse to myth and allegory—all the elements of his modernism—are shown in a textual economic reading of his text to be resolutely framed by the developmental narrative of a *colonial* modernity that makes a strange and hostile European reality more agreeable by valuing it in contrast to the even more strange and hostile reality of Africa. European praxis is contrasted to (the absence of) African praxis and thus invested with value.

If Conrad's fictional travel narrative can be said to have embraced a colonial modernity, Hurston's "factual" travel narrative attempts to ignore it. *Mules and Men* is both a counter to the textual economy of the colonialist travel narrative and an attempt at a journey beyond the ideological perimeter of a colonial modernity. The consequences of this brave journey, represented as the journey of Zora, are deeply ambiguous

in effect and raise other questions for modernism, understood as an ideological response to modernity. Caught on the other side of a colonial
modernity from Joseph Conrad, Hurston arrives at a different assessment of it. Participating in a "black discursive modernism" constituted
as a negotiation of what Houston Baker calls "mastery of form" and
"deformation of mastery"—negotiation of the form of the minstrel
mask, that any articulate African American had to master, and of the
subsequent transformation of such mastery—Hurston resists and
reflects modernity in very different ways.[25] Unlike Conrad's European
modernism, Hurston's black modernism aspires much more unambigu-
ously to participate in the countercultural opposition to a (colonial)
modernity. It would appear, however, that it remains incomplete in its
attempted transformation of the form of the mask of minstrelsy handed
down in traditional black accommodation to a (colonial) modernity.

CHAPTER FOUR

WRIGHT AND WRONG
IN A LAND OF PATHOS

The previous chapter inaugurated a substantial engagement with the argument regarding colonialism and modernity by taking up two texts from the period of high colonialism. On the one hand, we found that Joseph Conrad's *Heart of Darkness* reproduced colonialist ideology through an evaluative structure that transfers value in the direction of Europe. Zora Neale Hurston's *Mules and Men*, on the other hand, exemplified a textual economy counter to the colonialist travel narrative. Her account betrayed a desire to escape the colonialistic structures of evaluation of the dominant genre. This textual economic reading permitted us to recognize the colonial dimensions of modernity—a modernity founded on a presumption of radical racial alterity and racialized evaluation of varieties of (human) praxis—and also, consequently, the modes of praxis of which the texts of Conrad and Hurston are expressive. The current chapter expands this argument by turning to a travel account produced by an African American traveler to Africa in the middle of the twentieth century.

It is by now a commonplace of African American literary scholarship to compare the careers of Richard Wright and Zora Neale Hurston and find in their works two different (and opposing) expressions of African American attitude toward the effects of slavery, segregation, and oppression. If Zora Neale Hurston insisted on the autonomy and irreducible humanity of the African American experience in her novels and nonfictional writings, Wright in his most celebrated books, *Native Son* and *Black Boy*, delineated the relentless limitations imposed on African

Americans by the structure of segregation and racism within which they existed. In this way of thinking, Wright and Hurston symbolize contrasting traditions of African American literary practice.

Although Wright's work and career have never been marked by that obscurity and disinterest from which, as we saw in the previous chapter, Hurston's texts had to be rescued, his vision of the African American condition has been powerfully contested by important African American writers. Both James Baldwin and Ralph Ellison criticized, often in an excoriating manner, what they considered the deplorable limitations of Wright's artistic and political imagination. Echoing the sentiments of his own famous response, entitled "The World and the Jug," to Irving Howe's positive assessment of Wright, Ellison noted in an interview:

> When I came to discover a little more what I wanted to express I felt that Wright was overcommitted to ideology—even though I, too, wanted many of the same things for our people. You might say that I was much less a social determinist. But I suppose that basically comes down to a difference in our concepts of the individual. I, for instance, found it disturbing that Bigger Thomas [the protagonist of *Native Son*] had none of the finer qualities of Richard Wright . . . ("That Same Pain, That Same Pleasure" 16)

In a number of controversial essays on Wright, his erstwhile mentor, James Baldwin arrives at a similar assessment.[1]

It is the perception that Wright is a "programmatic" writer (initially, in the service of Communism) that has led to the discontent that these successors to Wright feel about his work.[2] Being contested here is the nature of the historical experience of African Americans—the very ground of Ellison's quarrel with Wright in the passage quoted above. When Ellison observes the lack of correspondence between Richard Wright and Bigger Thomas, he is suggesting that Wright's weddedness to certain programmatic social perspectives has made him distort an important aspect of the African American experience. Asking the question whether Bigger Thomas is an accurate symbolic representation of African American experience, Ellison finds himself forced to reply that he is not. "Much of the Afro-American literary tradition can, in a real sense," Henry Louis Gates has noted,

> be read as successive attempts to create a new narrative space for representing the recurrent referent of Afro-American literature—the

so-called black experience. Certainly, this is the way we read the relation of Sterling Brown's regionalism to Toomer's lyricism, Hurston's
lyricism to Wright's naturalism and, equally, Ellison's modernism to
Wright's naturalism. ("The Blackness of Blackness" 295)

Often, this issue of representation has been posed as a reductive choice
between affirmation and protest; but in "On Richard Wright and Zora
Neale Hurston: Notes Toward a Balancing of Love and Hatred," June
Jordan points out the falsity of such a forced choice, asserting "that the
functions of protest and affirmation are not, ultimately, distinct: that,
for instance, affirmation of Black values and lifestyle within the American context is, indeed, an act of protest. Therefore, Hurston's affirmative work is profoundly defiant, just as Wright's protest unmistakably
asserts our need for an alternative, benign environment" (8).

In *Black Power: A Record of Reactions in a Land of Pathos*
(1954), Richard Wright turns his protesting gaze on a dimension of the
black experience that he had not previously explored in any great detail.
Like *Mules and Men* in the previous chapter, *Black Power* is a travel narrative, an account of Wright's journey to the Gold Coast during the summer of 1953, four years before the achievement of Independence by that
country.[3] During his stay in the Gold Coast, Wright not only witnesses
at first hand the activities of Kwame Nkrumah's Convention People's
Party as it campaigns for the achievement of full independence, but also
explores (as the subtitle to the book suggests) his "reactions" to Africa.[4]

Wright's title to his book acquires an especial resonance for readers who come to the text after the sixties, when the "Black Power"
movement gave the term popular currency. Wright's text, of course, pre-
dates the Black Power movement by more than a decade. In Wright, the
term is meant to indicate the nationalist drive to achieve state power in
the Gold Coast. It is interesting to note in this context the nationalist
overtones of the Black Power movement of the sixties. Perhaps indepen-
dently, the same phrase is applied to the nationalist aspirations of two
different black populations which are, after all, linked by that diasporic
community Paul Gilroy has felicitously christened the black Atlantic.
What this correspondence also suggests is the continuities of language
and praxis in the African American political tradition. As C. L. R. James
asserted in a laudatory essay on Kwame Turé entitled "Black Power":
"Stokely [Kwame Turé] and the advocates of Black Power stand on the
shoulders of all that has gone before. . . . [T]oo many people see Black

Power and its advocates as some sort of portent, a sudden appari-
tion. . . . It is nothing of the kind" (367). The two uses of the same
phrase are linked by the complex evolution of political praxis in the
modern black world from Marcus Garvey to Nelson Mandela. Wright's
own "protest literature" is a part of this political praxis. The special
challenges posed for it by the Africa encountered by Wright the traveler
is the subject of this chapter.

TRADITION AND MODERNITY

In the previous chapter, it was argued that the valuation of the West (or
Europe in the case of *Heart of Darkness*) as modern in a colonialist textual economy is inextricably linked to the devaluation of the Rest as
mired in various stages of premodernity. The production of a Western
modernity renders it a colonial modernity, a modernity that has its
roots in colonialism, among other historical phenomena. This formulation, it can now be suggested, points to the inadequacy of understanding the roots of this modernity as exclusively capitalist. In *The Black
Atlantic: Modernity and Double-Consciousness*, Paul Gilroy makes a
similar argument. He proposes that the emergence of modernity in the
West is not separable from the history of modern slavery. Through a
brilliant reading of Hegel's famous passage on the master-slave dialectic, he locates the contest between the master and the slave at the very
root of modernity. Declaring his disagreement with Jurgen Habermas's
influential defence of the Enlightenment project of modernity, Gilroy
writes that he is drawn to the passage from Hegel because "it points
directly to an approach which sees the intimate association of modernity and slavery as a fundamental conceptual issue . . . and because it
provides an opportunity to re-periodise and reaccentuate accounts of
the dialectic of enlightenment which have not always been concerned to
look at modernity through the lenses of colonialism and scientific
racism" (53). In this same section of the book, he goes on to add that
Hegel's allegory simultaneously reveals the brutality and terror that is
foundational to modernity.

Proceeding from this critical reformulation of modernity, Gilroy
examines articulations of what he calls a counterculture to modernity
by intellectuals and artists of the black Atlantic who find themselves
within the modern West but not necessarily of it. These contestatory

expressions, by such figures as W. E. B. Dubois and Frederick Douglass, question such features of modernity as its rationalism and its universalism. Where, for example, Hegel's allegory suggests that the slave, out of rational calculation, prefers submission to death, Douglass, in the account of his struggle with Covey found in all three of his autobiographies, prefers death to submission. He thus reveals a structure of values different from the rational calculation typical of modernity. It can be seen from Gilroy's argument that Hurston's project in *Mules and Men* can also be understood as the elaboration of a counterculture to modernity.

Gilroy's examination of the Hegelian allegory and the various alternative perspectives on modernity that are opposed to it are insightful in revealing the agonism that lies encoded within ideas of modernity. Modernity, it appears from Hegel's allegory, is struggle ending in discipline. But we can also see how such a view of modernity can quickly shift to an endorsement of revolution, struggle to subvert discipline. It is to Gilroy's credit that in his reading of Hegel's allegory he makes visible in this fashion the significance of "revolution" to the experience of modernity. At the same time, Gilroy's reading of this allegory in his book also allows him to make a persuasive argument regarding the limits of the modern project, the inequality that is constitutively present at the core of modernity.

It must be said, however, that though Gilroy alludes critically a number of times to what he calls at one point "the mesmeric idea of history as progress" (53), he leaves unanalyzed for the most part the invention of historical pasts by the proponents of Western modernity themselves. What is meant by this may be explained in the following way. Toward the end of his book, Gilroy examines the invention of pre-modern pasts as forms of antimodernity by black intellectuals critical of modernity. In this case, premodernity is a challenge to modernity. However, Gilroy is more concerned, except for the initial stages of his argument, with the black countercultures of modernity rather than modernity itself, and so he does not examine how the invention of premodern non-Western pasts by Western apologists (like Conrad) can become corroborations of a Western modernity within a colonial context.

This lack of attention to what is after all a well-acknowledged feature of modernity is significant. It takes us directly to the issue of Gilroy's curiously dissatisfying reading of Wright's travel books, of

which *Black Power* is one. "I want to make some claims for the value of
these travel books," Gilroy writes, "which offer much more than a series
of failed attempts to make the condition of chronic rootlessness habit-
able. Without necessarily accepting any of Wright's conclusions, it seems
possible to view this body of work as an extended exercise in intercul-
tural hermeneutics. . . . In the case of the most controversial volume,
Black Power, he produced a deliberate, if ultimately unsuccessful,
attempt to articulate his critical self-understanding with the difficult
work of accessible political, social, and historical analysis" (150). The
second sentence in this passage betrays Gilroy's desire to retrieve Wright
from the indefensible positions that he recognizes Wright often adopts. I
wish to quarrel a little with the manner in which Gilroy goes about exe-
cuting this retrieval. This is so despite my general agreement with Gilroy's
concluding assessment of his subject in his chapter on Wright: "Perhaps
more than any other writer he showed how modernity was both the
period and the region in which black politics grew. His work articulates
simultaneously an affirmation and a negation of the western civilisation
that formed him. It remains the most powerful expression of the insider-
outsider duality which we have traced down the years from slavery"
(186). As the discussion of *Black Power* below will show, it is possible to
endorse this assessment of Wright. Where I differ is in assessing the
details of Wright's affirmation and negation of Western civilization.

      Gilroy is interested in Wright's assessment of himself as a modern
black man in as well as of the West. This interest is of a piece with
Gilroy's general concern in his book with a diasporic black community
spread out in the West. It leads him to track with great astuteness, as in
the case of the Hegelian allegory alluded to above, the racial relationships internally constitutive of a Western modernity. Thus, Gilroy writes
approvingly of Wright's work that "In Wright's mature position, the
Negro is no longer just America's metaphor but rather a central symbol
in the psychological, cultural, and political systems of the West as a
whole. . . . The transmutation of the African into the Negro is shown to
be central to western civilisation, especially to the primitive, irrational,
and mystical elements in European culture that Wright would seek to
explore in *Pagan Spain*" (159–60). In this fashion, Gilroy assimilates
Wright's work to his diasporic black canon of modernity's counterculture and suggests that this work offers a revision of Western modernity.
Admittedly, Gilroy recognizes Wright's ambivalence in this regard, but
he nevertheless underestimates the significance of this ambivalence.

What happens to the African who is not transmuted into a Negro, who is not transported by way of the middle passage to "America?" Gilroy is not interested in this question in *The Black Atlantic*. Such a lack of interest in the fate of the African who remains in Africa, which arises from Gilroy's theoretical commitment to the disentangling of a black diasporic community from a disabling obsession with Africa as origin, leads him then to ignore the many ways in which Wright's travel books also reproduce a rather clichéd, Western view of not only Africa but of the "Third World." In them, it becomes clear that "tradition," often opposed to modernity as its critical counterculture as Gilroy recognizes, can at the same time be used to justify a disciplining modernity. There is both sympathy for Africa and hostility to the West in Wright's travel books; but the full complexity of Wright's ambivalence in holding these attitudes are comprehensible only if we are attentive not only to the largely slave modernity that Gilroy explicates in *The Black Atlantic* but the colonial modernity explored in this book. The gaps in Gilroy's reading of *Black Power* suggest that "modernity" cannot adequately be grasped either according to its "internal" or its "external" relationships exclusively. Some of Wright's other works from the same period in his career give us clues to an exploration of precisely these gaps in Gilroy's account of *Black Power*.

OUTSIDE IN HISTORY

Richard Wright's *The Outsider* (1953) is the story of Cross Damon, a disillusioned black man in Chicago, who takes the opportunity of a train crash that he is involved in to change his identity and disappear in the attempt to remake his life. In New York, under an assumed identity, he joins up with some Communists and finds himself in the midst of a cynical contest for power between Communists and a segregationist. Watching the world with the new freedom that the veil of his assumed identity gives him, Damon comes to a number of realizations regarding the human condition and the exercise of power. Both the Communists and the segregationists, Damon realizes, have understood the meaninglessness of life. Their exercise of power is an attempt to fill the void of human existence. This insight into the meaninglessness of life, Damon concludes, is what permits the monstrously efficient exercise of power on the part of Communists and segregationists. In his anger at this situation, Damon kills both Herndon, the Southern racist, and Blount, the Communist. As these murders lead him on to other murders, Damon ironically begins to confront his own arbitrary exercise of power.

The Outsider, even echoing Camus's L'Etranger in its title, can be read as an existentialist novel. Published during Wright's exile in Paris, external evidence strongly invites such a reading. However, the specific concept of "the outsider" as it is set forth by Wright in his novel is more relevant to the argument in this book. In the novel, "the outsider" is posited by Wright as a historical category. Outsiders in the novel are people who have understood the meaninglessness of life and are, there-fore, able to detach themselves from the systemic functioning of power and view it from the "outside." Such outsiders may themselves engage in the cynical exercise of power, as do the Communists, or may struggle with the very cynicism of such power, as do Damon and Ely Houston, the humpbacked white district attorney who befriends Damon and then hunts him down.

In a long declamation toward the end of the novel about totalitar-ian systems and their attempt to fight against and restrict the meaning-lessness of life, Damon observes that "As long as this works, it's wonderful. The only real enemies of this system are not the rats [who are controlled] themselves, but those outsiders who are conscious of what is happening and who seek to change the consciousness of the rats who are being controlled" (The Outsider 362–63). The outsider, in Wright's novel, is the privileged possessor of an uncommon knowledge regarding power and society, as well as the agent capable of acting on this knowledge—the outsiders are agents of change. The consciously abstract and metaphysical nature of Wright's argument has led John M. Reilly to suggest in "Richard Wright and the Art of Non-Fiction" that The Outsider is the expression of Wright's disillusionment with politics. Reilly argues that, in the nonfictional texts (Black Power, The Color Curtain, 1956, and White Man Listen!, 1957) that succeed The Out-sider, the completely individualistic philosophy that Wright tested in the Cross Damon of The Outsider, during the time of his "crisis," is super-seded by his discovery of the "entry into conscious history" of the "Third World" (519).

Reilly's argument regarding an evolution in Wright's thought beyond the individualism of The Outsider to a renewed commitment to politics is certainly plausible. The enthusiasm with which Wright explores the politics of decolonization in the three nonfictional texts is evidence for Reilly's assessment. However, there is also a continuity between the metaphysical meditation of *The Outsider* and the interpretation of history in the later nonfictional works. This point can be best made by turning to Wright's dedication to *White Man, Listen!* The book is dedicated to Eric Williams, prime minister of Trinidad at that time and an important political figure in the black diaspora, and to "the Westernized and tragic elite of Asia, Africa, and the West Indies—the lonely outsiders who exist precariously on the clifflike margins of many cultures—men who are distrusted, misunderstood, maligned, criticized by left and right, Christian and pagan—men who carry on their frail but indefatigable shoulders the best of two worlds" (7). Like the outsiders of the novel, "the Westernized and tragic elite" of the "Third World," on whom Wright depends for leadership during the process of decolonization, possess privileged access to knowledge. This knowledge is a direct consequence of the elite's existence "on the margins of many cultures." Invoking the metaphor of home (whose significance is well-known to us by now) at this point, the dedication goes on to describe the elite as "men" who "seek desperately for a home for their hearts: a home which, if found, could be a home for the hearts of all men" (7). Alienation becomes the source not only of knowledge but also of political action of profound historical consequence.[5]

Wright's "tragic elite," it can now be seen, are ideological exiles. In this they mirror Wright's conception of himself. "I'm a rootless man," Wright tells his reader in the introduction to *White Man, Listen!*, ". . . I declare unabashedly that I like and even cherish the state of abandonment, of aloneness. . . . [I]t seems to me the natural, inevitable condition of man [sic], and I welcome it. I can make myself at home almost anywhere on this earth" (17). Living as an expatriate in Paris and exploring the politics of decolonization, Wright discovers in the metaphors of home and exile a semantic field through which to articulate the politics of decolonization. In his own physical and mental condition he finds a connection to the ideological condition of the "tragic elite" of the "Third World." This connection between himself and the "tragic elite" is rendered more meaningful because as a black man Wright too exists, in some important respects, outside the ambit of Western culture. Ely Houston, the district attorney, expresses this idea to Cross Damon in *The Outsider* when he suggests that "Negroes as they enter our [American] culture . . . are going to be both *inside* and *outside* of our culture at the same time" (129, italics in original). Recognizing the importance

of "the outsider" in Wright's later work, Wright's biographer Constance
Webb notes, "For many years the theme of the outsider was one of
Richard's favorites. . . . These [the outsiders] were the men dangerous to
the status quo, for the outsider was one who no longer responded to the
values of the system in which he lived" (313).

"Outsider," "home," "exile," "struggle"—these are some of the
key terms that make up the conceptual baggage that Wright takes to the
Gold Coast with him in 1953. These terms find resonance in two earlier
titles that Wright suggested for the text that was finally published as
Black Power. One of the titles was "Stranger in Africa"; the other was
"Ancestral Home" (Fabre, *Unfinished Quest* 401 and 404, respectively).
The two previous titles identify two important dimensions of *Black
Power*. The evaluative structures of Wright's travel narrative work to
bring the "stranger" to his "ancestral home" and suggest an interesting
resolution to his experiences there.

The Stranger in His Ancestral Home

Soon after his arrival in the Gold Coast, Wright drives into James Town,
the slum section of Accra, with Nkrumah. Here he witnesses from the
car some women dancing in a manner that seems strangely familiar to
him. "And then I remembered: I'd seen these same snakelike, veering
dances before . . ." Wright tells us. "Where? Oh, God, yes; in America,
in storefront churches, in Holy Roller Tabernacles, in God's Temples, in
unpainted wooden prayer-meeting houses on the plantations of the Deep
South . . ." (*Black Power* 56). Bewildered by this sudden echo from his
personal past, Wright is forced to confess, "I'd doubted that I'd be able
to walk into the African's cultural house and feel at home and know my
way around. Yet what I was now looking at in this powerfully impro-
vised dance of these women, I'd seen before in America!" (57). Thus,
Wright confronts early in *Black Power* the question of the meaning of
his African ancestry. The semantics of this ancestry are potent territory
for Wright. Thinking about the incident of the dancers the next day, he
writes, "That there was some kind of link between the native African
and the American Negro was undoubtedly true. But what did it mean?"
(66). The issue of a connection between Africa and African Americans
comes up often in *Black Power*. In the bus going from Takoradi to
Accra, the landscape with its "rich red" soil and black figures going

about their work reminds him of the American South (36). In the Old Slave Market Castle in Christianborg, Wright meets a Mr. Hagerson who is the descendant of slaves and finds in Mr. Hagerson's features and bearing the reflection of his grandfather (181).

A comparison can be made here with another book by an African American writer traveling in Ghana. In Maya Angelou's *All God's Children Need Traveling Shoes*, too, there is a scene similar to the one in which Wright recognizes his grandfather's features in Mr. Hagerson. *All God's Children Need Traveling Shoes* is the account of Maya Angelou's stay in Ghana in the early sixties, about a decade after Wright's own journey to the country when it was still called the Gold Coast.[6] Toward the end of her long stay in Ghana, Angelou travels to a part of the country that she has not been to before. In Eastern Ghana, Angelou undergoes two strange experiences. The scene of surprised recognition similar to Wright's occurs on the narrow stairs leading up to the raised market in the town of Keta. There, on the stairs, Angelou is confronted by a woman who mistakes her for the daughter of a friend. When Angelou does not respond to her repeated queries (in Ewe, which Angelou does not understand), the woman begins to get angry. Mr. Adadevo, one of Angelou's companions, has to intervene at this point and Angelou has to produce her California driver's license as evidence of her identity. The woman, finally convinced by the massive force of the California state authority's interpellation of Angelou as a subject, takes her then to be introduced to her friends as the descendant of lost slaves from that region. As the woman leads her up from the dark stairs into the light above, Angelou is astounded to recognize her grandmother's features in the woman's face (203–5). A similar scene had preceded this one— Angelou's unaccountable disquiet on approaching Keta bridge. As the car approaches the bridge, Angelou begins to get so uneasy that she finally makes the driver stop the car and walks across the bridge. Once on the other side, Mr. Adadevo asks her if she has heard of the story of the Keta bridge. When she replies in the negative, Mr. Adadevo tells her that until about a century before the bridges in the region were so badly constructed that people were afraid to cross them in any kind of conveyance. Since it was easier in the event of a mishap to reach the other side if you were on foot, the passengers would commonly dismount from the conveyance and walk across (199–200).

The remarkable similarity between the scenes of recognition recorded by Wright and by Angelou does not, however, lead to a similar interpretation of the scenes by the two writers. For Angelou, her two experiences in Eastern Ghana become evidence of a fundamental link between herself and her African past that goes beyond the rationalizing ground of "history." This is the implicit message of the incident on the bridge especially, when Angelou experiences a transhistorical, nonpersonal memory. Considering Angelou's presentation of her link to Africa serves to illustrate the immense difficulty that Wright experiences when faced by this same issue. The comfort that Angelou finds in the connection to Africa is never Wright's. In the conclusion to her book, Angelou writes with potent double-meaning as she describes her departure from Ghana: "Many years earlier I, or rather someone very like me and certainly related to me, had been taken from Africa by force. This second leave-taking would not be so onerous, for now I knew my people had never completely left Africa" (209).

The ground of Angelou's transhistorical link to Africa through "my people" is race and it is precisely race that Wright does not, cannot, have recourse to in his exploration of his link to Africa. This point is explicitly made by Wright in an exchange that he has with Dr. J. B. Danquah, author of *The Akan Doctrine of God* and one of Nkrumah's leading opponents. When Danquah says to Wright that if he were to "stay longer" he would "*feel*" his race and a "knowledge" of it would "come *back*" to him, Wright replies "I doubt that" and notes "I know that I'd never feel an identification with Africans on a 'racial' basis" (218–19, italics in original). And, indeed, such a feeling based on his race—a feeling that Maya Angelou experiences—never does "come back" to Wright in *Black Power*. What comes instead is an insight regarding culture. In culture, a ground contained within history, Wright finds the connection between himself as an African American from Mississippi and the Africans. "The question of how much African culture an African retains when transplanted to a new environment is not a racial, but a cultural problem, cutting across such tricks as measuring of skulls and intelligence tests," Wright notes (266). This is not a surprising resolution of the issue for Wright the rationalist. Wright's Marxist background leads him to look for a historical resolution to the question of the connection between Africa and himself. Successfully countering the seductions of the rhetoric of race, Wright remains a stranger in Africa in a way in which Maya Angelou, who discovers a mystic community through "race," does not.

There are other, related aspects to Wright's self-identification as a stranger in Africa that we can specify from various comments that

he makes in *Black Power*. Wright is of the West, as he himself repeatedly insists, and it is his acute consciousness of this aspect of his identity that causes him to adopt the attitude to Africa that he does.
Whatever his critical attitude to the West in other respects, Wright's
self-identification as someone *inside* the West is dramatically foregrounded in his travel books. Thus, in a statement like, "Today the
ruins of their [the Akan people's] former culture, no matter how cruel
and barbarous it may seem to *us*, are reflected in timidity, hesitancy,
and bewilderment," we find Wright ranging himself quite explicitly on
the side of the West, addressing a like-minded audience that is of the
West (153, italics added).

Another scene of dancing, also in James Town, serves to bring
home to Wright the Westerner this acute sense of his difference from the
Africans (125–27). Poking about in the alleyways of that slum area of
Accra, Wright discovers a compound in which men and women are
dancing in the dark to the beat of drums. "What's going on in there?"
he asks a man who is about to enter the compound. When the young
man observes, "You're a stranger, aren't you?" Wright's reply is, "Yes;
I'm an American." The young man invites Wright into the compound
and Wright observes the dancers "moving slowly, undulating their
abdomens, their eyes holding a faraway look." Wright wants to know
why they are dancing and is told that a girl has just died. Wright cannot
understand this explanation. "I still didn't know why they were dancing
and I wanted to ask him a third time," he writes. Some time later Wright
leaves, his confusion at the funeral dancers with "no sadness or joy in
their faces" uncleared. His final comment on this episode is, "I had
understood nothing. I was black and they were black, but my blackness
did not help me."

A comparison of this scene and the passage from *Heart of Darkness* discussed in the previous chapter—where Marlow pronounces
Africans prehistoric—illustrates what is at issue here. Conrad's narrator Marlow is also confronted by a sense of the incomprehensibility of
Africa and Africans. In Marlow's description of the jungles of Africa
is revealed a well-rehearsed method of managing alterity in colonialist discourse. The epistemological problem that the radical disjuncture of alterity poses for Marlow is managed by a particular narrative
that reassigns Africa and its constitutive difference-beyond-comprehension to a position outside the margins of a history regarded as a
record of (human) praxis. Asserting the chaotic incomprehensibility

of Africa, Marlow's narrative exiles Africa beyond the margins of ordered human existence. By simultaneously inserting Africa in a particular relationship with Europe, expressed in a particular linear conception of history, it establishes an evaluative structure that transfers value to Europe.

Although *Black Power* taken as a whole works toward a less reductive idea of Africa, we may find traces of a similar evaluative structure in Wright the Westerner's comments about Africa. Trying to make sense, like Marlow, of the difference of Africa, Wright suggests a resolution that is similar in some ways and different in others. "The tribal African's culture *is* primally human," Wright argues in theorizing the relationship of Africans to other peoples, and goes on to add— "that which *all* men [*sic*] once had as their warm, indigenous way of living, is his" (266, italics in original). Here, in Wright's idea of the primal or the primitive as some kind of a "common denominator" of humanity, the sense of Marlow's prehistory returns surreptitiously: the African is what all "men" are to some extent.[7] What is left unstated but dangerously implicit is the suggestion that that is all the African is but others, through a process of historical evolution, have become more. Thus, an echo of Conrad's endorsement of a colonial modernity is to be found in *Black Power*. This complex rendering of Africa and Africans is Wright's own way of "making sense" of all those incomprehensible details about Africa that confront him again and again. It allows him both to render Africa and Africans as different and to place them in a narrative of world evolution which, in its turn, allows him now to make greater sense of the West of which he ambivalently considers himself a part.

Wright's typographical insistence on a community between "*all* men" reveals his consciousness of how slippery indeed this evolutionary slope is. Yet, like many other Western travelers to Africa before him, he too evaluates, however self-reflexively, the continent in a stereotypical manner. "The distance today between tribal man and the West is greater than the distance between God and Western man of the sixteenth century" declares Wright at one point (117). Such is the distance that Wright both feels acutely as a Westerner himself and tries to overcome as a black man writing about other black people. Wright's rationalism suggests to him the problems in turning to "race" as a category for explaining his own relationship to Africa. At the same time, Wright has recourse to a certain conception of history. In both Walter Rodney's

How Europe Underdeveloped Africa and Richard Wright's *Black Power*, there is a linear conception of history derived from Marxism. Rodney's thesis hints at the critical reformulation to which such a conception of history lends itself, while Wright's reveals the allegiance that it owes to a colonial modernity.

A passage that appears toward the end of *The Color Curtain*, Wright's journalistic report on the Bandung conference of "Third World" nations, captures well his conception of the historical role of the West with which he aligns himself. He writes: "Is this secular, rational base of thought and feeling in the Western world broad and secure enough to warrant the West's assuming the moral right to interfere *sans* narrow, selfish political motives? My answer is, Yes" (185). Here Wright's confidence in the West as the fount of a valued rationality leads him to an open call for Western intervention in the "Third World." A similar apology for Western intervention in Africa is not in fact made in *Black Power*, but the idea of the West as the fount of rational thought is very much a part of Wright's narrative of world history in the earlier book. Thus, in *Black Power*, Wright is often horrified by the examples of religion and superstition that he finds himself confronted with in the Gold Coast. At one point, he records "the pathetic story" of a worker in a gold mine attempting to steal a bar of gold while reciting a magic formula that he thought had rendered him invisible (312–13). At another point, he describes himself as "com[ing] up for air, to take a deep breath" after going through Danquah's book on Akan religion with astonished disbelief (218).[8]

Black Power, then, is the ambivalent travel record of a stranger in his ancestral home. Confronted with the material signifiers of black bodies that visually remind him of his own, Wright struggles with the meaning that his ancestry has for him; and confronted by the "irrationality" of African cultural practice, he has recourse in a complex way to his self-identification as a rational Westerner. In situating himself at a tangent to both of these collective identities (of Africa and the West), Wright seems to critique both in a superficial reading. But this is precisely the point at which a linear conception of history as a movement from irrationalism to rationalism, from tribal to modern, appears in Wright the Western traveler's text to impose an evaluative structure on the relationship between "West" and "Africa." Sometimes, as in the case of the young men whose intimate dancing with one another produces homophobic anxiety in Wright, the "advanced" condition of the West is seen as being not necessarily better (108–10); but most often the West appears as a rational progression beyond "primitive" superstition.

One of the short stories in *Eight Men* (1961), a later collection of Wright's stories, explores extensively the relationship between the West and Africa. "Man, God Ain't Like That . . ." is the story of the relationship between John, a painter living in Paris, and Babu, an African whom John knocks down with his car one rainy day in Ghana. In the story, John is meant to be symbolic of the West and Babu of Africa. Wright's story, though it condemns the irrationality of John's racism at the same time that it condemns the irrationality of Babu's religion, sets up the West as "advanced." This advanced status of the West is implied in Babu's repeated question as to why God had given stone buildings to whites and only huts to blacks. Technology, the ability to produce stone buildings, is at issue here and becomes the sign of a superior human praxis. Wright makes no explicit answer to Babu's questions, but the West's technology represents (superstitious Babu does not understand this) a historically significant Western development of human praxis expressed as "science." This "science" is contrasted to the religion of the non-West. Even as the story criticizes racism as irrational, it continues to posit Western praxis as "advanced." Whether Babu's own praxis, his activities at the end of the story as a religious organizer in Africa, represents a significant challenge to this status of the West remains unclear.

"Man, God Ain't Like That . . ." clearly summarizes many of the dominant themes of *Black Power*.[9] *Black Power* too describes the contrast between the West and Africa as the difference between rationality and irrationality, science and religion. Indeed, this contrast is one of the persistent themes of Wright's later nonfictional works in general. In *The Color Curtain*, for example, Wright declares, after surveying the behavior of Asian delegates to the Bandung conference traveling in the same plane as him, "It was rapidly dawning on me that if the men of the West were political animals, then the men of the East were religious animals" (69). This contrast is precisely what is often conventionally rendered as the opposition between modernity and tradition, respectively. Rather than a tradition that is, as in Gilroy's examples, the counterculture of modernity, here tradition becomes a handmaiden serving to establish the superiority of modernity. A similar contrastive evaluation of modernity and tradition as different modes of human praxis is to be discerned in the depiction of Africans in *Black Power*.

BETWEEN AFRICAN DEPICTIONS AND POLITICAL EXPRESSIONS

Kwame Anthony Appiah in "A Long Way from Home: Wright in the Gold Coast" discovers in *Black Power* what he calls a "paranoid hermeneutic" (181). Since Wright discards the comforts of "racial explanation," Appiah argues, he has no reason for being in the Gold Coast— and "[b]ecause he has no reason for 'being there,' Wright's reactions seem to oscillate between condescension and paranoia" (180). Appiah finds *Black Power* an ungenerous book in its depiction of the Ghana in which he grew up. He discovers in it "Wright's desire not to understand," by which he seems to be referring to various examples of Wright's refusal to take up invitations by Ghanaians to follow them intellectually into the world of the Africans (183). It is because of this desire not to understand, Appiah implies, that the religions and myths of the Gold Coast appear in the guise they do. Such a "lack of understanding," we have seen, is also a part of the epistemological presumptions of a colonialist textual economy.

Appiah's assessment of *Black Power* is in contrast to that of John M. Reilly whom Appiah describes in his essay as "one of the book's more devoted readers" (176). Reilly, in "Richard Wright's Discovery of the Third World," arrives at a more positive evaluation of *Black Power*. He acknowledges the bewilderment Wright exhibits when confronted by "African survivals" in African American culture and his "ambivalence" (Reilly's word) regarding Western rationality (49). However, Reilly also concludes the following: "[W]ith confidence that Africans can *consciously* enter into historical change, Wright concentrates his attention on the liberating consequences of the escape from dependency on ritual and myth. Whatever else he found in Africa pales beside the renewed hope he gained" (51, italics in original). What is important to Reilly is that with the publication of *Black Power*, Richard Wright became an exponent of national liberation (52).

A close reading of *Black Power* and Wright's other nonfictional texts to do with the "Third World" (*White Man, Listen!* and *The Color Curtain*) shows Reilly's assessment of *Black Power* to be overly sanguine. Wright's turn to the politics of "Third World" liberation toward the end of his life is not unproblematic. Appiah's critical response to *Black Power* is but the latest in a long line of critical responses to *Black Power* and the later Richard Wright on the part of many scholars. Toward the end of Wright's life in Paris, Baldwin tells us, Africans had

turned their faces from him; Baldwin quotes an African as saying of
Wright—"I believe he thinks he's white" ("Alas, Poor Richard" 212).
"Third World" assessment of Wright's later nonfictional works was not
friendly. None of the three works—*Black Power, The Color Curtain*,
and *White Man, Listen!*—Edward Margolies notes,

> met with the unalloyed enthusiasm of anticolonialists. Kwame
> Nkrumah and Eric Williams were said to have been irritated. Nor
> were close European friends always in accord. Gunnar Myrdal,
> whom I interviewed in 1962, stressed that his Introduction to *White
> Man, Listen!* was carefully worded to avoid appearing to endorse
> Wright's text. ("Opposing Freedoms" 409)

Constance Webb, Wright's biographer, has also noted the critical hostility that greeted *Black Power* on its publication (338).

George Padmore was one of the few anticolonialists to endorse the
book, even if only in private. In *The World of Richard Wright*, Michel
Fabre quotes Padmore's assessment of *Black Power* in a letter to Wright
(202). "It needed saying," Padmore wrote in his letter, "and it is best
you said it. It will find popular endorsement among the younger
Africans who haven't got a vested interest in all this mumbo-jumbo. The
ju-ju won't work on people like us—detribalized blacks." Voicing a similar opinion, Dorothy Padmore, George Padmore's wife, wrote in a letter to Michel Fabre:

> [W]e both considered the book a pretty fair summing up of the soci-
> ety, with its aspirations and past and future perspectives. This was
> not how it was received, however, in the Gold Coast. . . . It was felt
> that part of the picture drawn fitted in too closely with the views of
> their critics that they were not yet ready for self-government. . . .
>
> Wright, I am sure, was disappointed in the book's reception in
> Africa, where opinion on it weighed against him for the future and
> precluded him from offering the contribution that he was so anx-
> ious to make to Africa's need of freedom and unification. (quoted in
> Fabre's *The World of Richard Wright*, 249)

More recently, Mary Louise Pratt has offered another sympathetic
reading of *Black Power* that overlooks many of the aspects of the book
being discussed here. She declares that "Wright [in *Black Power*] is trying to represent an experience of ignorance, disorientation, incompre-

hension, self-dissolution which does not give rise to terror or madness, but rather to a serene receptivity and intense eroticism" (*Imperial Eyes* 222). Pratt's argument is based on the evidence of a passage that appears in a section of the book where Wright acknowledges succumbing *momentarily* to "the spell of this land" and feeling the power of African superstitions (*Black Power* 263). At the end of this passage, in which the spellbound Wright considers giving in to such superstitions as belief in the ability of a line of ants to point to a guilty man, the sound of a lorry brings back to Wright "the world I know." The evidence of other passages in the book as well as Wright's acknowledgment here that his feeling of oneness with the land is momentary suggest that Wright, in fact, feels otherwise most of the time. Indeed, Wright's alienation from Africa is amply demonstrated by the appearance of the colonialist structure of evaluation noted above. Yet Pratt is also correct in stating that "in *Black Power* Wright directly set himself to work parodying and reworking the inherited tropology [of the colonialist travel narrative]" (*Imperial Eyes* 221). The critical responses to *Black Power* have assessed the book positively or negatively depending on whether they have focused on Wright's depictions of Africa and Africans (Appiah) or his overt political expressions (Reilly). Both, it can be argued, are a part of *Black Power*.

BECOMING MODERN IN A LAND OF PATHOS

At one point in *Black Power*, Wright describes addressing some Ghanaians at a political gathering held under the auspices of Nkrumah's Convention People's Party. Among the words he speaks to his audience are the following: "I'm one of the lost sons of Africa who has come back to look upon the land of his forefathers. In a superficial sense it may be said that I'm a stranger to most of you, but, in terms of a common heritage of suffering and hunger for freedom, your heart and my heart beat as one" (77). These words express both the tension between Wright's identity as a black man and as a Westerner and his attempt at a resolution of this tension. There is a hint of the dialectical in the construction of the passage. The first sentence, on the one hand, introduces Wright's acknowledgment of a common racial history between himself and his African audience. The beginning of the second sentence, on the other hand, emphasizes the historical gulf between them. However, abandoning any attempt to reconcile these two positions or even explain them further, Wright introduces a third position into the discussion. What binds his audience and himself, he says, is "a common heritage of suffering and a hunger for freedom." Abandoning both (black) race and (Western) culture, Wright chooses to make his stand on the ground of politics. The passage captures very aptly the trajectory of Wright's argument in *Black Power*, a trajectory also captured by the history of the title of Wright's text. Discarding "Stranger in Africa" and "Ancestral Home" (among others), Wright finally hits on *Black Power* as expressing that political sensibility that he so wished to emphasize.

It is possible to read *Black Power*, then, as the account of a journey not just into a spatial or cultural but also a political geography. Any travel account involves such a journey, but in *Black Power* it is an overtly expressed aspect. In the opening scene of the text, politics is offered as one of the reasons for journeying to the Gold Coast (3–7). It is Dorothy Padmore who suggests the Ghana trip to Wright in Paris, after an Easter Sunday luncheon. In the four-page-long scene that follows, a medley of questions regarding his African ancestry, Africa's underdevelopment, its pagan religion, the meaning of race and other such issues immediately occurs to Wright. Even in its brevity, the scene is riven by all those ambivalent tensions that make up the text of the book as a whole and that have led to its contrary assessments. Also present in the scene is the theme of "politics," understood as a contest for state power. "Kwame Nkrumah, the Prime Minister, is going to table his motion for self-government in July," is the most important reason that Dorothy Padmore gives Wright in attempting to persuade him to go to Ghana (3).

At first Wright does not pay much attention to this political aspect of a prospective journey to the Gold Coast. "I genuinely wanted to know about the political situation in the Gold Coast," he tells us, "yet another and far more important question was trying to shape itself in me. According to popular notions of 'race,' there ought to be something of me down there in Africa" (4). The scene however ends with the political part of the journey foregrounded. It is when he learns from Dorothy Padmore that there are African cabinet ministers in the Gold Coast with significant responsibilities that he makes his final decision to go.

When Wright departs, he leaves from Liverpool in England, "the city that had been the center and focal point of the slave trade" (7). The irony of this departure to Africa from Liverpool by a descendant of slaves follows immediately on the above scene which itself amends in important ways the premises of colonialist travel narratives. If Marlow and Indiana Jones profess to pursue only material treasures into colonial territories, Wright departs professing a quest of political treasure. If both Marlow and Jones have the security of a Home, respectively signified as Europe and the United States, behind them in their journeys into an Out There, Home is precisely one of the terms placed in question by Wright in *Black Power*. He is an African American living in exile in Paris, journeying to an Africa that it may be possible to regard as his ancestral home, but which position he is loathe to assume. Key to a comprehension of this homelessness of Wright is an understanding of his experience of life in the segregationist southern states of the United States. Black, western, and in exile, his bitterness at the African American experience in the U.S. south leaves him with nowhere to turn.

There is a passage in *Black Boy* that expresses the extent of Wright's alienation from the southern black experience. About a quarter of a century after his father had abandoned his family, Wright returns to the south to visit his father on a plantation on which he worked. Wright's narrative at this point raises his father to a figure symbolic of the bitter desolation of the segregationist south. "From the white landowners above him," Wright tells us of his father, "there had not been handed to him a chance to learn the meaning of loyalty, of sentiment, of tradition" (43). Observing his father standing before him in peasant clothes, Wright notes, "though there was an echo of my voice in his voice, we were forever strangers, speaking a different language [sic], living on vastly different planes of reality" (42). Wright's overwhelming feeling in this encounter is that of a vast distance between himself and his father, predicated primarily on the difference in class status between the two at this point.

Wright's experience of returning to the South is, of course, starkly different from that of Zora Neale Hurston's in *Mules and Men*. What is a warm homecoming as "Lucy Hurston's daughter" for Hurston is a realization of an unbridgeable difference between his father and himself for Wright. Unlike Hurston, the Wright who sets out for the Gold Coast in *Black Power* has no easily assumed "home" location to return to or set out from; he is "at home" nowhere. It is true that Hurston in *Mules and Men*, as discussed in the previous chapter, goes beyond simply celebrating the South as Home in contrast to New York; yet she never gives up the right to regard the South also as Home. For Wright, where there should be a location that he can evaluate as Home, there is only absence. Into this vacuum rushes in "politics" and it is in this sense that *Black*

Power can be described as a journey into a political geography. As the passage that opens this section of the chapter makes clear, a certain kind of politics becomes the ground for a shared community, a substitute home, for Wright.

Black Power revises the textual economy of the colonialist travel narrative in two significant ways. First, it puts forward a radically different understanding of what constitutes a "home." Second, and in this it shows some similarities to *Mules and Men*, it seems to set out to journey *to* a "home" rather than from it and back. "Home," as has been noted before, is the cryptic term for a point within the economy of a travel narrative to which value gravitates. It is the privileged site within the text at which value is accumulated by the dynamic, structural operation (evaluative structure) of the travel narrative. If the colonialist evaluative structure of *Heart of Darkness* transmits such value back toward "London," *Black Power*, through a radical transformation of such an evaluative structure, proceeds to accumulate value around a practice ("politics") rather than around a place or a cultural or national identity. Rather than colonialist praxis, it orients itself self-consciously to anticolonialist praxis. Indeed, its very attention to the significance of political practice is arguably counter to the colonialist travel narrative. But this revisioning is complicated by the simultaneous functioning of another evaluative structure that continues to privilege the West as the site of rationality and secular values in ways noted earlier in the chapter. *Black Power* is also a text in which Wright as a Westerner travels from the West to Africa and back. In the functioning of *this* evaluative structure the West is the home from which Wright sets out on his travel. Here, Wright's literary practice continues to orient itself according to the coordinates of colonialist praxis—Western rationality, Western civilization, Western modernity.

Black Power, then, is a textual economy in which (at least) two powerful evaluative structures, working in contrary ways, find equal play. The history of the book's title suggests only the structure of values Wright would like to foreground. The other evaluative structure continues to function in the text, and the contrary readings of the book can be attributed to the ambivalent tension within the text because of the simultaneous operations of both structures. In this respect, *Black Power* is both an anticolonialist and a colonialist travel narrative. However, there are ways in which the operations of the two evaluative structures intersect, not to resolve finally the resulting ambivalence, not to make it disappear, but to hold such ambivalence temporarily in abeyance. The presence of such points of intersection allow the textual economy of *Black Power* to appear a coherent, seamless totality to the reader. What is thus brought into being is the semblance of a single meaning.

The word "pathos," appearing a number of times in the text, is one of the points of intersection for the two evaluative structures. The importance of the word is emphasized by the subtitle to Wright's book, which is "A Record of Reactions in a Land of Pathos." The first time the word appears in the text, Wright uses it to describe the condition of a young African man who approaches Wright to ask him for money so that he may take a correspondence course in detective work from an institution in the United States (72). The African says his reason for taking the course is to track down all the criminal actions of the British colonialists: "Detective work's for catching criminals, sar. That's what the English are, sar" (72). Wright is appalled at what he considers the boy's "warped" "view of reality" (73). The second time the word occurs, Wright has just been propositioned by a female prostitute (165). The word describes Wright's response: "I shook my head, filled with pathos."

By the third time the word occurs, Wright is beginning to use the word to describe a generalized condition of "the African." The third occurrence of the word is at one of the key moments in the text, after Wright sitting in the galleries has watched Nkrumah make a speech before the Legislative Assembly "petitioning Her Majesty's Government to enact the necessary legislation for Gold Coast self-government" (169). Witnessing this political act is one of the primary reasons for Wright's journey to the Gold Coast. After the petition, Nkrumah is carried into the celebrating crowd outside. But Wright, watching the scene, is apprehensive. He writes:

> I could feel the fragility of the African as compared with the might of the British, the naiveté of the African when weighed against the rancid political insight the British possessed, the naked plea of the African when pitted against the anxieties of man [*sic*] holding the secrets of atomic power in their [*sic*] hands. . . . And a phrase from Nietzche welled up in me: the pathos of distance. (170)

Pathos, it appears from this passage, is that which Wright perceives as the vast difference between the British and the Africans, a difference worthy of being expressed in the grand metaphysics of Nietzchean language.

When the phrase "pathos of distance" appears next, it cannot but help draw on this particular meaning. Bibiani is a town centered around a gold mine up on a hill. Walking through the town, the sounds of the machinery of the mine audible even down below where "[i]n the mud huts life was being lived by the imperious rule of instinct," Wright comes across "a tall, naked black boy" defecating on "the porch of his hut" (310). Wright's comment on this scene is: "It was clear the industrial activity upon that hill, owned or operated by no matter what race, could not exist without the curbing and disciplining of instincts, the ordering of emotion, the control of the reflexes of the body. Again I felt the pathos of distance!" (310). The distance, the passage makes clear, is between an instinctual, emotional, reflexive life on the one hand and a rational, industrial life on the other. Now, with its Nietzchean allusion, Wright's narrative invests the historical distance between the African and the British with metaphysical weight.

What makes the simultaneously metaphysical and historical distance between Africa and Britain "pathetic" is their practical difference—the failure of one kind of praxis to transcend the instinctual. Clearly, rational life is superior to instinctual life, for it has successfully overcome the other in order to create such things as mining machinery. In this context, rational life appears as a more evolved praxis than the life of instinct. The word "pathos" appears in a number of different passages in *Black Power*. It appears in scenes involving not only a slum boy such as the one above, but also a member of the bourgeois elite such as Dr. Busia, Nkrumah's rival (229). The word always describes, however, the difference, with an implication of inferiority involved, between Africans on the one hand and the British or Westerners on the other. For Wright, the land of pathos is not only the land of emotions and instincts, but also pathetic in the other, more condescending sense of the term.

By rendering the Gold Coast "pathetic," Wright assimilates the country and its inhabitants to a powerful Western textual economy operating according to the dictates of ethnographic vision. It is possible to understand Wright's "pathetic" rendering of the Gold Coast as a perpetuation of colonialist evaluations of the colonized as "primitive," "feminine," "child-like," and so on. "Colonized" belongs in the same semantic field as these other terms by figuring as the devalued opposite for a transcendental Western subject constituted as rational and masculine.

The history and politics—the record of past and present praxis—that is portrayed in *Black Power* may be described as a movement from the premodern or traditional to the modern, from the tribal to the industrial, from the pathetic to the rational. Nkrumah's nationalist revolution is instrumental in carrying the people of the Gold Coast from the first set of terms to the second. The pathos of distance between the two terms is precisely expressed through the colonialist travel narrative's rhetoric of distance. The geographical distance between Europe and Africa, represented in Wright's narrative by a journey by ship from Liverpool to Takoradi, underwrites the pathetic distance between the two. This distance it is the business of Nkrumah's revolution to close. It must render the Gold Coast less "pathetic." The nationalist revolution appears then as an overdetermined stage in an evolutionary history.

The "single" meaning of *Black Power*, brought into being by the interplay of twin evaluative structures expressing colonialist and anticolonial perspectives, may now be formulaically rendered in the following manner: one (colonialist) evaluative structure operating through a rhetoric of distance works to signify the Gold Coast as a land of pathos, even as another (anticolonial) evaluative structure suggests the Gold Coast may be made to become less pathetic by the politics of revolutionary change. One evaluative structure transfers value to the West and the other to the politics of the Gold Coast, if not the Gold Coast itself. Both evaluative structures emerge out of Wright's practical representation of African praxis.

In this context an important contrast to the textual economy of *Black Power* is offered by C. L. R. James's *Nkrumah and the Ghana Revolution*. The book offers an evaluation by an influential figure of the same political events that Wright sets out to describe in his book.[10] In *Nkrumah and the Ghana Revolution*, James appears in the guise of a historian of revolutions. In 1938, James had written *The Black Jacobins*, a detailed examination of Toussaint L'Ouverture and the revolution that brought Haiti into being as an independent nation. The concluding pages of the book make connections between the Haitian revolution and the prospective (in 1938) anticolonial struggles of Africa. Referring to these pages in the preface to the 1963 Vintage edition of the book (written, that is, after he had already composed significant portions of the text that was to become *Nkrumah and the Ghana Revolution*), James writes, "I have retained the concluding pages which envisage and were intended to stimulate the coming emancipation of Africa. They are a part of the history of our time" (vii).

The Black Jacobins makes numerous references not only to the French Revolution, with which the Haitian revolution is roughly contemporary, but also to Europe in 1848 and Russia in 1917. In making these connections, James is at pains to tease out some common laws of revolution. "In a revolution," he notes, "when the ceaseless, slow accumulation of centuries bursts into volcanic eruption, the meteoric flares and lights above are meaningless chaos and lend themselves to infinite caprice and romanticism unless the observer sees them always as projections of the sub-soil from which they come" (x). That subsoil, for James, is world history itself. For him, as for Rodney after him, history is a record of (human) praxis. "Great men [*sic*] make history," James writes, "but only such history as it is possible for them to make. Their freedom of achievement is limited by the necessities of their environment" (x). It is in answer to the laws of this history that revolutions take place. In this regard, *Nkrumah and the Ghana Revolution* may be seen as a sequel to *The Black Jacobins*. In it, James extends the analysis of history as praxis—what better subject can there be for such analysis than revolutions?—to the earliest of the African revolutions.

Thus, James notes at one point in *Nkrumah and the Ghana Revolution*:

> In this organization for immediate ends under leaders of the old régime, the spontaneous outburst of political action, and the statement of the most ulterior aims of the revolution by unknown elements in the crowd, the readiness of larger provincial towns to act as soon as they heard the news from the capital, the people of the Gold Coast were following a pattern we have seen repeated often enough for nearly two hundred years: Ghana from the very start takes its place in the very vanguard of the middle of the twentieth century, and the future is established without possibility of argument by the actions of Nkrumah. (47)

The passage cogently expresses James's summary of the salient features of revolutions in modern times. Taken together, *The Black Jacobins* and *Nkrumah and the Ghana Revolution* conceive of modern history as a series of revolutions which take the world further along a particular trajectory. It appears there are formal laws to these revolutions which can be ascertained through rigorous scientific inquiry. It appears these laws can then be used to predict and to act. For James, the study of history is an eminently practical act.

James's purpose in *Nkrumah and the Ghana Revolution* appears similar, in a superficial reading, to Wright's in *Black Power*. Both set out to explain Kwame Nkrumah's political activities. There are, however, significant differences between the two texts. Where Wright often confesses a lack of comprehension, James writes with a self-confidence born out of his faith in the objective existence of the formal features of revolution. As a corollary to these aspects of the two texts, we find that Wright's concern in *Black Power* is as much with his own reactions as it is with the events unfolding in the Gold Coast. On the other hand, James's concern is almost exclusively with the practical history that is before him.

It is certainly possible to understand the differences between the two texts as generic. As much as the remarks of Wright, James's remarks regarding the Ghana revolution can be seen as a function of the constraints of the genre that he adopts. James's confidence that there are formal laws to revolutions to be ascertained is one consequence of the conventions of "scientific inquiry" invested with value by this particular generic economy. Thirty years later, loss of faith in both "revolution" and "science" seems to suggest that James's confidence was misplaced romanticism.

There are, however, other salutary consequences to James's adoption of this particular historiographic genre. It allows him to avoid focusing in an ahistorical and metaphysical way on the issue of his difference from the Africans he is examining. This issue of difference is precisely the one that leads Wright to the vexatious questions regarding his self-identity, the historico-ontological status of Africans and his access to any knowledge about them. The issue of difference between traveler and people traveled to in a colonial context arises directly out of the generic expectations of the typical colonialist travel narrative. In this regard, James's historiographical focus on revolutions as expressions of human praxis allows him to sidestep the problems that emerge in Wright's more "literary" narration of his journey to the Gold Coast.

Like *Nkrumah and the Ghana Revolution*, Richard Wright's *Black Power* sets out evaluate anticolonial praxis as it found expression in the events in the Gold Coast/Ghana. For C. L. R. James, as for Walter Rodney in *How Europe Underdeveloped Africa*, this African praxis is part and parcel of a broader human praxis. For Richard Wright, the issue is more clouded. On the one hand, he seems to share James's belief; on the other, he is unable to forego the seductions of cultural difference. Thus, his ambivalent and contradictory text comes to stage within the same textual economy a confrontation between colonialist and anticolonial evaluative structures. The contradiction between these two evaluative structures also offers us a clue to the project of modernity as it is revealed to us in *Black Power*. "[Richard Wright] saw," Wimal Dissanayake has written of *Black Power*, "in these Third World countries a clash between tradition and modernity, and he hoped, with the best intentions in the world, that the forces of modernity would win out" (488). Choosing intentionality, rather than praxis, as the ground for evaluation and leaving the content of Wright's "modernity" unexamined, this assessment of *Black Power* misses the contradictory impulses of Wright's narrative, which can by no means be said to be sympathetic to the "Third World" in some uncomplicated way. The evaluative structures of *Black Power* are comprehensible not according to the psychological details of Wright's best intentions but according to the historical details of his ambivalent practical contribution. It is crucial to an evaluation of *Black Power* that the practical content of Wright's modernity be properly understood. This a comparison with the views of African history advanced by James and Rodney helps us do.

If it is the modernity of a *particular* kind of developmentalist view of history that leads Wright to find the Gold Coast a land of pathos and thus premodern, it is the modernity-as-struggle, arising from this same view of history, that leads Wright to be optimistic of the Gold Coast. Despite its oversights, Paul Gilroy's reading, in *The Black Atlantic*, of the Hegelian allegory is invaluable in drawing attention to these aspects of modernity. Modernity as the latest stage in the evolution of human praxis lends itself to the hierarchical ranking of civilizations and the expression of the domination of one by another. But the very idea of a contest between master and slave, colonizer and colonized, that is encoded in this view of history also opens the door to the possibility that the slave, the colonized, can and will struggle back. It may be possible then to argue that even if the colonial dimensions of modernity reveal its problematic status for the colonized, modernity's expression of struggle invites the colonized to test the limits of this colonial modernity through anticolonial nationalist revolutions that themselves aspire to the status of modernity. In this chapter, attention to the economy of the text, by leading us to consider the paradoxes of Richard Wright's practice in writing *Black Power*, has permitted us to recognize in detail the paradox within "modernity" as a particular expression of praxis. The next chapter explores the historical consequences for the "Third World" of these apparently opposed—colonial and anticolonial—dimensions of modernity and returns, with these explorations in mind, to the discussion of the postmodern initiated in the first chapter.

V. S. NAIPAUL, MODERNITY, AND POSTCOLONIAL EXCREMENT

Attention to the textual economy of *Black Power* revealed Richard Wright's ambivalence regarding Africa, expressed in the form of two evaluative structures, one of which concentrates value in a political practice he calls "Black Power" while the other continues to transfer value in the direction of Europe. Thus, we came to recognize that Richard Wright's travel account—like *Indiana Jones and the Temple of Doom*, for example—may be described as an ensemble of evaluative structures, though here these structures do not work to reinforce each other. Through attention to these competing structures of evaluation, then, we identified Wright's distinctively ambivalent practical attitude to Africa and found a clue within it to certain aspects of "colonial modernity." We may note here yet again the manner in which a textual economic reading permits us to advance our insights into the relationship colonialism bears to modernity by focusing attention on the category of praxis, both as it is thematized within a text and as the cause of the effect that is the text. As the argument regarding colonialism and modernity winds to its conclusion in this chapter through a reading of V. S. Naipaul's India trilogy, we will certainly have reason to return to this aspect of textual economics.

Broad similarities between V. S. Naipaul's trilogy on India—*An Area of Darkness* (1964; henceforth *Area*, when abbreviated), *India: A Wounded Civilization* (1977; henceforth *Wounded Civilization*, when abbreviated), and *India: A Million Mutinies Now* (1990; henceforth *Mutinies*, when abbreviated)—and Richard Wright's *Black Power* are immediately evident. Both Naipaul and Wright write about their experiences as displaced persons traveling back to the lands from which their ancestors migrated or were taken forcibly generations earlier. Whereas Wright leaves for Africa from his exile in Paris, Naipaul does so from London. They are both nonwhite metropolitans struggling with the double legacy of being metropolitan *and* nonwhite.[1] Being of the "West" (a geopolitical entity as well as a particular, hegemonic history and culture constructed for this entity) for Wright is a question of birth as well as nationality, whereas, for Naipaul, born into a Hindu East Indian family in Trinidad, it is one of elective affinity. Naipaul portrays himself in his works as having graduated to membership in Western culture through the vocation of writing, "the career" which, he notes in "Prologue to an Autobiography," published in 1984, "wasn't possible in Trinidad" (19).[2]

It is the historical encounter between the West and the Rest that both Naipaul and Wright experience in different ways as an acute personal dilemma and repeatedly stage in the narratives of their travels to non-Western societies—Wright at the moment of decolonization and Naipaul during the post-/neocolonial period. Naipaul's trilogy, spanning nearly thirty years of post-Independence Indian history, offers itself as a coherent body of work through which to investigate the revision of the textual economy of the colonialist travel narrative in the neocolonial period which, we have already seen, has also been regarded by some as postmodern.

"QUALIFIED TO JUDGE AMONG CULTURES"

In his book-length study of V. S. Naipaul's nonfictional works, *London Calling*, Rob Nixon points out a divide in the response to Naipaul's career between "Third World" critics and "First World" critics (3). Naipaul is lionized by many "First World" critics, Nixon suggests, because he is viewed "as a neutral explainer of non-western cultures to Western audiences" (66); and, further, "by venturing into travel writing and journalism [Naipaul] has garnered a reputation of a different order [than that of simply "a writer"]. . . . In short, he has grown into an 'expert'" (4). In his book, Nixon illustrates in detail how Naipaul's cultivated pose of homelessness and exile is crucial to his emergence as a "neutral explainer." Not surprisingly, Paul Theroux's description of his friend and mentor—now erstwhile friend and mentor—in "V. S. Naipaul" repeatedly emphasizes this homelessness of Naipaul.[3] His portrait concludes with the approving citation of Naipaul's claim that he has no attachments and "fears no one" (454). Theroux's account of his former friend in Uganda, where he first met and got to know him, puts on fine display Naipaul's arrogance. Naipaul shows nothing but contempt for Africans, belittling the poems that African students show him and making fun of African names. This does not, however, dissuade Theroux from declaring that Naipaul "has considerable courage, a refined sense of order, and an answering literary and moral integrity" (454).

The links between the pose of homelessness that Naipaul strikes, his controversial attitude to non-Western cultures, and his reputation as a neutral and courageous observer of such cultures are easy to see.[4] Through an unacknowledged but nevertheless self-conscious manipulation of the politics of identity, Naipaul has come to serve a strategically useful role in neocolonial articulations of the "Third World." If a dark-skinned person makes pejorative remarks about dark-skinned people, then surely he must be fearless and objective. Through such a superficial invocation of racial identity, such an elision of the consequences of Naipaul's own privileged and specific subject position, Naipaul's reputation has come to be what it is. Naipaul, as Nixon illustrates conclusively in his book by drawing on a wealth of evidence, has assiduously encouraged a perception of his work as an "objective" commentary on the "Third World." In so doing, he has demonstrated his utility to what Nixon dubs "the dominant New York–London media axis" (80).

It is this utility that carried Naipaul to the cover of *Newsweek* in 1981, in the wake of the Iranian revolution and the publication of the account of his travels through four non-Arabic Islamic countries, including Iran, entitled *Among the Believers* (1981). Charles Michener wrote in his story on Naipaul in that issue of *Newsweek*: "Is Naipaul's vision, as critics have charged, too fixed on failure? Is his acerbity that of a dark-skinned man's too-zealous conversion to Western tastes? These questions are really political ones, raised to score political points. Such critics usually overlook one of the most salutary aspects of Naipaul's attitude toward the Third World—Naipaul refuses to condescend" (112). Michener's words reveal only too well the sleight of rhetoric and superficial invocation of identity through which Naipaul, dark-skinned man criticizing dark-skinned natives, is converted into courageous antagonist of cowardly liberals. It is not Naipaul who adopts problematic views in Michener's perception; on the contrary, he "refuses to condescend."

However, it can be argued that Naipaul, by refusing to note the innumerable ways in which the inhabitants of the countries he visits live with courage amid the devastation caused by global capitalism, does nothing but condescend. Simultaneously, he condescends by refusing to accept (as will be demonstrated in this chapter) the interpretations of the inhabitants themselves of the conditions they live in. The extent of the London–New York media axis's investment in the career of Naipaul and the particular use to which it has put him is nowhere illustrated better than in the endorsement of Naipaul by James Michaels when he was the editor of *Forbes*: "If any person is qualified to judge among cultures Naipaul is. He was born in Trinidad in 1932, the grandson of Hindu immigrants from India, lives in England and has probed the Muslim, Latin and African worlds" (10). Michaels concludes his ringing endorsement of Naipaul by writing: "And for entertaining and enlightening reading, get any Naipaul book" (10).

The critics of Naipaul have not always had the powerful support from influential media quarters that the lionizers of Naipaul have had, but Rob Nixon's book on Naipaul is only the most recent in a long line of critiques of Naipaul's gratuitous comments on the "Third World." One of the earliest of these was by fellow–West Indian author George Lamming, who, in *The Pleasures of Exile* (1960), responded hostilely to Naipaul's description of West Indian society as philistine and noted "I reject this attitude; and when it comes from a colonial who is nervous both in and away from his native country, I interpret it as a simple confession of the man's inadequacy" (30). Similarly, in an essay on Naipaul written in 1985, Salman Rushdie referred to "the dark clouds that seemed to have gathered over Naipaul's inner world" in alluding to his later works ("V. S. Naipaul" 148). And, A. Sivanandan, surveying Naipaul's career, has written:

> Failing to come to terms with the historical experience of racism, [Naipaul] is diminished as a man. Diminished as a man, he is diminished as a creator. Ultimately there is only his craft, and it is that craft that bridges the gap between man and writer. . . . The man is subsumed under the writer. And so the thinking becomes less profound, less truthful, even as the writing gets finer, more truth-like. (43)

Only by ignoring the complexities of history understood, as it repeatedly has been in this book, as a record of human praxis has Naipaul the literary practitioner managed to pursue assiduously his version of the vocation of writing. His India trilogy offers the opportunity to demonstrate this argument.

The Excremental Reality of India

In an essay from the same period as *An Area of Darkness*, his first book on India, Naipaul confesses to experiencing moments of "near-hysteria" in India ("In the Middle of the Journey" 41). It is this same near-hysteria, it would seem, that Naipaul expresses when he declares in *Area*, "Indians defecate everywhere. They defecate, mostly, beside the railway tracks. But they also defecate on the beaches; they defecate on the hills; they defecate on the river banks; they defecate on the streets; they never look for cover" (74). During the next four or five pages the lack of hygiene of Indians is described at some length. Indeed, Naipaul's near-hysteria at the sight of fecal matter is not a momentary lapse in this section but forms one of the central motifs of the book. Thus, on the pilgrimage to the cave of Amarnath (with an ice lingam of Shiva in it) in the North, Naipaul finds his journey spoiled by the defecating pilgrims (171). And again, amid the ruins of "the great city of Vijayanagar" in the South, he writes, "A child was squatting in the mud of the street; the hairless, paleskinned dog waited for the excrement. The child, big-bellied, rose; the dog ate" (215). Such obsession with fecal matter on the part of Naipaul is not confined to *Area*. It is repeated in *India: A Wounded Civilization*, written about thirteen years later.[5] Responding to this obsession, Austen Delaney, in a review of *Area of Darkness* entitled "Mother India as Bitch," declared Naipaul's vision that of a compulsive "turd-watcher" (50). In Naipaul's near-hysterical description of the lack of hygiene in India, excrement becomes a marker of the ontological status of India. It begins to define India.

Excrement is not alone in playing this role in Naipaul's first two books. Consider this passage from *Area*:

> The flat now seems to hang in a void. India is a stone's throw away, but in the flat it is denied: the beggars, the gutters, the starved bodies, the weeping swollen-bellied child black with flies in the filth and

cowdung and human excrement of a bazaar lane, the dogs, ribby,
mangy, cowed and cowardly, reserving their anger, like the human
beings around them, for others of their kind. (65)

The flat belongs to a rich boxwallah (company executive) and Naipaul
finds himself listening to the enervating gossip among the boxwallahs.
What is interesting is the way India is defined exclusively in terms of the
beggars and the gutters, as if the flat were not also a part of Indian reality. It is poverty that is definitive of India; indeed, it is so definitive of
India, apparently so special to Indians in Naipaul's opinion, that
Naipaul is able to refer at another point in *Area* to the Indian "attitude
to poverty as something which, thought about from time to time in the
midst of other preoccupations, releases the sweetest of emotions" (47).
Poverty is so definitive of India that that which is not poor, such as the
flat of the boxwallah, is not India.

Again, a similar sensibility can be seen to inform Naipaul's comments on India in *Wounded Civilization*. In his account of the beggars
who throng the streets of Bombay, he refers glibly to the "Hindu function" performed by the beggars (55–57). He describes the attempts at
change that take the form of "rounding up all the beggars, of impound-
ing them, expelling them, dumping them out of sight somewhere, keeping them out," without either explaining how specifically the function
of beggary is Hindu or noting that these violent methods of dealing
with beggars were a direct result of Indira Gandhi's draconian Emer-
gency regulations.

And so a particular scene of India comes to be composed by
Naipaul—a scene in which excrement and poverty as definitive, constitutive elements are complemented by yet another crucial element, primitive technology. At the very beginning of Naipaul's discursive
engagement with India, on the very first page of *Area*, the first book of
the trilogy, technology (or rather the lack of it) is alluded to. Coelho, the
contact that the travel agency had sent to meet Naipaul's ship, Naipaul
tells us, "required cheese. It was a delicacy in India. Imports were
restricted, and the Indians had not yet learned how to make cheese, just
as they had not yet learned how to make newsprint" (11). Later, as
Naipaul prepares to move into the Hotel Liward in Srinagar, where he
is to stay for many months, he describes the primitive implements and
skills with which Mr. Butt and his assistant Aziz set about improving the
conditions of the hotel (107–10).

The brief allusions to the primitive technology of India in *Area* become an extensive, explicit discussion in *Wounded Civilization*. In the chapter entitled "Synthesis and Mimicry," there is a long account of India's attempts to experiment with "appropriate technology" (124–33). Naipaul has nothing but derision for these attempts. Attempts to improve the efficiency and performance of the bullock cart are swept away—why don't they simply fit the cart with a little engine? Confident of his superior wisdom in suggesting this solution, Naipaul does not stop to consider environmental degradation or India's dependence on foreign nations for the oil that would go into the engine or India's balance of payment problems or the economic significance of India's large bullock population or the ultimately lower cost of improving cart design as opposed to producing an entirely new vehicle driven by an engine. Later, having scornfully described the experiments and innovations being attempted at the newly established National Institute of Design, Naipaul declares with sure confidence, "An elementary knowledge of the history of technology would have kept that student [designing agricultural tools]—and the teachers who no doubt encouraged him—off the absurdity of his tools; even an elementary knowledge of the Indian countryside, elementary vision. Those tools were designed in an institute where there appeared to have been no idea of the anguish of the Indian countryside" (132). However, many of Naipaul's examples—a new kind of reaping instrument, a spraying machine—seem precisely to be responding to this countryside (129–31). Even though Naipaul parodies these inventions so completely that it is not possible to ascertain what they were really like, whether they represent genuine attempts at technological innovation or not, the fact that they respond to the needs "of the Indian countryside" emerges clearly.

Naipaul's mockery of Indian attempts at technological innovation has a particularly significant part to play in his textual economy. Ernest Mandel points out in his analysis of late capitalism that "belief in the omnipotence of technology is the specific form of bourgeois ideology in late capitalism. This ideology proclaims the ability of the existing social order gradually to eliminate all chance of crises, to find a 'technical' solution to all its contradictions" (*Late Capitalism* 501). Naipaul is giving expression to this ideology of late capitalism when he uses "technology" to measure the difference between India and the named or unnamed but ever-present West. In the ideological regime of late capitalism, mastery over technology comes to the forefront as another important signifier of modernity.

There is, then, much continuity between *An Area of Darkness* and *Wounded Civilization*. At the same time, the latter book acknowledges now and then that change may perhaps be afoot in India. Thus, Naipaul writes at the very end of the book, "in the present uncertainty and emptiness there is the possibility of a new beginning, of the emergence in India of mind, after the long spiritual night" (191). India is still evaluated as excremental in *Wounded Civilization* but its meaning is now a little different. India is no longer simply a stagnant society. However, Indian attempts at modernization are nevertheless imitative, fantastic, misguided. In Naipaul's own words, they are "a mixture of mimicry and fantasy" (138).

Excrementality, poverty, primitive technology: these are chief among the devalued terms of Naipaul's textual economy in the first two books of the trilogy. Collectively, these terms indicate the overdetermined nature of Naipaul's near-hysterical response to India. From the external markers of excrement and of primitive and inappropriate technological inventions, the cultural and intellectual inadequacy of India is discovered. The argument in this book has suggested that the deployment of such terms in a certain textual economy has its origin in a certain praxis, contributes to a certain praxis and describes a certain praxis. The praxis the terms describe in the Naipaul books under discussion is Indian. The terms evaluate such praxis as inferior. Naipaul declares at the end of *Wounded Civilization*: "The poverty of the land [of India] is reflected in the poverty of the mind; it would be calamitous if it were otherwise" (189). Excrement, for Naipaul, is only the most visible marker for the constitutive excrementality of all facets of Indian praxis. Walter Rodney's reference to "the element of *conscious activity* that signifies the ability to make history, by grappling with the heritage of objective material conditions and social relations" has been cited before in this book (280, italics in text). Rodney's "conscious activity," it has been suggested, refers to nothing other than praxis. For Naipaul, in the first two volumes of the trilogy, Indian ability to act consciously has only produced poverty, excrement and primitive technology.

Practically India

In *Area* and *Wounded Civilization*, devalued Indian praxis is contrasted to the actions, ideas, and opinions of Naipaul himself. Naipaul is convinced he knows and sees that which Indians themselves do not. In a "model village" in Rajasthan, Naipaul sits and discusses matters with the villagers (*Wounded Civilization* 22–23). He writes:

> So handsome, these men of Rajasthan, so self-possessed: it took time to understand that they were only peasants, and limited. The fields, water, crops, cattle: that was where concern began and ended. They were a model village, and so they considered themselves. There was little more that they needed, and I began to see my own ideas of village improvement as fantasies. Nothing beyond food—and survival—had as yet become an object of ambition; though one man said, fantastically, that he would like a telephone, to find out about the price of grain in Kotah without having to go there. (23)

Even in this model village, Naipaul is eager to discover economic poverty and its corresponding poverty of praxis—peasants who are "limited." The discovery is achieved by the willful reinterpretation of evidence that he himself provides. Thus, "fantastically" (the most important word in the passage, a word that takes the contradictory evidence that follows and converts it into supporting data) a peasant "would like a telephone." Why is this desire for a telephone fantastic? Why is this not, on the contrary, the sign of a peasant who, in all the limitations of his condition, understands the importance of immediate access to information regarding the economic forces (market capitalism, indicated by "the price of grain in Kotah") that determine that same condition? Ignoring such questions, Naipaul dismisses the peasant's ability to act consciously. "Fantastically" is a comforting word for Naipaul. It allows his vision of the excremental reality of India to remain undisturbed. Any evidence *against* is converted into evidence *for* by the reduction of the evidence to comic absurdity.

A similar example may be cited from *Area*. In the first fifteen pages of the book (entitled "Traveller's Prelude: A Little Paperwork"), Naipaul describes in great comic detail his attempt to get a permit for a bottle of alcohol that he had brought with him to India (11–26). Waiting in a room in the humid Bombay heat for the permit, Naipaul's "companion" faints and has to be revived with water. Later, when this incident is recounted to "a friend of our friend," the friend of the friend (notice how Naipaul distances himself from this person) responds: "It isn't the heat at all. Always the heat or the water with you people from outside. There's nothing wrong with her. You make up your minds about India before coming to the country. You've been reading the wrong books" (24–25). Naipaul does not comment on the words of this friend of a friend because he does not need to. His narrative of his and his fainting companion's trials and tribulations in obtaining the alcohol permit has already prepared the ground for the evaluation of the friend of a friend's remark as insensitive. In the process, a valid objection to Naipaul's strategies of assigning or denying value is effectively neutralized. The idea that Naipaul has made up his mind before coming to India is reduced to absurd peevishness—Naipaul is always true to what he encounters.

The veracity of his comments on the countries that he travels through is defended by Naipaul to Charles Michener (author of the *Newsweek* article on Naipaul) in the following words:

> *Nothing* was falsified. I'm very, very scrupulous about that. And I have seldom been misled by people because in every new situation I'm always with the other man. I'm always looking at the world through *his* eyes. . . . It's a matter of observing where people are made by false hopes, political beliefs, tribal causes. People with causes inevitably turn themselves off intellectually. (110, italics in original)

Immediately afterwards, oblivious to the irony, Naipaul responds to Michener's question whether he himself has a cause by declaring that he "is interested in the spread of humane values" and proceeds to define these humane values as "the Christian idea of love, added to the Roman idea of laws and contracts" (110). Naipaul's cause is a particular construction of Western civilization and it is the ideology of this cause that Naipaul carries with him as a traveler to India. It is, then, by no means absurd to suggest that Naipaul had indeed made up his mind before coming to India, had indeed, in his own words, turned himself "off intellectually." Naipaul, arriving in India with certain ideas of its literal and metaphorical excrementality, proceeds to explain this excrementality as a deviation from the Western values (Christian love/Roman law) that he espouses. Moving near-hysterically through the external excremental landscape of India, Naipaul leads his reader directly to a deeper excrementality, the degeneration of Indian culture. Thus, he declares at the end of *Wounded Civilization*, as noted above, "The poverty of the land [of India] is reflected in the poverty of the mind; it would be calamitous if it were otherwise" (189).[6] This is the conclusion that Naipaul is eager to demonstrate in the first two books of his trilogy. The foregone nature of the conclusion is indicated by the second portion of the sentence.

Such imputations of inferiority are not made only of India by Naipaul. In his very first travel book *The Middle Passage* (1962), an account of his return to the Caribbean after many years spent in England, Naipaul notes in a key passage: "Again and again one comes back to the main, degrading fact of the colonial society; it never required efficiency, it never required quality, and these things, because unrequired, became undesirable" (58). One might believe such a statement would be a criticism of the brutality of colonialism itself, but, as Naipaul's comments in the text repeatedly make clear, it is instead a symptomatic blaming of the victims of colonialism. Thus, *The Middle Passage* ends on a critical note, with Naipaul emphasizing the irrelevance, as he sees it, of the West Indies in the world (230–32).

From *The Middle Passage* to *Mutinies*, Naipaul consistently portrays the "Third World" as third rate, though in the latter book the form of the portrayal begins to change significantly. Such a portrayal of the "Third World" has its connections to his personal reactions to Trinidad early in his life. In *The Middle Passage*, Naipaul notes that Trinidad was a nightmare to him, both when he was growing up there and after he had moved to England (41). In "Prologue to an Autobiography," he describes how his father, also an aspiring writer, was acutely conscious of the limitations of Trinidad—his father, Naipaul says, passed on his fear of extinction (a fear that is to be combatted by the vocation of writing) to him (72). Letters between Naipaul and his father, recently published in *Between Father and Son*, demonstrate these aspects of Naipaul's early life in detail. Naipaul's personal ambition and his conviction regarding the limits faced by that ambition in Trinidad leads him to a deeply personalized and decontextualized understanding of the "Third World." Naipaul's trilogy on India, masquerading as a disinterested examination of India, is an extensive and interested demonstration of an already-assumed third-rateness as it is expressed in the excremental reality.

Describing his strategy when writing travel books in "The Crocodiles of Yamoussoukro," Naipaul writes, "I travel to discover other states of mind. And if for this intellectual adventure I go to places where people live restricted lives, it is because my curiosity is still dictated in part by my colonial Trinidad background" (90). A little later he continues, "The intellectual adventure is also a human one. I can move only according to my sympathy. I don't force anything; there is no spokesman I have to see, no one I absolutely must interview. The kind of understanding I am looking for comes best through people that I get to like" (90). Beginning, by his own confession, from the template of his adolescence in Trinidad, he travels to "Third World" societies he has already defined as restricted. Despite his insistence that he does not "force anything," there is "a kind of understanding" that he likes that he gets only from people that he likes (who agree with him? whom he agrees with?). In "The Crocodiles of Yamoussoukro" the people that he likes are expatriate residents of Ivory Coast. As Rob Nixon notes in *London Calling*, this leads Naipaul "to recycle the hoariest myths of the imperial encounter" (77).[7]

Naipaul's construction of his identity as a colonial in residence in metropolitan London is crucial to the structures of evaluation put on display in his travel books. So is his lack of reflection on the possible consequences of his gender identity. Naipaul does not acknowledge the limitations that his masculine identity places on his access to the societies that he is traveling through and reconstructing for a metropolitan audience. Thus, in *Among the Believers*, as he travels through Islamic countries, he introduces us to a succession of male interpreters and guides and never stops to reflect on the gendered nature of the resultant view.

Paul Theroux in his portrait of V. S. Naipaul writes that Naipaul's English wife was—at that time—an important factor in his writing. Even though she hardly ever appears in his writing, "[s]he has traveled great distances with him. . . . She is behind every word he writes," Theroux remarks in his former capacity as a personal friend of Naipaul (452). Theroux himself does not find this worthy of any further comment, but we may note here that it is precisely the erasure of his wife (or someone like her) from the narrative that allows Naipaul to construct his travel books as the adventures of a lonely, male protagonist among other, mostly male, counterparts. It allows him to recuperate in a postcolonial setting the colonialist textual economy of earlier travel narratives of exploration. Naipaul remakes himself in his travel books as a neocolonial successor to earlier male explorer protagonists of the genre (such as David Livingstone, Mungo Park, or Henry Morton Stanley) as well as the protagonists of the male quest romance. In this respect, V. S.

Naipaul's India trilogy is a variation of a theme already encountered in *Indiana Jones and the Temple of Doom.*

The scene from the beginning of *Area* in which the fainting of Naipaul's female companion (his wife?) is discussed by Naipaul and the male friend of a friend has already been cited. In the scene, the one person to remain silent, while Naipaul and the friend of a friend contest the meaning of the fainting, is the female companion herself. This silence of the anonymous companion is immediately symptomatic of the erasure of gender in Naipaul's travel writing in general. At the same time, it indicates how conventional his narratives of travel really are. Throughout most of Naipaul's travel writing, the challenge of intellectual engagement is replaced by the dangerous banality of an intellectually turned-off predetermined demonstration of the excrementality of the "Third World." The politics implied in such a demonstration is the corollary to Naipaul's clichéd presentation of himself as lone traveler–protagonist. In the textual economy of Naipaul's travel books, both that colonialist aspiration to subjective transcendence that Swift challenged centuries before and that masculinist bias at the heart of the colonialist travel narrative find renewed expression.

Even if, in the first instance, Naipaul himself as traveler-protagonist is invested with that value that is denied to India and Indians, finally this value is delivered to the West with which Naipaul has elected to affiliate himself. Thus, the familiar trajectory of Home-Out There-Home is once again deployed and the textual economy of the colonialist travel narrative falls in place. Like Indiana Jones, V. S. Naipaul brings a superior praxis to bear on India. Unlike Jones, however, Naipaul is not a heroic adventurer. The superiority of his praxis is demonstrated not through his heroic actions but rather through his keen ability to see the true nature of things. Naipaul's knowledge complements Jones's actions, reuniting in this complementarity at the level of ideology often dichotomized aspects of (human) praxis.

That Naipaul, a brown descendant of India, announces these opinions and is himself the agent of a superior praxis would seem to indicate that race is no longer an issue in the differential evaluation of the West and the Rest. Naipaul repeatedly says what Lucas/Spielberg would not make Jones say—that Indian peasants are limited, that Indian technology is absurd, that Indian excrementality is not only external. It would seem the encoding of practical value in the postcolonial age has been delinked from ideas of race. However, quite to the contrary, Naipaul and Jones are also ideological complements to each other in their racial difference. *Indiana Jones and the Temple of Doom* reveals what Naipaul's trilogy tries to obscure—that Naipaul's Christian love and Roman law retain racial connotations. If Naipaul's references to technology reveal "the specific form of bourgeois ideology in late capitalism," the depiction of Jones in *Temple* betrays the continued relevance of race for the differential evaluation of various forms of praxis. Naipaul might be of Indian descent himself, but the relevant issue has never been individual identity or individual intention. As was noted in a previous chapter, Joseph Conrad's motivations or beliefs are less interesting as symptoms of an individual psychology, perhaps worth discussing in another context, than as clues to the functioning of a particular textual economy. A similar point may be made with regard to V. S. Naipaul. *Temple* and Naipaul's trilogy, along with a host of other textual economies, draw from, contribute to, and complement one another in a neocolonialist praxis that in a context of domination and resistance attempts to attain ever more thorough forms of hegemony over the "Third World."

HOPE AND WHOLENESS IN A LAND OF MUTINIES

So far, the discussion has concerned the first two books of the trilogy. In *India: A Million Mutinies Now*, the third volume of his trilogy on India, Naipaul seems to want to break with the structures of evaluation elaborated in the previous volumes. This attempt on the part of Naipaul is, perhaps, what leads Rob Nixon to call *Mutinies* "the most decisive new departure in Naipaul's career" (169). Nixon's reading of *Mutinies* is essentially sympathetic, though he acknowledges its many limitations. Appearing in a chapter entitled "A Kinder, Gentler Naipaul?" Nixon's reading suggests an author mellowed with age. "The book could not have been written at any other point in his career," Nixon notes, and goes on to describe Naipaul a little later as "Newly whole, in the sense of having made peace with the places of his past" (171). But what kind of peace has Naipaul made? *Mutinies* is, indeed, a different kind of travel narrative than either of the first two books of the trilogy; the nature of this difference, however, bears some close examination. Closer scrutiny may discover that Naipaul still continues in *Mutinies*, albeit in a modified guise, a project that he had set in train in his very first travel book, *The Middle Passage*. Such scrutiny would be led to dissent from Nixon's sympathetic reading of *Mutinies*.

At the beginning of *Mutinies*, Naipaul writes that what he experienced in India in 1962, the year of the journey that is narrativized in *Area*, is "a feeling of alienation" (6). Because of the idea of India that was introduced to him in Trinidad, Naipaul notes, "the India from which my ancestors had migrated to better themselves became in my imagination a most fearful place" (7). It is this fear and alienation, Naipaul declares some five hundred pages later, that had caused him not to understand in 1962 "the extent to which the country had been remade" (517). But now, at the time of writing the last few pages of *Mutinies*, matters are different—"In twenty-seven years I had succeeded in making a kind of return journey, shedding my Indian nerves, abolishing the darkness that separated me from my ancestral past" (516). In 1962, the darkness in his imagination and knowledge, that had hung like a veil between himself and India, had, erroneously, been found by him to be constitutive of the land itself. In 1990, Naipaul is ready to acknowledge that the darkness was exclusively within himself. Finally, it seems, he is beginning a process of distancing himself from his earlier, obsessive characterization of India as excremental.

In *Mutinies*, Naipaul continues to deploy an excremental language, but now it is deployed to evaluate a new reality. Some passages in *Mutinies* are reminiscent of *Area* or *Wounded Civilization*; in others a change is suggested. One example seems to illustrate the kind of attitude exhibited by Naipaul in the earlier books. At one point, he comments on the procedure by which "an unturbanned Sikh" in Punjab fixed the punctured inner tube of Naipaul's hired car by covering the tear with a patch—"The procedure sent me back to my childhood; it made me think of the way we used to mend bicycle punctures; I had thought it was something that had passed out of my life forever" (425). Here the focus on the "backwardness" of India seems familiar. It seems recognizable from earlier books. Yet the evaluative structure within which the comment is situated is very different. We expect Naipaul to use this example of primitive technology to devalue India and Indians. He does not.

There are other passages in the book where "technology," continuing to operate as the ideological currency of late capitalism, provides the language to express a new India. The old language is put in the service of a new reality. Thus, at one point in the book, Pravas (one of

Naipaul's informants) notes the limitations of experience imposed on his grandfather because he did not have the benefit of mobility provided to Pravas by his scooter (170–71). "He [grandfather] was part of a static society," Pravas says (170). Naipaul approves of Pravas's "technological" approach to social history and remarks, "The bike—Pravas had been talking of the Bangalore traffic and his own motor-scooter. I liked the metaphor: it made the static past understandable" (170). Similarly, when later in the book another of his informants remarks that machines had changed the people of Punjab by making them "more modern," again Naipaul approves: "I said that what he was saying about machinery was true of other parts of India as well, in villages and cities. It was an aspect of the Indian industrial revolution" (443). This is indeed a different Naipaul than the one who had poured derision on inventors and experimenters in *Wounded Civilization.*

In the same mood, Naipaul is able to say, "People had a little more money now. It showed in the Karnataka countryside on the road south from Goa. Indian poverty was still visible . . . [but] . . . [t]here was nothing like the destitution I had seen twenty-six years before" (149). Time and again Naipaul compares his experience of India in 1962 with his experience of it now and finds the poverty, excrement, and technological lack of the earlier trip disappearing. It is in this practical context that he acknowledges that his earlier description of the country as an area of darkness reveals more his own failure of imagination, his own lack of understanding, than a historical reality, because the positive change he was witnessing now must have already been in process then—"It was a kind of regeneration that could have come only slowly" (149).

The conclusion of the book captures in an allusive way Naipaul's narrative approach to the new forces of transformation in India. After journeying through India for many months, Naipaul returns to Bombay, where he had begun this particular encounter with the country, and once again meets Paritosh, whom he had met and interviewed earlier. Paritosh is a film director. When Naipaul returns to Bombay, he has just finished shooting for a film set in a slum. For this film, an entire slum had been reconstructed: "For legal reasons they couldn't use a real place. They had taken photographs of various real places, and they had created a kind of composite Bombay slum. While the film was being shot, they had all lived in the various huts of the set. Just the day before, Paritosh said, they had begun to dismantle the make-believe slum they had lived in for many weeks. It had given him a pang" (520). These are the concluding lines of the book. They summarize well Naipaul's thesis in *Mutinies*—the excremental reality of India is finally undergoing transformation, but the process is not without its painful moments.

Between the first two books of the trilogy and the third book, then, there is a change in Naipaul's (ethnographic) vision of India. The argument thus far suggests that at the root of this change in vision is a particular view of the modernity of the "underdeveloped" or the (neo)colonized (not to be confused with what is being referred to as colonial modernity) as partial, inauthentic, incomplete. In this view, an authentic modernity becomes the fulfillment of history. What Naipaul is at pains to demonstrate in the third book of the trilogy is the historical process by which India is acceding to such an authentic modernity, is becoming "whole":

> Excess was now felt to be excess in India. What the mutinies were also helping to define was the strength of the general intellectual life, and the wholeness and humanism of the values to which all Indians now felt they could appeal. And—strange irony—the mutinies were not to be wished away. They were part of the beginning of a new way for many millions, part of India's growth, part of its restoration. (518)

The passage suggests a specific understanding of modern Indian history and of the modernity of this history. The details of this understanding as they appear in *Mutinies* bear close scrutiny, a scrutiny we may begin by turning to three reviews of *Mutinies* that suggest three different approaches to Naipaul's thesis.

Ian Buruma in "Signs of Life" raises *Mutinies* for generously showing an India that is beginning to modernize itself. By modernization Buruma means Westernization or, the Naipaulian term that Buruma approvingly quotes, assimilation to a *universal civilization* (3). Buruma's positive reading of the book is opposed to the evaluations of the book made by Firdaus Kanga and Akeel Bilgrami from deeply divergent positions. In a hard-hitting review of the book entitled "Seeing and Looking Away," Kanga declares that *Mutinies* exposes a Naipaul who has surrendered to "the despairing Indian sense of life as an illusion" (1059). "A writer cannot look away from what he sees; to do that is to create his own area of darkness—a tragic thing for a man whose intellectual clarity and courage have floodlit the literary landscape of our time,"

Kanga writes (1059). The earlier Naipaul, the Naipaul of the first two books of the trilogy, is much more to Kanga's liking. That Naipaul wished to represent India as it was. The new Naipaul has succumbed to the seductions of illusion.

In "Cry, the Beloved Subcontinent: Naipaul Fiddles while India Burns," Akeel Bilgrami is equally critical of *Mutinies*, but from a very different vantage point. Bilgrami finds *Mutinies* a superficial book. He notes that the kind of critic who disliked the earlier books on India simply for being harsh in their judgments about the country will like this book, while the kind of critic who disliked the earlier books for their superficial commentary will continue to dislike this book (30). What is lacking in *Mutinies*, Bilgrami asserts, is any adequate historical contextualization for the numerous life-stories that Naipaul presents. Bilgrami acknowledges that Naipaul's suggestion that things are finally moving in the right direction in India *may* be correct, but notes that there is no evidence in his book to prove it (34).[8] Most of Bilgrami's review is taken up in giving precisely the kind of historical detail (regarding the Punjab situation, the Babri Masjid-Ram Janmabhumi affair, etc.) that the approximately five hundred pages of *Mutinies* leave out.

Akeel Bilgrami identifies a weakness of *Mutinies* that both Buruma and Kanga in their desire to recuperate a particular idea of Naipaul ignore. While *Mutinies* purports to provide "glimpses of the Indian century," it does so in a manner particularly insensitive to the practical context to which it refers.[9] *Mutinies* functions very much as a sequel to the first two books of the trilogy. It carries forward and completes a sweepingly generalized historical argument begun in these books and persists in extending their superficialities. Its conclusions have been assumed a priori.

A detour through Jawaharlal Nehru's *The Discovery of India* (1946) will help us explore this point. The choice of this particular book is not arbitrary. In *The Discovery of India*, as is well known, Nehru set out to give an account of India's history from a nationalist perspective. Composed while Nehru was in Ahmadnagar Fort prison for five months in 1944, the book is a series of brief essays that moves from the prison through incidents in Nehru's life that brought him to "the discovery of India" to a historical narrative of the most important events and periods (as Nehru sees it) of Indian history. At the center of this narrative is "India," conceived of as a unified nation. "Some kind of a dream of unity has occupied the mind of India since the dawn of civilization,"

Nehru declares early in the book (50). Much later, Nehru defines nationalism as follows: "Nationalism is essentially a group memory of past achievements, traditions, and experiences" (526).

Nehru's definition of nationalism leads him directly to an idiom of "wholeness" and "decay." The terms indicate opposed conditions. "Wholeness" means not only the political unity of India, but also the continued vigor and creativity of national intellectual and spiritual life, of Indian praxis. Since Nehru assumes a "whole" Indian nation that reaches back to the earliest moments of history, he must explain the ups and downs of Indian history in terms of the condition of this "wholeness." And so, attempting to suggest reasons for India's "decay" or decline from "wholeness," Nehru writes, "Why this should have happened so is more difficult to unravel, for India was not lacking in mental alertness and technical skill in earlier times. One senses a progressive deterioration during centuries. The urge to life and endeavor becomes less, the creative spirit fades away and gives place to the imitative" (42). Nehru's obsessive quest in *The Discovery of India* is to identify the reasons for what he calls the "internal decay" of India (219). For him, it would seem, Indian decline refers to a decline in practical ability, the ability to transform the world. "The creative spirit fades." Most tellingly, the urge to life itself becomes "less."

Nehru takes the moment in time when the decay of India begins as the end of the first millennium after Christ (218). This is significant because it is about this time that Muslim invaders appear along the northwestern reaches of the subcontinent. The Muslim invaders, however, are not the reason for India's decay, in Nehru's eyes, but rather those who benefit from it; India was stagnant before Muslim invasions (261–62). Simultaneously, Nehru writes that the Muslim invasions, as opposed to the British invasions centuries later, led to Indian rulers (who thought of themselves as Indians and ruled from India) (233–34). This last move on the part of Nehru, his desire to include Muslims as Indians, must be seen as part of his attempt to build and consolidate a multireligious, all-India secular constituency. Yet, at the same time, Nehru's nationalism remains susceptible to a North Indian and Hindu conception of "India." He spends very little time on South Indian (leave alone, say, North-East Indian) history and thus continues a well-entrenched political and cultural bias toward the Hindi speaking North and against the Dravidian South. And even though he does not make the Muslim invasions the reasons for India's decay, Nehru discovers a "whole" India only in the pre-Muslim period and dismisses the Muslim periods of rule as continuing a decline (with the temporary exception of Akbar) that had already begun earlier. Nehru's nationalism, despite all its attempts at inclusiveness, devalues both non-Hindus and regions outside the Gangetic plain.[10]

Naipaul's trilogy contains ideas startlingly similar to Nehru's. The idea that India is a "decayed civilization" underlies the narrative of *Wounded Civilization* and impels him to ask the question "Renaissance or Continuity?" in the last chapter of the book (183). When he writes "Hinduism hasn't been good enough for the millions. It has exposed us to a thousand years of defeat and stagnation," he seems remarkably like Nehru in his sense of the stages of Indian history, though Nehru would have been less dismissive of Hinduism than Naipaul (50). Later he writes in a similar vein, "Indians say their gift is for synthesis. It might be said, rather, that for too long, as a conquered people they have been intellectually parasitic on other civilizations" (144). Again, in this section of the book, Naipaul is much less careful than Nehru in defining India in a manner that excludes Muslims, but the echoes are still strong enough to be unmistakable.

In *Mutinies*, however, Naipaul is intent on portraying a reawakening civilization as opposed to the "lesser civilization" that he declares India to be in *Wounded Civilization* (186). Not surprisingly, in Naipaul's evaluation of Indian praxis in this book the echoes of Nehru's nationalism are even stronger. A passage from the end of the book in which Naipaul has recourse to the language of "wholeness" has already been quoted. Earlier in the book, in his reference to "an unvarying impression [when looking at Indian history before the mid-nineteenth century] of a helpless, trampled-over country, never itself since the Muslim invasions," he echoes Nehru's sense of a break in Indian history occurring at the time of the Muslim invasions (396). Naipaul's education included, as he himself tells us in *Area*, reading about India:

> The India, then, which was the background of my childhood was an area of the imagination. It was not the real country I presently began to read about and whose map I committed to memory. I became a nationalist. . . . But this came almost at the end. The next year India became independent; and I found that my interest was failing. (44)

From this brief assumption of a nationalist stance as an adolescent, Naipaul quickly passes on to what can only be called a neocolonialist position. This is the position that is articulated in *Area* and *Wounded Civilization*.

Does *Mutinies* represent a renewed journey on the part of Naipaul toward a nationalist perspective on Indian history? The strong echoes of Nehru found in Naipaul suggest that this might indeed be the case. "The freedom movement . . . ," Naipaul notes in *Mutinies*, "turned out to be the truest kind of liberation" (517). Certainly, Naipaul does not shower praise on the "greatness" of India as Nehru does, but a conception of Indian history as moving from a vital civilization through a period of decay under foreign occupation (though Nehru would not explicitly characterize the Muslim rulers as foreign) to a period of renewal in the twentieth century (though Naipaul would credit the British with helping to revitalize India far more than Nehru) is shared by both writers.[11] To make a comparison between Naipaul and Nehru in this fashion is not to equate the two. Though he shows himself sympathetic to certain nationalist perspectives, Naipaul does not become a nationalist. Nor is Nehru's significant contribution to the independence struggle in India reducible in its totality to the problematic view of Indian history he advances in *The Discovery of India*.

It is possible, however, to see how a certain form of nationalism, such as Nehru's, remains connected to a colonialist conception of history. Such nationalism leaves unquestioned many of the historical premises that colonialist discourse postulates. This disturbing conceptual congruence between colonialism and a powerful strain of nationalism, despite their political animosity to each other, requires us to scrutinize nationalism anew. Such a scrutiny is indeed being urgently attempted in India. The meaning of nationalism and its practical potentialities have again become significant areas of discussion. One cogent intervention in the debate is Partha Chatterjee's *Nationalist Thought and the Colonial World: A Derivative Discourse?* In a passage that is especially relevant to the argument in this book, Chatterjee writes:

> Nationalism denied the alleged inferiority of the colonized people; it also asserted that a backward nation could "modernize" itself while retaining its cultural identity. It thus produced a discourse in which, even as it challenged the colonial claim to political domination, it also accepted the very intellectual premises of 'modernity' on which colonial domination was based. (30)

The connection between modernity and nationalism suggested here by Chatterjee has already been encountered by us in the discussion in the previous chapter of Richard Wright's evaluation of Nkrumahism.

The renewed debate around the meaning of nationalism in India is taking place in the aftermath of the relative decline of Nehruvian nationalism as the official ideology of the Indian nation-state and the concomitant rise of the Hindu right.[12] *Mutinies* was researched and written by Naipaul between December 1988 and February 1990, even as the Hindu right made impressive gains by focusing public attention on a mosque in Ayodhya, the reputed birthplace of the god Rama. The mosque, the Hindu right claimed, had been built some four hundred years ago by destroying a temple that stood in its place.[13] Naipaul's only reference to this practical context in *Mutinies* is a brief paragraph (362). Such oversight is especially curious since Naipaul has a personal association with Ayodhya. It is the town from which his father's family migrated to Trinidad ("East Indian" 36). This is the kind of erasure about which Akeel Bilgrami complains.[14] At the same time that Naipaul's text excludes such crucial details, it stages a version of a tired nationalist history. From the neocolonialist historical vision of the first two books of the trilogy, Naipaul passes in *Mutinies* to a version of nationalism. However, Naipaul does not, as it has been noted above, become a nationalist. The new directions that *Mutinies* moves in actually broach a larger, global agenda.

In a talk entitled "Our Universal Civilization," given at the Manhattan Institute in 1991 (that is, at about the time *Mutinies* was completed) and later published in *The New York Review of Books*, Naipaul argues that a universal civilization beginning in Europe has spread all over the world. "So much is contained in it [the universal civilization]" Naipaul declares,

> the idea of the individual, responsibility, choice, the life of the intellect, the idea of vocation and perfectibility and achievement. It is an immense human idea. It cannot be reduced to a fixed system. It cannot generate fanaticism. But it is known to exist; and because of that, other more rigid systems in the end blow away. (25)

It is clear that such a universal civilization is only comprehensible, paradoxically enough given its universality, in relationship to a "Third World" (as well as a disappeared "Second World") of "rigid systems" that lies outside it. Naipaul defines the universal civilization as it appears above by noting first that he began to formulate this idea during the course of his travels through non-Arab Muslim countries. The account of these travels finally became *Among the Believers*. *Among the Believers*, as much as the texts of the India trilogy, sets out to explain an already assumed thesis in true Naipaulian style. Naipaul's thesis in *Among the Believers* is of the rigidity and parasitic nature of Islamic societies. Islamic societies, in Naipaul's eyes, are parasitic on a dynamic world outside them for the commodities and communication systems that are necessary for them to survive and that they are incapable of generating themselves (e.g., 81 and 401). This outside world is referred to by Naipaul in the concluding section of *Among the Believers* as a "universal civilization":

> The life that had come to Islam had not come from within. It had come from outside events and circumstances, the spread of the universal civilization. It was the late twentieth century that had made Islam revolutionary, given new meaning to old Islamic ideas of equality and union, shaken up static or retarded societies. It was the late twentieth century—and not the faith—that could supply the answers—in institutions, legislation, economic systems. (429)

The narrow provenance of this "universal civilization" is made clearer when Naipaul refers in passing in *Among the Believers* to "[t]he West, or the universal civilization it leads" (168). Thus, the West as the apotheosis of a universal civilization is opposed to all the restricted, limited places located in what is conventionally called the "Third World."

Indeed, it can be specified further that Naipaul's "universal civilization" is nothing else than late capitalism and the culture of Western bourgeois society. Hence, Naipaul's continual recourse to "technology" in giving expression to, as noted above, the ideology of late capitalism. Naipaul's rhetorical attempts at dissimulation ("*our* universal civilization," the conflation of this civilization with history itself in the cryptic reference to "the late twentieth century") cannot obscure this fact. Naipaul's neocolonial travel narratives stage again and again what he considers the parasitic relationship between the "Third World" societies to which he journeys and the "universal civilization." Although he never uses the term "universal civilization" in his trilogy on India (not even in *Mutinies*, which is written after *Among the Believers*), the same understanding of history and global relations underlies the trilogy. If Naipaul had encountered only an excremental Indian reality in the first two books of the trilogy, it is because he had then perceived India as lying outside the purview of what he later came to call "our universal civilization." In *Mutinies* he began to consider the possibility that India was becoming a part of such a "civilization." Ian Buruma recognizes as much in his reverential review of *Mutinies* cited earlier in this chapter.

It has been suggested above that *Mutinies* propounds a version of nationalist history. It is being argued now that, at the same time, *Mutinies* depicts an India being drawn into Naipaul's universal civilization. We are led thus to observe a complementarity between bourgeois, modernizing nationalism and global capitalism. Ali Mazrui in his essay "Exit Visa From the World System: Dilemmas of Cultural and Economic Disengagement" characterizes the world system as a Westphalian nation-state system and suggests that decolonization is a process by which societies enter the system (62–63). The implication: if a society is to enter the global political order that is the expression of global capitalism, it must do so in the guise of a nation-state. Partha Chatterjee comes to a similar conclusion at the end of *Nationalist Thought and the Colonial World*: "Conservatory of the passive revolution [of capitalism], the national state now proceeds to find for 'the nation' a place in the global order of capital, while striving to keep the contradictions between capital and the people in perpetual suspension" (168). There is no contradiction, then, between Naipaul's "nationalist" perspective on Indian history and his endorsement of a "universal civilization." Both come together in *Mutinies* as the process by which the "imagined community" of the Indian nation regains a lost wholeness even as it progressively integrates itself into the culture and economy of the global capitalism that Naipaul cryptically calls "our universal civilization."[15] *Mutinies* is an enthusiastic celebration of this process.

ALL THAT IS WHOLE TURNS INTO WEST

The argument in this book makes clear that the alleged Indian accession to a "universal civilization" described in *Mutinies*—with its cryptic endorsement of a Western, capitalist model of "advanced" society—is really the description of an accession to a "universal modernity." A further exploration of what is entailed here might begin with Marshal

Berman's important book *All That Is Solid Melts Into Air*, one of the most influential treatments of such a "universal modernity."

"There is a mode of vital experience . . ." Berman begins his book, "that is shared by men and women all over the world today. I will call this body of experience 'modernity.' To be modern is to find ourselves in an environment that promises us adventure, power, joy, growth, transformation of ourselves and the world—and, at the same time, that threatens to destroy everything we have, everything we know, everything we are. . . . To be modern is to be part of a universe in which, as Marx said, 'all that is solid melts into air'" (15). A constitutive contradictoriness is, thus, the chief characteristic of modernity for Berman. As Berman's title makes clear, his understanding of this contradictoriness is indebted to Karl Marx and he devotes the second chapter of the book to an extended analysis of *The Communist Manifesto*. Berman emphasizes in this analysis what he sees as Marx's celebration of the achievements of an ascendant bourgeoisie. However, in so doing, Berman is less attentive to the many qualifications by which Marx hedges such a celebration. In *The Communist Manifesto,* Marx and Friedrich Engels do indeed sing the glory of the bourgeoisie but only to illustrate the manner of its growth into a hegemonic and exploitative class. Berman's reading disregards, for the most part, the latter portion of their argument.

Such a selective reading of *The Communist Manifesto* is symptomatic of Berman's perspective on modernity in general. Although he continually refers to the contradictory nature of modernity, its capacity both for good and evil, he finally tends to regard the modern project as a heroic one. Berman engages in "a celebration," as John Tomlinson remarks in commenting on Berman's book, "of modernity" (148). The conclusion to *All That Is Solid Melts into Air* makes this clear: "The process of modernization, even as it exploits and torments us, brings our energies and imaginations to life, drives us to grasp and confront the world that modernization makes, and to strive to make it our own. I believe that we and those who come after us will go on fighting to make ourselves at home in this world, even as the homes we have made, the modern street, the modern spirit, go on melting into air" (348). It may be noted here that Berman's sweeping reference to modernity's exploitation of "us" would seem to indicate his location outside a critical tradition of Marxism (at least in this book). Any analysis of modernity that is sensitive to the class dimensions of society will recognize the differentially exploitative character of (capitalist) modernity. It is only by casting "modernity" as an abstract existential condition in *All That Is Solid Melts into Air* that Berman can make of it something heroic and universalize a particular experience of it.

Berman also makes a distinction in his book between the modernities and modernisms of "advanced" and "backward" nations. His chief example of a backward (another of Berman's terms here is "underdeveloped") nation is Russia during the nineteenth century which, he declares, can be seen "as an archetype of the emerging twentieth-century Third World" (175). For Berman, the history of which nineteenth-century Russia is an example is "distinctively modern from the start, but modern in a twisted, gnarled, surreal way" (272). Whereas the modernism of advanced nations has the reality of an achieved modernity to refer to, "the modernism of underdevelopment is forced to build on fantasies and dreams of modernity. . . . In order to be true to the life from which it springs, it is forced to be shrill, uncouth and inchoate" even if it is also possessed of a "desperate incandescence" that Western modernism "can rarely hope to match" (232). This contrast between the modernities and modernisms of developed and underdeveloped nations is fundamental to Berman's argument in his book; but given the space he devotes to elaborating this contrast, it is significant that he does not explore the historical connections between the so-called developed and underdeveloped countries. To Berman's mind, the "twisted, gnarled, surreal" modernism of underdevelopment is simply the result of a disjuncture between consciousness and reality within underdeveloped countries. He does not consider the role that "developed" countries might have played in bringing about such a condition. If he were to venture into this territory, he would have to consider the role of colonialism in the creation of a particular kind of modernity in "underdeveloped" countries. The relevance of this theme with regard to Russia cannot be commented on here; but we have already seen how important it is with regard to the modernity of the "Third World" of which Berman makes Russia premonitory.

Both Berman's selective reading of *The Communist Manifesto* and his selective understanding of the relationship between developed and underdeveloped countries become comprehensible in the context of the overarching ideology in which his book is couched. It is clear, even from the passages above, that Berman conceives of the West and its modern culture in normative terms—the modern culture of the "underdeveloped" countries in contrast is twisted, gnarled, surreal (the preface to the Penguin edition of Berman's book begins by discussing Brazil in similar terms), in a word, abnormal. It is true that the modernism of the West is itself contradictory but nevertheless Berman can refer approvingly to "the modernism of advanced nations, building directly on the materials of economic and political modernization and drawing vision and energy from a modernized reality . . . even when it challenges that reality in radical ways" and contrast it to "a modernism that arises from backwardness and underdevelopment . . . a truncated and warped modernization" (231–32). Even in all its contradictoriness, the modernity of the West is whole in a way that the modernity of the "underdeveloped" countries, full of wishful fantasizing because it has no modernized reality to draw from, cannot be.

It is interesting in this context to compare Marshall Berman and Walter Rodney. Both Rodney and Berman draw inspiration from Marx in their works. Where Berman is more attentive to those aspects of Marx's work that celebrate the bourgeoisie, Rodney is more attentive to the critical dimensions. Rodney's central thesis in *How Europe Underdeveloped Africa*, so compelling at many different levels, insists that the relationship between "developed" and "underdeveloped" (nations, societies, theoretical categories) be understood in dynamic and critical terms. Consequently, Rodney is able to write "that development and underdevelopment are not only comparative terms, but . . . they also have a dialectical relationship one to the other" (75). Berman, so compelling and insightful in other respects in his book, is only able to understand the relationship between "developed" and "underdeveloped" as comparison.

Reading V. S. Naipaul's travel books in the context of Marshall Berman's argument reveals the pervasiveness of a particular historical amnesia regarding the project of modernity. It has been suggested above that what Naipaul calls "universal civilization" is really the capitalist modernity of the "developed" countries. Despite their many differences, both Naipaul and Berman ignore the colonial dimension of this modernity or universal civilization.[16] They show no understanding of the ways in which the origins of modernity lie, just as much, in colonialism. It is because of this amnesia that Berman is able to elide the agency of the "developed" countries in the appearance of what he regards as the grotesque if also brilliant modernism of the "underdeveloped."

It is again because of this amnesia that Naipaul is able to construct the relationship of the "Third World" to what he calls "universal civilization" in the way he does. In *Wounded Civilization*, he portrays Indian experiments with modernity as imitative and futile. By the time he comes to write *Mutinies*, he is more sanguine about the modern project in India and views Indian accession to the "universal civilization" as an imminent and desirable possibility. But is the accession that Naipaul desires really possible (leave alone desirable)? Can the modernity of the underdeveloped that Berman identifies ever be transformed into the modernity of the developed? It would seem that the answer to these questions is simple—if the appropriate social, economic and political policies are followed, then indeed "underdeveloped" will become "developed" and those who have been outside the purview of universal civilization will be brought within it. If, however, the history of modernity is inextricable from the history of not only capitalism but also colonialism, it is possible that "modernity" is constitutively incapable of accommodating a "universal civilization."[17] The project of modernity must then be recognized as constitutively inegalitarian.

In *The Wretched of the Earth*, Frantz Fanon discusses Western bourgeois ideology in a colonial context and notes:

> Western bourgeois racial prejudice as regards the nigger and the Arab is a racism of contempt; it is a racism which minimizes what it hates. Bourgeois ideology, however, which is the proclamation of an essential equality between men [*sic*] manages to appear logical in its own eyes by inviting the sub-men to become human, and to take as their prototype Western humanity as incarnated in the Western bourgeoisie. (163)

But Fanon's point in *The Wretched of the Earth* is that the "sub-men" can never in fact "become human" in the way human is understood by bourgeois ideology. The "sub-men" can never aspire to anything but the status of third-rate copies or imitations of the "men." Cannot Naipaul's invitation to the "Third World" to accede to a universal civilization be understood in a similar way? If "universal civilization" is nothing other than "modernity," and this modernity (drawing on the argument in the book as a whole) is to be understood as a "(neo)colonial modernity," can the colonized or the formerly colonized ever become a part of it?

At the end of the last chapter, Wright was seen to oppose (apparently) the agonistic politics of nationalism to the politics of colonial modernity in the two evaluative structures that were discovered in his text. It was noted then that we could therefore regard nationalism as aspiring to the status of an anticolonial modernity. In this chapter, it has been suggested that the politics of nationalism in the "Third World" hopes to achieve the objective of helping those outside of "universal civilization" accede to it, of closing the gap between the weak modernity of the colonized or the formerly colonized and the strong modernity of the (neo)colonizers. Through the forced fabrication of the sociopolitical form of the nation, such a politics aspires to move its constituency from the realm of the premodern or the wrongly modern to the realm of the modern. However, whether such a journey is at all possible under the aegis of what remains a modernity that maintains itself by marking the distinction between colonizer and colonized, between West and Rest, between modern and premodern or wrongly modern, remains a crucial question for critical theories of modernity.

Partha Chatterjee in *The Nation and its Fragments* suggests an answer to this question. Drawing on Michel Foucault, he argues that "a modern regime of power" is one "in which power is meant not to prohibit but to facilitate, to produce" (15) and that "the principal justification for the modern regime of power is that by making social regulations an aspect of the self-disciplining of normalized individuals, power is made more productive, effective and humane" (17). In Chatterjee's view, such a modern regime of power, however, must necessarily remain an incomplete project in a colonial situation because it implies the conferral of a *legal* equality of status on the people who fall within its purview. If the establishment of a modern regime of power were pursued to its proper conclusion, the subjects of the empire would be converted into citizens, an impossibility for what Chatterjee calls "the rule of colonial difference" which specified the irreconcilability of brown and white, colonized and colonizer (16).

Thus, in Chatterjee's argument, although the colonial state introduced a modern regime of power, indeed modernity itself, into colonial India, the project of modernity could only be advanced any further through the ultimate abolition of the colonial situation. Chatterjee's argument suggests that the ambition of the colonial authority to import efficient regimes of power into its territory through the fashioning of a modern state is contravened by its simultaneous commitment to the rule of colonial difference. There would seem to be a contradiction, then, between modern regimes of power (might we say modernity?) and colonialism. In such a reading, the nationalist contestation of colonial power is almost an inevitable product of this contradiction. By abolishing the rule of colonial difference, anticolonial nationalism aspires to give "modernity" itself greater scope for play.

The arguments in this and the previous chapters, however, suggest that there is no contradiction between colonialism and modernity, that even if nationalism aspires to the status of an anticolonial modernity, "modernity" may be incapable of accommodating it. So inextricable may be the connection between the history of colonialism and the history of modernity that "Third World" nationalism's aspiration to the status of an anticolonial modernity, a modernity whose lineaments are not dissimilar to Naipaul's universal civilization at the same time that it is resolutely anticolonial, may be an absurdly paradoxical project. For such a modernity is fundamentally colonial—encoded in every, visible and invisible, aspect of its culture is a distinction between modern and premodern, colonizer and colonized. There can be no such achieved historical condition as an anticolonial modernity. Critical perspectives, it may be suggested at this point, rather than separating out "modernity" and "colonialism" as analytical categories, as Chatterjee seems to do, need to recognize how integral these categories are to each other.

If such is the case, how are we to understand the postcolonial aspiration to modernity? The above discussion allows us to get at an answer. The discussion suggests that following anticolonial struggle, the postcolonial nation, seeing itself as whole again, eagerly rises up from its "decayed" condition—but only to find that the rules have changed. The game of modernity is played in a different way now. The paradox that Chatterjee recognized in the colonial situation has now been, to use a currently favored term, globalized. The paradox of the colonial world is now the paradox of the "global village." Globalization corresponds historically—the publication of *Mutinies* in the period of India's economic "liberalization" or entry into a globalized economy makes clear—to the creeping advance of Naipaul's "universal civilization." If globalization were pursued to its logical end, equality would have to be conferred on all within its purview. But the very terms of this universal civilization (really a capitalist Western culture masquerading as the vanguard of history) suggests that such equality can never be conferred. Thus, the specific contradiction noted by Partha Chatterjee in the colonial situation reappears, transformed, at the global level, in the guise of *a neocolonial rule of difference*. Like the colonized, the neocolonized are still pathetic. Now, their pathos is not marked by their race alone, a reading of *Mutinies* makes clear, but also by their poverty and by their backward technology. Once again, their modernity is incomplete and it can be only be completed by a struggle to achieve an impossible (within the terms of this modernity) equality—for, even as the "backward" nations "catch up" economically, culturally and technologically, the "advanced" have once again slipped into the future. The "backward nations" find they have not "caught up" at all. This is not just a matter of semantics, a matter of discourse; for the eagerness of the "backward nations" to "catch up" helps define—for better and for worse—the nondiscursive praxis in which they engage. This was the way the game of modernity was always played.

Postmodernity by Any Other Name

And so we return to the question of postmodernity, a term which would seem to imply a transcendence of the very game of modernity. Perry Anderson in his admiring survey of Jameson's comments on postmodernity writes: "His theorization of postmodernism, starting in the early eighties, takes its place among the great intellectual monuments of Western Marxism" (71). It is not necessary to take exception to this assessment of Jameson's magisterial performance to disagree with his notion of the postmodern. As it appears in Fredric Jameson's influential formulation, the term is closely linked to the narrative of modernization. Jameson argues repeatedly in *Postmodernism, or the Cultural Logic of Late Capitalism* that while the modernisms were characterized by a sense of the radical difference of the past (a fairly conventional understanding of the modern), archaic features of the premodern persisted into the modern period. For Jameson, the modernity of the modern age was an incomplete one and it is only in the postmodern age that the process of modernization is completed. From Jameson's perspective, postmodernity is the fulfilled condition of modernity. However, the argument in this book suggests that modernization (understood as more than a technological process) has not been completed, cannot be completed; that modernity was incomplete, is incomplete. Clearly, the issue requires further review.

Jurgen Habermas in "Modernity—An Incomplete Project" launches a spirited critique of the very idea of the postmodern. The "project of modernity," Habermas argues, is not yet complete. In eighteenth-century Europe, "the philosophers of the Enlightenment" exerted their efforts toward the development of "objective science, universal morality and law, and autonomous art according to their inner logic" (9). Whereas this effort aimed at the fuller development of these realms, the result was a problematic separating out of them. The various antimodernisms, of which postmodernism is one, are responding to the many crises engendered by a sundering of the three realms. The question for Habermas is whether these antimodernisms are prescient and the time has come for the abandonment of the project of modernity as such. Habermas's answer to this question is emphatically in the negative. Rather, Habermas believes that efforts must be made to complete the project of modernity, which

> aims at a differentiated relinking of modern culture with an everyday praxis that still depends on vital heritages, but would be impoverished through mere traditionalism. This new connection, however, can only be established under the condition that societal modernization will also be steered in a different direction. The life-world has to become able to develop institutions out of itself which set limits to the internal dynamics and imperatives of an almost autonomous economic system and its administrative complements. (13)

Habermas, though not optimistic regarding the chances for a completion of the project of modernity, remains convinced that a subscription to its objectives is preferable to the neoconservative antimodernism that is postmodernism.

Habermas's response to the contemporary historical conjuncture, then, is to reassert the relevance of the project of modernity. Terry Eagleton, however, takes a more skeptical view of modernity that is at the same time wary of devolving into a postmodernism. In a critical review of two of Jean-François Lyotard's books, entitled "Awakening from Modernity," Eagleton observes: "'modernity' for Lyotard would seem *nothing but* a tale of terroristic Reason, and Nazism little more than the lethal terminus of totalizing thought. This reckless travesty ignores the fact that the death camps were among other things the upshot of a barbarous irrationalism which, like some aspects of post-modernism itself, junked history, refused argumentation, aestheticized politics and staked all on the charisma of those who told the stories" (194, italics in original). Eagleton refuses to endorse either modernity or postmodernity with the enthusiasm of either a Habermas, on the one hand, or Lyotard, on the other. "In the end," writes Eagleton, "Lyotard's work offers its reader a choice between the politics of the ageing hippie and those of the arch-Hegelian. It would seem doubtful that these are the only options available" (194). In a more detailed examination of the postmodern, entitled "Capitalism, Modernism and Postmodernism," Eagleton expands on this thesis, observing, "[a] whole traditional ideology of representation is in crisis, yet this does not mean [for modernism] that the search for truth is abandoned. Postmodernism, on the contrary, commits the apocalyptic error of believing that the discrediting of this particular representational epistemology is the death of truth itself" (144). It will be readily apparent from these passages that Eagleton's claims with regard to both postmodernism and postmodernity are quite modest.

David Harvey writes in a similar spirit in *The Condition of Postmodernity*. He argues that postmodernism is the result of a transitional moment within capitalism. Like earlier such moments, this transition involves what Harvey calls "a new round of 'time-space compression' in the organization of capitalism" (vii). The condition of postmodernity, he then argues, is the historical experience of this reorganization of capitalism; the feelings of fragmentation and disorientation to which many postmodern commentators as well as commentators on postmodernism have testified, whether in a celebratory or a critical spirit, arises out of this experience. Harvey's argument is convincing because it acknowledges the apocalyptic sensibility of postmodernism while more modestly and firmly locating this sensibility within a historical conjuncture. His argument makes it possible for us to see how postmodernism is really not some irresistible historical departure *from* modernism but rather an emergence (or, more accurately, the reemergence) into the foreground of a particular tendency within capitalism. Harvey titles chapter 22 of his book "Fordist modernism versus flexible postmodernism, or the interpenetration of opposed tendencies in capitalism as a whole." To see modernism and postmodernism in this fashion, as opposed tendencies within a capitalism conceived of as a whole, Harvey suggests, "helps us dissolve the categories of both modernism and postmodernism into a complex of oppositions expressive of the cultural contradictions of capitalism. We then get to see the categories of both modernism and postmodernism as static reifications imposed upon the fluid interpenetration of dynamic oppositions" (339).

Harvey's argument in *The Condition of Postmodernity*, it must already be clear, is made through an analysis of what he calls "the logic of capital" (343). "Capital," he notes, "is a process and not a thing. It is a process of reproduction of social life through commodity production. . . . Its internalized rules of operation are such as to ensure that it is a dynamic and revolutionary model of social organization, restlessly and ceaselessly transforming the society within which it is embedded" (343). Postmodernity appears here as a transitional phase within a historical evolution of capitalism. Postmodernism as a tendency, we may then infer, comes to be foregrounded during postmodernity as a phase. Postmodernity, characterized (we can suggest, drawing on Harvey) by "the anarchical flux, change, and uncertainty to which capitalist modernity is always prone," is not an irresistible departure from modernity (any more than postmodernism is such a departure from modernism) but rather a particular expression of it (108). This is, in the first instance, a question of semantics; but in the choice of how to semanticize postmodernity lies buried a particular evaluation of it. Resemanticizing postmodernity as a particular expression of modernity allows us to articulate yet again a disagreement with Jean-François Lyotard's rather breathless account (reviewed in the first chapter) of the postmodern condition.

Though David Harvey's account of postmodernism and postmodernity is suggestive within its terms, there are oversights in it. Harvey's description of modernity in the passage quoted above as a *capitalist* modernity indicates where his emphasis lies. In this book, the argument has rather concerned a *colonial* modernity. The objective has been to explore the ways in which modernity is not separable from the history of colonialism. A sense of the colonial dimensions of modernity conveys to us the problems with both Jameson's conclusion that modernization has been completed and Habermas's conclusion that the objective should be the completion of the project of modernity. Modernity, it has been argued in this book, is constitutively incapable of being completed.

We embarked on the exploration of a colonial modernity because of the riddle posed by *Indiana Jones and the Temple of Doom*: Is it a postmodern text? Is it a neocolonial text? If it is both, how do we reconcile the postmodernity with the neocoloniality? Already in the first chapter, an answer was suggested. *Temple*, it was noted, contravenes many of the formulations of the contemporary critical commentary on the postmodern because it is a neocolonial text. Postmodernity, as the term for a transcendence of modernity, we found, cannot be reconciled with neocolonialism.

The argument proceeded then to find that the ethnographic vision that was examined critically in *Gulliver's Travels* is unhappily reproduced centuries later in *Temple*. The presumption of transcendent subjectivity critiqued by Jonathan Swift is presumed once again. The primitivism, in its various forms, at work in Joseph Conrad's *Heart of Darkness*, Richard Wright's *Black Power* and V. S. Naipaul's India trilogy is at work in *Temple* too. And the resistance to dominant formulations of modernity advanced in different ways in *Black Power* and Zora Neale Hurston's *Mules and Men* is indicative of the global historical situation of struggle to which *Temple* is responding. *Temple* aspires to delegitimize the anticolonial Indian nationalism that contested the British Raj as well as its postcolonial successor. As noted in the first chapter, nothing gestures more clearly to the practical context within which *Temple* operates than the manner in which the movie was greeted—by censorship—by the institutional successor to anticolonial nationalism in India—the postcolonial state. In many different ways, *Temple* is best regarded as a text that expresses a (neo)colonial modernity. Thus, the comparativism enabled by the discussion of three different geographical areas, abetted by the notions of praxis recuperated here, allows us to signal in an illustrative way the vast global and practical context in which *Temple* is to be placed.

In the first chapter, it was suggested that the so-called postmodernity of the West may be understood as (postcolonial) crisis and (neocolonial) management. The argument of the book has traced the antecedents of this crisis and management through a number of key texts. Modernity, it has been argued, necessarily presumes a premodern—represented by the colonized in the colonial period and by the "Third World" in the neocolonial. While the premodern under colonialism is strongly marked by racial characteristics, under neocolonialism technological and economic characteristics come to the foreground. Only hinted at in *Heart of Darkness*, a textual economy involving the latter characteristics can be seen emerging in Richard Wright's ambivalent comments in *Black Power*. In V. S. Naipaul's India trilogy, such a textual economy is fully articulated. It would seem then that discourses of race, contested by the various anticolonial resistances, are no longer dominant in neocolonialism. *Temple* serves to remind us, however, that racial economies have not been abandoned in the neocolonial period. While drawing on "technology" and "poverty" in the portrayal of India, *Temple* also continues to have recourse to race as a way of explaining the difference between Indiana and Indian. That the movie allows such explanation to flow from the narrative itself rather than some metanarratival racialized commentary cannot obscure the salience of this recourse to race. It is in these ways that *Temple*, working in complementarity with texts such as Naipaul's trilogy, attempts to manage the crises forced on the scene by anticolonial resistances. The evaluative structures on display in *Temple* and Naipaul's trilogy are clues to a general historical condition that is visible in a host of cultural phenomena from U.S. television news to European tourism to African magazine advertisements to the celebration of Mother Theresa to the global division of literary labor between "First World" theory and "Third World" poems, plays, and novels, and so on, and on. To label this historical condition postmodern—rather than modern in the sense suggested in this book—is really to miss its *practical* complexity.

And it is just such a complexity that is foregrounded by an attention to the notion of a textual economy, broached in the first chapter. In making the case for a textual economics and a cultural politics of praxis there, I explored the ways in which a text produces and distributes "value." This exploration led us to see both how a specific text is the expression of a specific praxis and how praxis is thematized within a text; but of course the connection between expression and thematization is intimate. Following this lead, then, Part II set out to explore the thematization of both the colonized and the colonizers as *practical* beings in a variety of texts and thus came to recognize the politics expressed by the texts (as suggested in the recapitulation above). It was thus too that the argument arrived at a recognition of the manner in which notions of praxis lie embedded within the discourse of modernity. That the argument was primarily concerned with *colonial* modernity let us see beyond the dissimulating innocence of much of this discourse. For, finally, differing *evaluations* of (human) praxis are at issue here. In the so-called postmodern period—or, to introduce a different language, in these times of globalization—the chief features of a modern (differential) evaluation of praxis remain in place, finding a variety of practical expressions as well as contestations.[18] "Modernity," then, is the valued name reserved for certain (Western and white) kinds of praxis. And, while the centuries of colonialism may in a superficial sense be behind us, in the game of (neocolonial) modernity, the ball is still very much in play.

How are we to imagine an end to the game?

NOTES

CHAPTER ONE: INTRODUCTION

1. I have in mind here Tania Modleski's distinction between "'popular art,' which arises 'from the people,' and 'mass art,' which is imposed from above" (x). I am aware that this distinction is a highly contested one in contemporary criticism; but an overhasty dismissal of the distinction makes it impossible for us to understand the different ways in which different texts are produced, disseminated, and received. To my way of thinking, "popular culture" and "mass culture" do not indicate mutually exclusive categories but rather two poles of a theoretical continuum in terms of which texts and cultural practices can be situated.

2. For a sampling of other relevant work in this context, see G. Thomas Goodnight's essay, in which he too argues that Spielberg is a postmodern filmmaker (though he does not touch on *Temple*) and Pauline Kael's review of the film which, though she does not use the word postmodern, finds recognizably postmodern characteristics in it.

3. A few statistics may be cited here to illustrate my point. Two hundred and sixty-two movies were made in the United States in 1984, the year in which *Indiana Jones and the Temple of Doom* was released. There were 1,190 million paid admissions within the United States amounting to $4,036 million. The earnings of *Temple* were on an epic scale—$109,000,000, making it the eighth most lucrative movie in history. The Indiana Jones movie that preceded it, *Raiders of the Lost Ark*, had earned $115,598,000 in North American rentals and was seventh in rank in terms of all-time earnings. The most lucrative film in history in 1984 was also directed by Steven Spielberg. *ET-The Extra-Terrestrial* had earned $209,976,989 in 1982 in North American movie house rentals. *Temple*'s single-day gross earning of $9,324,760 at 1,687 sites on Sunday, 27 May 1984 was a record. Its opening week gross of $45,709,328 was also a record. It is estimated that weekly cinema attendance for 1984 in the United States was 229 million.

These statistics help us get a sense not only of the enormity of the Hollywood film industry but also of the success and centrality of Spielberg and Lucas within this industry. Lucas's *Star Wars* was the largest money earner in its time and was still the second largest grosser in history in 1984. Most of the figures cited are for the United States or North America. The estimation is that movies generally earned approximately the same overseas as they did within the United States (Robertson 37). In addition, these movies continue to enjoy through videotape distribution a continually renewed currency. The Indiana Jones format has since also been successfully adapted for television in *The Young Indiana Jones Chronicles*. Arguably, Lucas and Spielberg have been (and remain) among the handful of most important figures in Hollywood during the so-called postmodern age. Their cultural productions, then, offer a good opportunity to explore the meanings of postmodernity.

4. There have been a number of recent allusions to "economy" among theorists concerned with culture or literature. Jean-François Lyotard titles his book *Libidinal Economy* to suggest both what he considers the weaknesses of Marx's theorization of a *political* economy and the manner in which Marx's biases and desires structure his arguments. Perhaps the most sustained recent theorization of "economy," however, is by Jean-Joseph Goux in his essay "Numismatics." Beginning with Marx's example, Goux in "Numismatics" sets out to demonstrate the "economic" functioning of different sectors of social life. In a different vein, Stephen Greenblatt, among recent cultural critics, has been influential in establishing a methodological approach that insists on analyzing the text or cultural practice in relationship to the society in which it "circulates." Greenblatt's indebtedness to an "economic" understanding of society and aesthetic processes is apparent in his language of "exchange," "appropriation," "negotiation," and so on (see *Shakespearean Negotiations*). Two literary critics who have explored many different resonances of the word "economy" for "literature" in greater detail in book-length studies are Marc Shell and Kurt Heinzelman. Kurt Heinzelman in *The Economics of the Imagination* demonstrates not only the economic valence of literary texts but also the literary valence of economic texts. At its broadest, Heinzelman's argument can be understood as an "economic" theory of the relationship (sustained through the instrumentality of the text) between a reader and an author. In the conclusion to his book *The Economy of Literature*, Marc Shell writes, "We have seen that literary works are composed of tropic exchanges . . . , some of which can be analyzed in terms of economic content and all of which can be analyzed in terms of economic form. The economy of literature seeks to understand the relationship between literary exchanges and the exchanges that constitute a political economy" (152). While Shell's book concerns itself with the economy of language (of which a text is made) or a social economy (in which the text exists), it does not concern itself with the text itself *as* an economy. A similar comment may be made of Heinzelman's arguments in *The Economics of the Imagination*.

Perhaps the most influential recent treatment of "value" in literary criticism is Barbara Herrnstein Smith's *Contingencies of Value*. Smith's work is mainly an attempt to demonstrate how it is that literary value, as it comes to be embodied in the canon, is produced. A perceptive critique of Smith's argument is to be found in John Guillory's *Cultural Capital*, which is concerned with similar issues. Other works that may be mentioned here (and whose concern is also largely with the value bestowed on a text) are Tony Bennett's "Really Useless 'Knowledge': A Political Critique of Aesthetics," Terry Eagleton's *Literary Theory: An Introduction* (especially the first chapter) and *Ideology of the Aesthetic*, and Jane Tompkins's *Sensational Designs* (especially the introductory and final chapters).

5. It is clear that Marx's interest in asserting that the political-economic origin of value lies in labor and labor alone is calculated to forward the worker, the bearer of labor power, as the rightful owner of the increased value (surplus value) that resides in the commodities that emerge at the end of the productive process. Many economists, bourgeois and otherwise, have contested this assertion of Marx, suggesting that the source of economic value is to be found rather in a human psychology that expresses itself in the supply-demand relationships of the marketplace. Other economists complain that Marx's theory regarding the origins of economic value in labor is ultimately useless from the perspective of an economic *science* because it does not express itself in an empirically verifiable way. For perspectives on what is at issue here, see Leszek Kolakowski, *Main Currents of Marxism* (vol. 1, chapters XII and XIII, section 6), "Value," *A Dictionary of Marxist Thought* (507–11) and especially Ernest Mandel's perceptive defence of the labor theory of value in "Introduction," *Capital* (vol. 1), 44–46.

6. Ernest Mandel's comments on the extent to which Marx's argument in *Capital* may be generalized bear repeating here. Asserting that, "*Capital* is . . . not 'pure' economic theory at all," Mandel notes:

> In *Capital* Marx's fundamental aim was to lay bare the laws of motion which govern the origins, the rise, the development, the decline and the disappearance of a given social form of economic organization: the capitalist mode of production. He was not seeking *universal* laws of economic organization. Indeed, one of the essential theses of *Capital* is that no such laws exist. ("Introduction," *Capital*, vol. 1, 12, italics in original)

Mandel means by "economic organization" what may be more narrowly construed, for our purposes here, as the realm of "political economy."

7. In this context, see also Erich Fromm on "labor" as an ontological category in *Marx's Concept of Man*, especially pages 29 and 40.

8. Part of the debate on the theme of praxis and its importance in the work of Marx has revolved around the question of the young Marx and the old

Marx, the philosophical Marx and the scientific Marx, the Marx of the *Economic and Philosophical Manuscripts* and of *Capital*. The debate has often taken the shape of a clarification of Marx's relationship to Hegel. It has been suggested that the category of praxis with its voluntaristic and subjectivist implications disappears from *Capital* because Marx has moved beyond his Hegelian phase to a more systematic, structural understanding of history. This is not the place to comment on this debate in any great detail. However, my own arguments tend in the direction of finding a continuity between the young Marx and the later Marx.

9. See such essays as "Poststructuralism, Marginality, Postcoloniality and Value" and "Scattered Speculations on Value."

10. See the chapter on "The Chicago School" in Leitch's *American Literary Criticism from the Thirties to the Eighties*.

11. For other introductory works on ideology, see Jorge Larrain's *The Concept of Ideology*, David McLellan's *Ideology*, Mike Cormack's *Ideology* and Raymond Williams's chapter of the same title in *Marxism and Literature*.

12. See *Beyond Postcolonial Theory* and, especially, *Hegemony and Strategies of Transgression*.

13. See "Economic and Philosophic Manuscripts of 1844." For some different perspectives on the issues at stake in references to "materialism," see "Materialism," in Tom Bottomore, ed., *A Dictionary of Marxist Thought*, Jean-Paul Sartre's "Materialism and Revolution," Richard Bernstein's *Praxis and Action*, Raymond Williams's *Problems in Materialism and Culture* and his entry for "Materialism" in *Keywords*.

14. It is possible that this exchange itself is apocryphal. What is more to our purpose here is the widely held belief in the authenticity of it and its appearance on the postcard as a political statement.

15. See "Awakening from Modernity."

16. In his more recent *The Geopolitical Aesthetic*, Jameson seems to take a more nuanced view of this issue. See, for example, page 77.

17. See also Von Gunden (124–26) and Zimmerman (37).

18. For an apt summarization of a postmodernism thematized as irony and play see Eagleton's essay "Awakening from Modernity" (194).

19. Aside from the works cited below, this section also draws on the following: William Henry Sleeman's *Rambles and Recollections of an Indian Official*, Iftikhar Ahmad's dissertation, and essays by Radhika Singha and Parama Roy.

20. William Henry Sleeman's *The Thugs or Phansigars of India*, published in 1839, gathered together the most important of this material in two volumes and demonstrated the elaborateness of the discourse around "thuggee" at that

time. Publication information given in the preface to the first volume notes that the two volumes were compiled from Sleeman's volume published in Calcutta in 1836. Pages 13–48 of the first volume are Dr. Sherwood's account of "phansigars" from 1816 (predating Sleeman and mentioned in the next paragraph). Pages 48–75 consist of text prepared, apparently, from Sleeman's accounts and that of an unnamed author of an article in volume forty-one of *Foreign Quarterly Review* (see footnote on page 49, vol. 1). The text from pages 75 to 118 is explicitly ascribed to Sleeman. Pages 119–227 are conversations held "by Capt. Sleeman with Thug informers while preparing his vocabulary of their language" (119). Pages 6–33 of the second volume continue the conversations between Sleeman and his informers from the first volume. Pages 35–112 consist of the "ramaseeana" or vocabulary of "thugs" prepared by Sleeman. Pages 113–228 consist of official papers (prepared by different administrative personages) relating to the trials of "thugs." I have taken the ascription of the two volumes to Capt. Sleeman at face value and have assumed the author of the text to be Sleeman, unless made perfectly clear otherwise.

The books by Thornton and Taylor alluded to in the previous sentence of the text are *Illustrations of the History and Practice of the Thugs* (1837) and *Confessions of a Thug* (1839) respectively. "Fraternity" is a word commonly applied by these writers to "thuggee."

21. The sequence in which the three semitic religions are listed may also capture their relative valuation in contemporary Western culture.

22. In this popular novel published soon after India's independence, the hero John Savage is based on the historical William Henry Sleeman. There is also a more recent cinematic version of this novel.

23. See, for example, pages 54, 68–69, and 107 of Sleeman's *The Thugs* (vol. 1).

24. This scene involves, among other things, the serving of such grotesque dishes as soups with eyeballs floating in them and monkeys' heads. Willie Scott's horrified response is supposed to represent civilized behavior. Such a crude mapping of cultural difference in this scene is especially problematic since it involves a country in which vegetarianism has greater currency than most others.

25. See *The Yellow Scarf*, Francis Tuker's biography of Sleeman for this reference (xi).

26. This portrayal of the relationship between Christianity and India does scant justice to the millennia-long presence of Christianity there. The idea of Christianity in *Temple* is, however, consistent with the self-image of Western missionary Christianity.

27. A note regarding my use of the terms "postcolonial" and "neocolonial" may be in order here. The terms are often employed in imprecise ways. Though both terms refer to the same historical phenomenon, the emergence of

the "Third World," they emphasize different aspects of this phenomenon. "Post-colonial" conveys a sense of the newly achieved autonomy of formerly colonized countries, and "neocolonial" a sense of the continuation of an uneven relationship of dominance and control between former colonizers and former colonized. The two conditions indicated by the terms are not mutually exclusive and it is possible to use both terms simultaneously to emphasize different aspects of the same situation. I should also note here the distinction between "colonial"—signifying a historical condition—and "colonialist"—an ideological position. Therefore, in the book, I have preferred the term *(neo)colonialist travel narrative* for what is often more loosely termed *colonial travel narrative*.

28. For more on decolonization, see my entry for the term in the forthcoming *Encyclopedia of Postcolonial Studies*.

29. Jones does cross over to become one of "them" when he is forced to drink Kali's blood by Mola Ram, but this is not a deliberate crossing over. Compare Kurtz in *Heart of Darkness*. For my discussion of the depiction of Willie Scott as a racist see below.

30. Hollywood cinema's ethnographic preoccupations in representing non-Western cultures is fully visible, for example, in *King Solomon's Mines*, cited above. The camera frequently dwells with obsessive curiosity on the ornamented faces of "natives," while the narrative movement stands suspended. See for example the entry of Allen Quartermain and party into the Kaluana village. The camera moves with deliberate voyeurism from face to face of gathered Africans. The movie's attempt to achieve an ethnographic realism begins, as the movie progresses, to overtake its narratival impulse with increasing force.

31. The paired relationships between adults and children in the movie are of great significance. The "good" pair of Jones and Shorty is contrasted by the "bad" pair of Mola Ram and the boy maharajah. In a different way, the (colonially) functional pair of Jones and Shorty is contrasted to the dysfunctional pair of Blumburrt and the boy maharajah. It should be noted that the children in the movie are all nonwhite. Two texts which have suggestive discussions of the homology between the colonial and the adult-child relationships are Ashis Nandy's *The Intimate Enemy* and Ariel Dorfman's *The Empire's Old Clothes*.

32. For an useful overview of cinema and colonialism, see the already-cited "Colonialism, Racism and Representation: An Introduction" by Robert Stam and Louise Spence (12–14).

33. See Laura Mulvey's classic "Visual Pleasure and Narrative Cinema" for a feminist analysis of an audience's relationship to a film.

34. See "Index/Index" *Index on Censorship* (38) and "Banned" *The Times* of London (12).

CHAPTER TWO: TRAVEL NARRATIVES AND GULLIVER'S TRAVELS

1. For other examples that illustrate the point that criticism has largely foregone a full engagement with Swift's anticolonialism until recently, see the anthology *Fair Liberty Was All His Cry*, edited by A. Norman Jeffares (especially the essay "A Modest Appraisal: Swift Scholarship and Criticism, 1945–65" by Ricardo Quintana), and the anthology *Swift*, also edited by A. Norman Jeffares.

2. Exemplary works that may be cited as evidence in this regard are Laura Brown's "Reading Race and Gender: Jonathan Swift," Ann Cline Kelly's "Swift's Explorations of Slavery in Houyhnhnmland and Ireland," Edward Said's *The World, The Text, and the Critic*, and Clement Hawes's "Three Times Round the Globe: Gulliver and Colonial Discourse."

3. This is so despite *GT*'s problematic status in other respects. See Laura Brown's essay "Reading Race and Gender: Jonathan Swift" for a discussion of the treatment of women in *GT*.

4. In writing the word in this fashion, de Certeau means to emphasize a characteristic colonialist treatment of the speech of the "savage" not germane to my argument.

5. José Límon reminds me that anthropologists customarily speak of writing "up" people.

6. Among the canonical, pre-"predicament" anthropologists that Clifford discusses in his book are Margaret Mead and Bronislaw Malinowski. A sense of the urgent need to question the nature of ethnographic authority and practice is quite widespread in anthropology and among commentators on anthropology today. Talal Asad's edited volume *Anthropology and the Colonial Encounter* is important in this regard. In addition to this book and the work of those whom I cite in the body of the chapter, the following far from comprehensive list of names may be mentioned to indicate the diversity of positions from which an interrogation of anthropology is being carried out: Michael Herzfeld, George Marcus, Stefania Pandolfo, Kathleen Stewart, and Smadar Lavie.

7. For a useful review of what is at issue in such a term as "race," see the first two chapters of Kwame Anthony Appiah's *In My Father's House*.

8. Although material from the two essays reappears in the book, as Pratt tells us in the Preface (xii), it does so in a very different form. Hence, I have continued to cite the two essays separately in the discussion that follows.

9. Of course, there is another kind of travel, a travel that is linear in its trajectory. Such travel goes under such names as "exile" or "immigration" or "expatriation." For one example of a discussion of these terms, see Anannya

Bhattacharjee's "The Habit of Ex-Nomination: Nation, Woman and the Indian Immigrant Bourgeoisie" (21–22). Those texts that are generically labeled "travel narratives" are overwhelmingly accounts of circular travel.

10. Johannes Fabian has written at length of this "denial of co-evalness" in *Time and the Other* (e.g., 31).

11. Although Pratt has labeled this section "1750–1800," she includes analysis of texts written earlier.

12. The extent of this mimicry may perhaps be illustrated by two incidents mentioned by John Arbuthnot in a letter to Swift, one of a sailor and another "of an old gentleman," in which GT is taken to be a true account. It is possible that these incidents are apocryphal. But in any case the impact of Swift's ironic mimicry of travel narratives must have had a freshness (which is lacking for us) for the eighteenth-century reader.

13. For a summary of different assessments of the accuracy of Swift's geography in *Gulliver's Travels*, see Milton Voigt (84–86).

14. See especially pages 230–31.

15. Gulliver presumes this reader to be English. This can be seen from the very first paragraph of the text, which plunges directly into details of English political life (xi). Swift too presumes this reader to be English, but for quite different reasons, as will emerge below.

16. The "soft school-hard school" debate over Part IV of GT, that is, the debate over whether the representation of the horses is positive (hard school) or negative (soft school), is summarized in James L. Clifford's "Gulliver's Fourth Voyage: 'Hard' and 'Soft' Schools of Interpretation."

17. The section citing the English as possible ancestors for the Yahoos appears as an emendation at the back of the book in the Herbert Davis edition of *Gulliver's Travels*. It is included in the body of the text in most editions. Most commonly, of course, the Yahoos have been taken to be modeled on the Irish or the Hottentots rather than the English (see Ann Cline Kelly and Laura Brown). But this is in an attempt to find historical models that Swift might have used. My reading does not ignore such scholarship but points to the text itself, where Gulliver repeatedly refers to his family and English compatriots as Yahoos. This use of the perceived traits of non-English ethnic groups ("Others") to describe the English is itself strong evidence for the argument I am making.

18. For a convenient summary of what is at issue here, see Clement Hawes's essay (187–88 and note on 211).

19. See chapter 1 for a reference to the New Critics William Wimsatt and Monroe Beardsley in this context.

20. Of related interest is Norah Carlin's demonstration that the English constitution of the Irish as a savage Other has a long tradition. Amongst other

suggestive comments, Carlin shows in detail how the Irish were compared to animals and "natural men" during the seventeenth century. An interesting reference she makes is to an English theory that the Irish were descended from the Scythians, which would ascribe to them an Oriental origin (95–96 and 99). In the context of *GT*, her reference to an English belief in Irish cannibalism as late as Spenser is especially significant for a reading of Part IV (99).

21. For another overview of Swift's politics, see Irvin Ehrenpreis's essay "Swift on Liberty."

CHAPTER THREE: INTO DARKNESS AND OUT OF IT

1. See Zdislaw Najder for some of the connections between the diary Conrad kept at the time of his journey to the Belgian Congo and *Heart of Darkness*.

2. The other two "important events" that Kimbrough identifies are the release of the film *Apocalypse Now* and the publication of Ian Watt's *Conrad in the Nineteenth Century*.

3. Some of these works do not mention Achebe directly, but all of them were written after Achebe's comments were made. Said's first published book was *Joseph Conrad and the Fiction of Autobiography*, but was written much earlier.

4. The extent to which Hurston's reputation has been reestablished may be judged by the fact that "In 1990 the Association to Preserve the Eatonville Community . . . decided to embark on a five-year cycle of festivals to focus on the life and work of Zora Neale Hurston" (Abbott 179–80).

5. I am thinking here of the editions put out by Harper and Row as part of a series edited by Henry Louis Gates. See Bibliography for full reference.

6. The year of Hurston's birth on the marker is probably wrong.

7. See, for example, Albert Guerard's essay "The Journey Within."

8. See, for example, Garrett Stewart's essay "Lying as Dying in *Heart of Darkness*."

9. See especially pages 32–33.

10. The relevant passage from the Hawkins essay is to be found on page 296.

11. Hurston identifies herself as "Zora" in *Mules and Men*. When I refer to Zora below, I mean this persona that appears in the book.

12. See pages 8–10 of the autobiography. Hurston writes that Eatonville was started in the late nineteenth-century after an African American was elected mayor of Maitland. Although black mayor and white colleagues cooperated amicably in the administration of the city of Maitland, Hurston writes, the black mayor could not help thinking of setting up an all-black town. The

all-black town of Eatonville is soon established with the financial help of prominent white citizens of Maitland. This history, which may be regarded as an originary story of mythic proportions, captures well both Hurston's racial self-pride and the peculiar blindness that characterized her vision when it came to the politics of segregation.

13. Hemenway writes of Hurston in his biography that "she tried to reconcile high and low culture by becoming Eatonville's esthetic representative to the Harlem Renaissance" (56) and "[w]here [other Harlem Renaissance writers] were Los Angeles or Cleveland, [Hurston] was Eatonville. She was the folk" (62).

14. Hurston's most famous novel, *Their Eyes Were Watching God*, for example, opens with the protagonist Janie Crawford returning to her hometown witnessed by a gathering of people on porches (9–11). That the store porch with which *Mules and Men* opens is also a gendered space appears much more clearly from *Their Eyes Were Watching God*. Janie's conflict with her second husband, Jody Starks, partly revolves around what she may or may not do on the store porch among the men of the town gathered there. See, for example, pages 84 to 86 of *Their Eyes Were Watching God*.

15. See Hemenway, pages 159–63.

16. See page 151 of *Mules and Men* for the description of the camp.

17. Cited in Hemenway, page 219.

18. A point made in one of the notes to the first chapter bears repeating here. "Migration" suggests a different kind of travel from that which is the focus of this book. Migration, in contrast to the assumed circularity of travel in the colonialist travel narrative, is linear. It is the product not of privilege but of historical compulsions. It is the displacement of groups of people as opposed to individuals.

19. See also "From Physics to Ethnology" and "The Critique of Racial Formalism" in the same collection of essays, *Race, Culture and Evolution*, by George Stocking, and Stocking's introduction to *A Franz Boas Reader* for useful commentary by an important interpreter of Boas. The *Reader* brings together representative material from Boas.

20. Hurston herself was accused by her second husband in a divorce suit of practicing hoodoo (Hemenway 274).

21. See, for example, Ashis Nandy, ed., *Science, Hegemony and Violence*, Vandana Shiva's *Staying Alive* and Claude Alvares's *Science, Development and Violence*.

22. See page 63.

23. See especially pages 109–59.

24. See, for example, Fredric Jameson's *Political Unconscious* (206). In *Modernist Fiction*, Randall Stevenson considers Conrad a transitional figure with regard to modernism (22).

25. The references are, of course, to Houston Baker's *Modernism and the Harlem Renaissance*.

CHAPTER FOUR: WRIGHT AND WRONG IN A LAND OF PATHOS

1. See especially the essays "Everybody's Protest Novel," "Many Thousands Gone," and "Alas, Poor Richard." In *Blues, Ideology and Afro-American Literature*, Houston Baker finds "Baldwin's evaluation of Wright incomparably more malevolent than Ellison's" (140).

2. As is well known, Richard Wright went from being a member of the Communist Party in the early part of his career to disillusionment with Communism. He describes some of his experiences with Communism in the second part of his autobiography, entitled *American Hunger*. See also his contribution ("Richard Wright") to *The God That Failed: Six Studies in Communism*, ed. R. H. S. Crossman.

3. In "Black Power Revisited: In Search of Richard Wright," Jack B. Moore presents his discoveries from his journey to Ghana some years after Wright to interview some of the people who appear in *Black Power*. Moore interviews James Moxon, Hannah Kudjoe, and Kofi Baako. All three challenge some of what Wright says in *Black Power* about incidents that took place. Moore's conclusion based on this (a conclusion he also suggests in "The Art of *Black Power*") is that *Black Power* "is sometimes profitably read as a novel" (185).

4. "What Is Africa to Me?" was one of the earlier suggested titles for *Black Power*. See Michel Fabre's *The Unfinished Quest of Richard Wright* (401). The Countee Cullen poem from which this title is taken continues to appear as an epigraph to the book.

5. Wright's faith in the "Westernized elite" is in stark contrast to the innumerable African writers (such as Chinua Achebe, Ayi Kwei Armah, Wole Soyinka, Ngugi wa Thiong'o, and Chinweizu, to name only a few) who have, on the contrary, expressed deep disillusionment with such an elite. However, it is also true that the careers of most of these writers are later than that of Wright.

6. In this matter of names ("Gold Coast" and "Ghana"), we can find conveniently summarized the relationships that colonialism and nationalism bear to the territory, geographical and otherwise, that they contest. Colonialism identifies the land by the commodity it produces; nationalism, casting its glance backwards, reclaims a history by appropriating the name of an ancient kingdom.

7. For a detailed discussion of the role that the category of the "primitive" has played in Western thought see Marianna Torgovnick's *Gone Primitive: Savage Intellects, Modern Lives* (especially pages 8–9 and 99).

8. This is not to say that Christianity goes uncriticized in *Black Power*. Wright in fact finds the Christianity of the Gold Coast both anemic when compared to the pagan religion and the instrument of colonialism (132–35).

9. Jack B. Moore, in his article "Richard Wright's Dream of Africa," looks at many different passages dealing with Africa in Wright's works. Curiously, he leaves out the story "Man, God Ain't Like That. . . ."

10. James and Wright knew each other. In 1945, in New York, they had worked together on a prospective popular magazine "to clarify the personality and cultural problems of minority groups" and on a book tentatively titled *The Meaning of Negro Experience in America* (see Webb 219 and 210–15 respectively). James was also present at the farewell party thrown for Richard Wright when he went into exile (Webb 263). Perhaps more indicative of the intimacy between Wright and James, James advised Wright in 1947 to always have his tickets for the United States ready. "If the Russians entered Paris," Webb notes, "it was James' belief, that they would execute Richard forthwith" (283).

Chapter Five: V. S. Naipaul, Modernity and Postcolonial Excrement

1. Naipaul refuses identification as a metropolitan despite his long residence in England.

2. In "Our Universal Civilization" (1991), Naipaul repeats this argument, remarking that the vocation of writing is possible in no culture except the Western (22).

3. Theroux has given more virulent expression to his opinion of Naipaul recently in a book, *Sir Vidia's Shadow*.

4. For an especially interesting example of Naipaul's problematic views, see his encounter with a racist Sikh in *Area* (234–46). Naipaul's relationship to the Sikh is self-consciously complicated. He recognizes often that the Sikh is a racist in the comments the Sikh makes about darker South Indians, yet he declares himself drawn to the Sikh. See especially pages 240, 241, and 245.

5. See, for example, pages 6 and 68.

6. At the end of his essay "East Indian," Naipaul describes an encounter with a fellow Trinidadian Indian in India. The essay is a comic investigation of the peculiar status of being an East Indian from Trinidad and the dynamics of such a person's relationship to the "metropolitan" country (in this case India).

At a meeting in a Delhi club, the two Trinidadians find themselves agreeing that they are "way ahead of this bunch [Indians]" (38).

7. See especially pages 153–55 of "The Crocodiles of Yamoussoukro" in this context.

8. Bilgrami's review was written in mid-1991 when it was still possible to see the historical conjuncture in India as finally compelling the emergence of a much needed but elusive center-left front led by V. P. Singh. Such a front could still be effective but the Hindu right's continued gains over the last few years while the center-left remains fragmented tempers expectations.

9. The second chapter is entitled "The Secretary's Tale: Glimpses of the Indian Century." It is interesting to note that Nehru's other well-known historical work (other than *The Discovery of India* which I discuss below) is entitled *Glimpses of World History* (1939).

10. Compare in this context the opening of this book, where I describe the responses of some of my students. Nehru's book is, of course, a reminder—if such reminder were needed—that the easy and problematic conflation of India and Hinduism is not a characteristic to be found only outside India.

11. It is interesting to speculate that the tracing of such a historical trajectory may be a fundamental discursive feature of nationalism in colonial countries in general, since nationalism in such countries typically involves the recuperation of an "imagined community," in Benedict Anderson's words in *Imagined Communities*, from the fallen condition of foreign rule.

12. Another interesting book which is part of this debate and provides a critique of Nehruvian nationalism, albeit from a different political perspective, is Ashis Nandy's *The Intimate Enemy* (1983). *The Intimate Enemy* is an attempt to recuperate Gandhism as an indigenous idiom of expression that avoids the pitfalls of Nehruvian secular nationalism.

13. In December of 1992, the Hindu right successfully destroyed the mosque in Ayodhya, with the complicity of sections of the Indian state.

14. Four works that provide some of the important information and contextualization that is lacking in *Mutinies* are *Khaki Shorts and Saffron Flags*, ed. Tapan Basu et al., *Mirrors of Violence: Communities, Riots and Survivors in South Asia*, edited by Veena Das, *Anatomy of a Confrontation: The Babri Masjid-Ram Janmabhumi Issue*, edited by Sarvepalli Gopal, and the video documentary *Ram ke Nam*, by Anand Patwardhan. None of these texts covers the most recent incidents, following December 1992.

15. The reference is, of course, once again to Benedict Anderson's analysis of nationalism in *Imagined Communities*.

16. Among other differences, Berman understands this modernity as constitutively contradictory in ways that Naipaul shows no signs of acknowledging.

17. Similarly, an argument could surely be made that notions of modernity are inextricable from notions of gender/sex difference.

18. A nondiscursive example: the different values assigned to labor in different parts of the world, so that the labor of an automobile worker in Madras is less than that of one in Detroit, also represents a differential evaluation of praxis, here in the realm of political economy.

BIBLIOGRAPHY

Abbott, Dorothy. "Recovering Zora Neale Hurston's Work." *Frontiers* 12.1 (1991): 175–81.

Achebe, Chinua. "An Image of Africa: Racism in Conrad's *Heart of Darkness.*" *Heart of Darkness.* By Joseph Conrad. Ed. Robert Kimbrough. 3rd ed. New York: W. W. Norton, 1988. 251–62.

——. Interview. *Bill Moyers' A World of Ideas.* With Bill Moyers. Videocassette. PBS Video. 1988.

——. "Viewpoint." *Times Literary Supplement* 1 Feb. 1980: 113.

Adams, Percy. *Travel Literature and the Evolution of the Novel.* Lexington, KY: UP of Kentucky, 1983.

Adorno, Theodor. *Aesthetic theory.* Trans. C. Lenhardt. Boston: Routledge and Kegan Paul, 1983.

Ahmad, Aijaz. *In Theory: Classes, Nations, Literatures.* London: Verso, 1992.

Ahmad, Iftikhar. "Thugs, Dacoits, and the Modern World-System in Nineteenth-Century India." Diss. SUNY-Binghamton, 1992.

Alvarez, Claude. *Science, Development and Violence: The Revolt Against Modernity.* Delhi: OUP.

Amin, Shahid. "Gandhi as Mahatma." *Selected Subaltern Studies.* Eds. Ranajit Guha and Gayatri Chakravorty Spivak. New York: OUP, 1988. 288–348.

Anderson, Benedict. *Imagined Communities: Reflections on the Origin and Spread of Nationalism.* 1983. rev. ed. London: Verso, 1991.

Anderson, Perry. *The Origins of Postmodernity.* London: Verso, 1998.

Angelou, Maya. *All God's Children Need Traveling Shoes.* New York: Random-Vintage, 1987.

Apocalypse Now. Dir. Francis Ford Coppola. MGM/United Artists, 1979.

Appiah, Kwame Anthony. *In My Father's House: Africa in the Philosophy of Culture.* New York: OUP, 1992.

——. "A Long Way from Home: Wright in the Gold Coast." *Richard Wright.* Ed. Harold Bloom. New York: Chelsea House, 1987. 173–90.

Arbuthnot, John. "Letter to Swift." *Swift: The Critical Heritage.* Ed. Kathleen Williams. New York: Barnes and Noble, 1970. 61–62.

Asad, Talal, ed. *Anthropology and the Colonial Encounter.* London: Ithaca, 1973.

Baker, Houston A. *Blues, Ideology and Afro-American Literature.* Chicago: U of Chicago P, 1984.

———. *Modernism and the Harlem Renaissance.* Chicago: U of Chicago P, 1987.

Baldwin, James. "Alas, Poor Richard." *Nobody Knows My Name.* New York: Dial, 1961. 200–15.

———. "Everybody's Protest Novel." *Notes of a Native Son.* 1955. Boston: Beacon, 1990. 13–23.

———. "Many Thousands Gone." *Notes of a Native Son.* 1955. Boston: Beacon, 1990. 24–45.

"Banned." *Times of London.* 20 Feb. 1986: 12.

Barthes, Roland. *Mythologies.* 1957. Selected and Trans. Annette Lavers. New York: Noonday, 1972.

Basu, Tapan, et al. *Khaki Shorts and Saffron Flags.* New Delhi: Orient Longman, 1993.

Beckett, James Camlin. *Literature and Society in the Ireland of Swift and Grattan.* New Orleans: The Graduate School–Tulane University, 1977.

———. *A Short History of Ireland.* London: Hutchinson's University Library, 1952.

Berger, John. *Ways of Seeing.* Harmondsworth, Eng.: Penguin, 1972.

Berman, Marshall. *All That Is Solid Melts into Air: The Experience of Modernity.* 1982. With a New Preface. New York: Penguin, 1988.

Bernstein, Richard J. *Praxis and Action: Contemporary Philosophies of Human Activity.* Philadelphia: U of Pennsylvania P, 1971.

Bennett, Tony. "Really Useless 'Knowledge': A Political Critique of Aesthetics." *Outside Literature.* London: Routledge, 1990.

Bhattacharjee, Anannya. "The Habit of Ex-Nomination: Nation, Woman, and the Indian Immigrant Bourgeoisie." *Public Culture* 5.1 (Fall 1992): 19–44.

Bilgrami, Akeel. "Cry, the Beloved Subcontinent: Naipaul Fiddles while India Burns." *The New Republic* 10 June 1991: 30–34.

Blunt, Alison. *Travel, Gender, and Imperialism: Mary Kingsley and West Africa.* New York: Guilford, 1994.

Boas, Franz. *A Franz Boas Reader: The Shaping of American Anthropology, 1883–1911.* 1974. Chicago: U of Chicago P, 1982.

Brady, Frank, ed. *Twentieth Century Interpretations of* Gulliver's Travels. Englewood Cliffs, N.J.: Prentice-Hall, 1968.

Brantlinger, Patrick. "*Heart of Darkness*: Anti-Imperialism, Racism, or Impressionism?" *Criticism* 27.4 (Fall 1985): 363–85.

Brink, J.R. "From the Utopians to the Yahoos: Thomas More and Jonathan Swift." *Journal of the Rutgers University Libraries* 42 (1980): 59–66.

Brown, Laura. "Reading Race and Gender: Jonathan Swift." *Eighteenth Century Studies* 23.4 (Summer 1990): 425–43.

Buruma, Ian. Rev. of *India: A Million Mutinies Now* by V. S. Naipaul. *The New York Review of Books* 14 Feb. 1991: 3–5.

Camus, Albert. *The Stranger*. Trans. Stuart Gilbert. New York: A. A. Knopf, 1946.

Carby, Hazel. *Reconstructing Womanhood: The Emergence of the Afro-American Woman Novelist*. New York: OUP, 1987.

Carlin, Norah. "Ireland and Natural Man." *Europe and Its Others*. Ed. Francis Barker et al. Proceedings of the Essex Conference on the Sociology of Literature. Colchester: U of Essex, 1985. 91–111.

Chatterjee, Partha. *The Nation and Its Fragments: Colonial and Postcolonial Histories*. Princeton, NJ: Princeton UP, 1993.

———. *Nationalist Thought and the Colonial World: A Deriviative Discourse?* London: Zed, 1986.

Clifford, James. *The Predicament of Culture: Twentieth Century Ethnography, Litertaure and Art*. Cambridge, MA: Harvard UP, 1988.

Clifford, James L. "Gulliver's Fourth Voyage: 'Hard' and 'Soft' Schools of Interpretation." *Quick Springs of Sense: Studies in the Eighteenth Century*. Ed. Larry S. Champion. Athens: U of Georgia P, 1974. 33–49.

Collins, Glenn. "In 'Indiana Jones,' it's the stunts that steal the limelight." Rev. of *Indiana Jones and the Temple of Doom*. *The New York Times* 20 May 1984, sec. 2: 1+.

Conrad, Joseph. *Heart of Darkness*. 1899. 3rd ed. New York: W. W. Norton, 1988.

———. *Lord Jim*. Garden City, NY: Doubleday, Doran, 1920.

Cormack, Mark. *Ideology*. 1992. Ann Arbor: U of Michigan P, 1995.

Crane, R. S. *The Languages of Criticism and the Structure of Poetry*. Toronto, Can.: U of Toronto P, 1953.

Danquah, J. B. *The Akan Doctrine of God: A Fragment of Gold Coast Ethics and Religion*. London: Lutterworth, 1944.

Das, Veena, ed. *Mirrors of Violence: Communities, Riots and Survivors in South Asia*. Delhi: OUP, 1992.

The Deceivers. Dir. Nicholas Meyer. Cinecom, 1988.

de Certeau, Michel. "Ethno-graphy—Speech, or the Space of the Other: Jean de Lery." *The Writing of History*. Trans. Tom Conley. New York: Columbia UP, 1988. 209–43.

———. "Montaigne's 'Of Cannibals': The Savage 'I.'" *Heterologies*. Trans. Brian Massumi. Minneapolis: U of Minnesota P, 1986. 67–79.

Defoe, Daniel. *Robinson Crusoe*. New York: Norton, 1975.

Delaney, Austen. "Mother India as Bitch." *Transition* 26 (1966): 50–51.

Derrida, Jacques. *Dissemination*. Trans. Barbara Johnson. Chicago: U of Chicago P, 1981.

Dissanayake, Wimal. "Richard Wright: A View from the Third World." *Callaloo* 9.3 (Summer 1986): 481–89.

Dorfman, Ariel. *The Empire's Old Clothes*. New York: Pantheon, 1983.

Eagleton, Terry. "Awakening from Modernity." *Times Literary Supplement* 20 Feb. 1987: 194.

———. "Capitalism, Modernism and Postmodernism." *Against the Grain*. New York: Verso, 1986.

———. *Ideology: An Introduction*. London: Verso, 1991.

———. *Ideology of the Aesthetic*. Cambridge, MA: Basil Blackwell, 1990.

———. *Literary Theory: An Introduction*. Minneapolis: U of Minnesota P, 1983.

"Economy." *Oxford English Dictionary*. 2nd ed. 1989.

Ehrenpreis, Irvin. "Swift on Liberty." *Swift*. Ed. A. Norman Jeffares. London: Aurora, 1970. 59–73.

Ellison, Ralph. "That Same Pain, That Same Pleasure (Interview)." *Shadow and Act*. New York: Random-Vintage, 1972. 3–23.

———. "The World and the Jug." *Shadow and Act*. New York: Random-Vintage, 1972. 107–43.

Escobar, Arturo. *Encountering Development: The Making and Unmaking of the Third World*. Princeton, NJ: Princeton UP, 1995.

Fabian, Johannes. *Time and the Other: How Anthropology Makes Its Object*. New York: Columbia UP, 1983.

Fabre, Michel. *From Harlem to Paris: Black American Writers in France, 1840–1980*. Urbana: U of Illinois P, 1991.

———. *The Unfinished Quest of Richard Wright*. New York: William Morrow, 1973.

———. *The World of Richard Wright*. Jackson: UP of Mississippi, 1985.

Fabricant, Carole. *Swift's Landscape*. Baltimore: Johns Hopkins UP, 1982.

Fanon, Frantz. *The Wretched of the Earth*. Trans. Constance Farrington. 1961. New York: Grove, 1968.

Fromm, Erich. *Marx's Concept of Man*. New York: Frederick Ungar, 1963.

Gandhi. Dir. Richard Attenborough. With Roshan Seth. Columbia, 1982.

Gates, Henry Louis. "Afterword—Zora Neale Hurston: 'A Negro Way of See-ing.'" *Mules and Men*. By Zora Neale Hurston. New York: Perennial-Harper & Row, 1990. 287–97.

———. "The Blackness of Blackness: A Critique of the Sign and the Signifying Monkey." *Black Literature and Literary Theory*. Ed. Henry Louis Gates, Jr. New York: Methuen, 1984. 285–321.

———. "Zora Neale Hurston and the Speakerly Text." *Southern Literature and Literary Theory*. Ed. Jefferson Humphries. Athens: U of Georgia P, 1990. 142–69.

Gilroy, Paul. *The Black Atlantic: Modernity and Double Consciousness*. Cambridge, MA: Harvard UP, 1994.

Goodnight, G. Thomas. "The Firm, the Park and the University: Fear and Trembling on the Postmodern Trail." *The Quarterly Journal of Speech* 81.3 (August 1995): 267–90.

Gopal, Sarvepalli, ed. *Anatomy of a Confrontation: The Babri Masjid-Ram Janmbhumi Issue*. New Delhi: Penguin, 1991.

Gordon, Stewart N. "Scarf and Sword: Thugs, Marauders and State-Formation in Eighteenth Century Malwa." *Indian Economic and Social History Review* 6 (1969): 403–29.

Goux, Jean-Joseph. "Numismatics: An Essay in Theoretical Numismatics." *Symbolic Economies: After Marx and Freud*. Trans. Jennifer Curtiss Gage. Ithaca, NY: Cornell UP, 1990. 9–63.

Greenblatt, Stephen. *Shakespearean Negotiations: The Circulation of Social Energy in Renaissance England*. Berkeley: U of California P, 1988.

Grewal, Inderpal. *Home and Harem: Nation, Gender, Empire and the Cultures of Travel*. Durham, NC: Duke UP, 1996.

Guerard, Albert. "The Journey Within." *Heart of Darkness*. By Joseph Conrad. Ed. Robert Kimbrough. 3rd ed. New York: W. W. Norton, 1988. 243–50.

Guillory, John. *Cultural Capital: The Problem of Literary Canon Formation*. Chicago: U of Chicago P, 1993.

Gunga Din. Dir. George Stevens. RKO/Radio, 1939.

Habermas, Jurgen. "Modernity—An Incomplete Project." Trans. Seyla Ben-Habib. *The Anti-Aesthetic.* Ed. Hal Foster. Port Townsend, WA: Bay Press, 1983. 3–15.

Harlow, Barbara. *Resistance Literature.* New York: Methuen, 1987.

Harris, Wilson. "The Frontier on Which *Heart of Darkness* Stands." *Heart of Darkness.* By Joseph Conrad. Ed. Robert Kimbrough. 3rd ed. New York: W. W. Norton, 1988. 262–68.

Harvey, David. *The Condition of Postmodernity.* Cambridge, MA: Blackwell, 1990.

Hawes, Clement. "Three Times Round the Globe: Gulliver and Colonial Discourse." *Cultural Critique* 18 (Spring 1991): 187–214.

Hawkins, Hunt. "Conrad's Critique of Imperialism in *Heart of Darkness.*" *PMLA* 94 (1979): 286–99.

Heinzelman, Kurt. *The Economics of the Imagination.* Amherst: U of Massachusetts P, 1980.

Hemenway, Robert. *Zora Neale Hurston: A Literary Biography.* Urbana: U of Illinois P, 1977.

Hoberman, J. "White Boys: Lucas, Spielberg, and the Temple of Dumb." *Village Voice* 5 Jan. 1984: 1+.

Hurston, Zora Neale. *Dust Tracks on a Road.* 1942. New York: Perennial-Harper & Row, 1991.

———. *Mules and Men.* 1935. New York: Perennial-Harper & Row, 1990.

———. *Tell My Horse: Voodoo and Life in Haiti and Jamaica.* 1938. New York: Perennial-Harper & Row, 1990.

———. *Their Eyes Were Watching God.* 1937. Urbana: U of Illinois P, 1978.

Hutcheon, Linda. *A Poetics of Postmodernism: History, Theory, Fiction.* New York: Routledge, 1988.

Hymes, Dell, ed. *Reinventing Anthropology.* New York: Vintage-Random, 1974.

———. "The Use of Anthropology: Critical, Political, Personal." *Reinventing Anthropology.* Ed. Dell Hymes. New York: Random-Vintage, 1974. 3–79.

"Index/Index." *Index on Censorship* 15.4 (1986): 37–41.

Indiana Jones and the Temple of Doom. Dir. Steven Spielberg. Story by George Lucas. With Harrison Ford, Kate Capshaw, Ke Huy Quan, Roshan Seth, and Amrish Puri. Paramount, 1984.

James, C. L. R. *Black Jacobins: Toussaint L'Ouverture and the Santo Domingo Revolution.* New York: Vintage-Random, 1963.

———. "Black Power." *The C. L. R. James Reader*. Ed. Anna Grimshaw. Oxford, UK: Blackwell, 1992. 362–74.

———. *Nkrumah and the Ghana Revolution*. Westport, CT: Lawrence Hill, 1977.

———. *Nkrumah Then and Now*. Ms. U of Chicago Library, Chicago.

Jameson, Fredric. "Foreword." *The Postmodern Condition: A Report on Knowledge*. Jean-François Lyotard. Minneapolis: U of Minnesota P, 1984. vii–xxi.

———. *The Geopolitical Aesthetic: Cinema and Space in the World System*. Bloomington: Indiana UP, 1992.

———. *The Political Unconscious*. Ithaca, NY: Cornell UP, 1981.

———. *Postmodernism, or the Cultural Logic of Late Capitalism*. Durham, NC: Duke UP, 1991.

JanMohamed, Abdul R. "The Economy of Manichean Allegory: The Function of Racial Difference in Colonial Literature. *"Race," Writing and Difference*. Ed. Henry Louis Gates Jr. Chicago: U of Chicago P, 1986. 78–106.

Jeffares, Norman A, ed. *Fair Liberty Was All His Cry*. London: Macmillan, 1967.

———, ed. *Swift*. London: Aurora, 1970.

Johnson, Barbara. "Thresholds of Difference: Structures of Address in Zora Neale Hurston." *"Race," Writing and Difference*. Ed. Henry Louis Gates, Jr. Chicago: U of Chicago P, 1986. 317–28.

Jordan, June. "On Richard Wright and Zora Neale Hurston: Notes Toward a Balancing of Love and Hatred." *Black World* 23.10 (August 1974): 4–8.

Kael, Pauline. "The Current Cinema." *The New Yorker* June 11 1984: 100–11.

Kanga, Firdaus. "Seeing and Looking Away." Rev. of *India: A Million Mutinies Now* by V. S. Naipaul. *Times Literary Supplement* Oct. 5 1990: 1059.

Kelley, Robin. *Hammer and Hoe: Alabama Communists During the Great Depression*. Chapel Hill: U of North Carolina P, 1990.

Kellner, Douglas. *Herbert Marcuse and the Crisis of Marxism*. Berkeley: U of California P, 1984.

Kelly, Ann Cline. "Swift's Explorations of Slavery in Houyhnhnmland and Ireland." *PMLA* 91 (1976): 846–55.

Kimbrough, Robert. "Introduction." *Heart of Darkness*. By Joseph Conrad. Ed. Robert Kimbrough. 3rd ed. New York: W. W. Norton, 1988. ix–xvii.

King Solomon's Mines. Dir. Compton Bennett and Andrew Marton. MGM, 1950.

Kolakowski, Leszek. *Main Currents of Marxism*. Vol. 1. New York: OUP, 1978. 2 vols.

Lamming, George. *The Pleasures of Exile*. London: Michael Joseph, 1960.

Larrain, Jorge. *The Concept of Ideology*. Athens: U of Georgia P, 1979.

Leitch, Vincent B. *American Literary Criticism: From the Thirties to the Eighties*. New York: Columbia UP, 1988.

Lévi-Strauss, Claude. *Tristes Tropiques*. 1955. New York: Atheneum, 1984.

Lloyd, David. *Anomalous States: Irish Writing and the Post-Colonial Moment*. Durham, NC: Duke UP, 1993.

Lukacs, Georg. "The Ideology of Modernism." *Realism in our Time: Literature and the Class Struggle*. Trans. John and Necke Mander. New York: Harper and Row, 1964.

———. "Reification and the Consciousness of the Proletariat." *History and Class Consciousness*. Trans. Rodney Livingstone. Cambridge, MA: MIT P, 1971. 83–222.

Lyotard, Jean-François. *The Libidinal Economy*. Trans. Iain Hamilton Grant. London: Athlone P, 1993.

———. *The Postmodern Condition: A Report on Knowledge*. Trans. Geoff Bennington and Brian Massumi. Minneapolis: U of Minnesota P, 1984.

Macdonell, Diane. *Theories of Discourse: An Introduction*. Oxford, UK: Basil Blackwell, 1986.

Mandel, Ernest. *Late Capitalism*. Trans. Joris de Bris. London: NLB, 1975.

———. "Introduction." *Capital*. Vol. 1. By Karl Marx. Trans. Ben Fowkes. New York: Vintage-Random, 1977. 3 vols.

Marable, Manning. *How Capitalism Underdeveloped Black America: Problems in Race, Political Economy and Society*. Boston, MA: South End, 1983.

Marcuse, Herbert. "The Foundation of Historical Materialism." 1932. *Studies in Critical Philosophy*. Boston: Beacon, 1973. 1–48.

———. "Freedom and the Historical Imperative." *Studies in Critical Philosophy*. Boston: Beacon, 1973. 209–23.

———. "On the Philosophical Foundation of the Concept of Labor in Economics." *Telos* 16 (Summer 1973): 9–37.

Margolies, Edward. *The Art of Richard Wright*. Carbondale: Southern Illinois UP, 1969.

———. "Richard Wright's Opposing Freedoms." *Mississippi Quarterly* 42.4 (Fall 1989): 409–14.

Marx, Karl. *Capital*. 1867–94. Trans. Ben Fowkes. New York: Vintage-Random, 1977. 3 vols.

———. "Economic and Philosophic Manuscripts of 1844." *The Marx-Engels Reader*. 1972. New York: W. W. Norton, 1978. 66–125.

———. "The *Grundrisse*." 1857–58. *The Marx-Engels Reader*. 1972. New York: W. W. Norton, 1978. 221–93.

———. "Theses on Feurbach." 1845. *The Marx-Engels Reader*. 1972. New York: W. W. Norton, 1978. 143–45.

Masters, John. *The Deceivers*. New York: Viking, 1952.

"Materialism." *A Dictionary of Marxist Thought*. 2nd ed. Ed. Tom Bottomore. Oxford: Blackwell, 1991. 369–73.

Mazrui, Ali A. "Exit Visa from the World System: Dilemmas of Cultural and Economic Disengagement." *Third World Quarterly* 3.1 (1981): 62–74.

McLellan, David. *Ideology*. Minneapolis: U of Minnesota P, 1986.

Memmi, Albert. *The Colonizer and the Colonized*. Boston: Beacon, 1965.

Michaels, James. "Shakespeare, Plato and Other Racist Pigs." *Forbes* 1 April 1991: 10.

Michener, Charles. "The Dark Visions of V. S. Naipaul." *Newsweek* 16 Nov. 1981: 104–15.

Minh-ha, Trinh T. "The Language of Nativism: Anthropology as a Scientific Conversation of Man with Man." *Woman, Native, Other*. Bloomington: Indiana UP, 1989. 47–76.

Modleski, Tania. *Loving with a Vengeance*. New York: Methuen, 1982.

Mohanty, Satya P. *Literary Theory and the Claims of History: Postmodernism, Objectivity, Multicultural Politics*. Ithaca, NY: Cornell UP, 1997.

Monaco, James. *How to Read a Film*. Rev. ed. New York: OUP, 1981.

Montag, Warren. *The Unthinkable Swift: The Spontaneous Philosophy of a Church of England Man*. New York: Verso, 1994.

Moore, Jack B. "The Art of *Black Power*: Novelistic or Documentary" *Revues Française d'Etudes Américaines* 31 (Feb. 1987): 79–91.

———. "Black Power Revisited: In Search of Richard Wright." *Mississippi Quarterly* 41 (Spring 1988): 161–86.

———. "Richard Wright's Dream of Africa." *Journal of African Studies* 2.2 (Summer 1975): 231–45.

Mulvey, Laura. "Visual Pleasure and Narrative Cinema." *Screen* 16.3 (Autumn 1975): 6–18.

Myrdal, Gunnar. "Foreword." *The Color Curtain*. By Richard Wright. London: Dennis Dobson, 1956. 7–8.

Naipaul, V. S. *Among the Believers: An Islamic Journey*. 1981. New York: Vintage-Random, 1982.

――――. *An Area of Darkness*. 1964. New York: Vintage-Random, 1981.

――――. *Between Father and Son: Family Letters*. Ed. Gillon Aitken. New York: Alfred A. Knopf, 2000.

――――. "The Crocodiles of Yamoussoukro." *Finding the Center: Two Narratives*. 1984. New York: Vintage-Random, 1986. 73–176.

――――. "East Indian." *The Overcrowded Barracoon*. New York: Alfred A. Knopf, 1973. 30–38.

――――. *India: A Million Mutinies Now*. 1990. New York: Penguin, 1992.

――――. *India: A Wounded Civilization*. 1976. New York: Vintage-Random, 1978.

――――. "In the Middle of the Journey." *The Overcrowded Barracoon*. New York: Alfred A. Knopf, 1973. 41–46.

――――. *The Middle Passage*. London: Russell-Andre Deutsch, 1962.

――――. "Our Universal Civilization." *The New York Review of Books* 31 Jan. 1991: 22–25.

――――. "Prologue to an Autobiography." *Finding the Center: Two Narratives*. 1984. New York: Vintage-Random, 1986. 1–72.

Narayan, R, K. *The Ramayana*. 1972. New York: Penguin, 1977.

Najder, Zdislaw. "Introduction to 'The Congo Diary' and the 'Up-river Book.'" *Heart of Darkness*. By Joseph Conrad. Ed. Robert Kimbrough. 3rd Ed. New York: W. W. Norton, 1988. 155–59.

Nandy, Ashis. *The Intimate Enemy*. Delhi: OUP, 1983.

――――, ed. *Science, Hegemony and Violence: A Requiem for Modernity*. 1988. Delhi: OUP, 1990.

Nazareth, Peter. "Out of Darkness: Conrad and Other Third World Writers." *Conradiana* 14 (1982): 173–87.

Nearing, Scott. *Black America*. 1929. New York: Johnson Reprint, 1970.

Nehru, Jawaharlal. *The Discovery of India*. New York: John Day, 1946.

――――. *Glimpses of World History*. 1939. New York: J. Day, 1942.

Nixon, Rob. *London Calling: V. S. Naipaul, Postcolonial Mandarin*. New York: OUP, 1992.

Pratt, Mary Louise. "Fieldwork in Common Places." *Writing Culture*. Ed. James Clifford and George Marcus. Berkeley: U of California P, 1986. 27–50.

――――. *Imperial Eyes*. London: Routledge, 1992.

――――. "Scratches on the Face of the Country; or, What Mr. Barrow Saw in the Land of the Bushmen." *"Race," Writing, and Difference*. Ed. Henry Louis Gates, Jr. Chicago: U of Chicago P, 1986. 119–43.

"Praxis." *A Dictionary of Marxist Thought*. 2nd ed. Ed. Tom Bottomore. Oxford: Blackwell, 1991. 384–89.

Quintana, Ricardo. "A Modest Appraisal: Swift Scholarship and Criticism, 1945–65." *Fair Liberty Was All His Cry*. Ed. Norman A. Jeffares. London: Macmillan, 1967. 342–55.

Rabasa, José. "Allegories of the *Atlas*." *Europe and Its Others*. Ed. Francis Barker et al. Proceedings of the Essex Conference on the Sociology of Literature. Colchester: U of Essex, 1985. 1–16.

Radhakrishnan, R. "Postmodernism and the Rest of the World." *Organization* 1.2 (1994): 305–40.

Ram ke Nam. Dir. Anand Patwardhan. Anand Patwardhan, 1992.

Rampersad, Arnold. "Foreword." *Mules and Men*. By Zora Neale Hurston. 1935. New York: Perennial-Harper & Row, 1990. xv–xxiii.

Reilly, John M. "Richard Wright and the Art of Non-Fiction: Stepping Out on the Stage of the World." *Callaloo* 9.3 (Summer 1986): 507–20.

———. "Richard Wright's Discovery of the Third World." *Minority Voices* 2 (1978): 47–53.

Roberts, John. Rev. of *Mules and Men* and *Their Eyes Were Watching God* by Zora Neale Hurston. *Journal of American Folklore* 93 (1980): 463–66.

Robertson, Patrick. *Guiness Book of Film Facts and Feats*. New edition. London: Guiness Superlatives, 1985.

Rodino, Richard H. *Swift Studies, 1965–1980: An Annotated Bibliography*. New York: Garland, 1984.

Rodney, Walter. *How Europe Underdeveloped Africa*. Washington, DC: Howard UP, 1982.

Rowe, John Carlos. "Postmodern Studies." *Redrawing the Boundaries: The Transformation of English and American Literary Studies*. Ed. Stephen Grennblatt and Giles Gunn. New York: MLA of America, 1992. 179–208.

Roy, Parama. "Discovering India, Imagining *Thuggee*." *The Yale Journal of Criticism* 9.1 (1996): 121–45.

Rushdie, Salman. "Outside the Whale." *American Film* 10.4 (Jan.-Feb. 1985): 16+.

———. "V. S. Naipaul." *Imaginary Homelands*. London: Granta-Viking, 1991. 148–51.

Said, Edward. *Culture and Imperialism*. New York: Alfred A. Knopf, 1993.

———. *Joseph Conrad and the Fiction of Autobiography*. Cambridge, MA: Harvard UP, 1966.

———. *Orientalism*. New York: Vintage, 1979.

————. *The World, the Text, and the Critic.* Cambridge, Mass.: Harvard UP, 1983. 72–89.

San Juan, Jr., E. *Beyond Postcolonial Theory.* New York: St. Martin's, 1998.

————. *Hegemony and Strategies of Transgression: Essays in Cultural Studies and Comparative Literature.* Albany: SUNY, 1995.

Sartre, Jean-Paul. "Materialism and Revolution." *Literary and Philosophical Essays.* Trans. Annette Michelson. London: Rider, 1955.

Sarvan, C. P. "Racism and the *Heart of Darkness.*" *Heart of Darkness.* By Joseph Conrad. Ed. Robert Kimbrough. 3rd ed. New York: W. W. Norton, 1988. 280–85.

Scott, Temple. "Introduction." *The Prose Works of Jonathan Swift: Vol VII.* Ed. Temple Scott. London: George Bell, 1905. ix–xx.

Shell, Marc. *The Economy of Literature.* Baltimore, MD: Johns Hopkins UP, 1978.

Sherwood, Richard C. ["General Notice on Phansigars."] *The Thugs or Phansigars of India.* [Ed. and] By W. H. Sleeman. Vol. 1. Philadelphia: Carey and Hart, 1839. 13–48. 2 vols.

Shiva, Vandana. *Staying Alive: Women, Ecology and Survival in India.* New Delhi: Kali for Women, 1988.

Shohat, Ella. "Gender and the Culture of Empire: Towards a Feminist Ethnography of the Cinema." *Quarterly Review of Film and Video* 13.1–3 (1991): 45–84.

————. "Imaging Terra Incognita: The Disciplinary Gaze of Empire." *Public Culture* 3.2 (1991): 41–70.

Showalter, Elaine. *Sexual Anarchy: Gender and Culture at the Fin de Siecle.* New York: Viking, 1990.

Singh, Frances B. "The Colonialistic Bias of *Heart of Darkness.*" *Heart of Darkness.* By Joseph Conrad. Ed. Robert Kimbrough. 3rd ed. New York: W. W. Norton, 1988. 268–80.

Singha, Radhika. "'Providential' Circumstances: The Thuggee Campaign of the 1830s and Legal Innovation." *Modern Asian Studies* 27.1 (1993): 83–146.

Sivanandan, A. "The Enigma of the Colonised: Reflections on Naipaul's Arrival." *Race and Class* 32.1 (July–Sept. 1990): 33–43.

Sleeman, William Henry. *Rambles and Recollections of an Indian Official.* London: J. Hatchard and Son, 1844. 2 vols.

————. *The Thugs or Phansigars of India.* 2 vols. Philadelphia: Carey and Hart, 1839.

Smith, Barbara Herrnstein. *Contingencies of Value: Alternative Perspectives for Critical Theory.* Cambridge, MA: Harvard UP, 1988.

Smith, Frederik N. "Afterword: Style, Swift's Reader, and the Genres of *Gulliver's Travels*." *The Genres of* Gulliver's Travels. Ed. Frederik Smith. Newark: U of Delaware P, 1990. 246–59.

Spivak, Gayatri Chakravorty. *A Critique of Postcolonial Reason: Toward a History of the Vanishing Present*. Calcutta: Seagull, 1999.

———. *In Other Worlds: Essays in Cultural Politics*. New York: Methuen, 1987.

———. "Poststructuralism, Marginality, Postcoloniality and Value." *Literary Theory Today*. Ed. Peter Collier and Helga Geyer-Ryan. Ithaca, NY: Cornell UP, 1990. 219–44.

———. "Scattered Speculations on the Question of Value." *In Other Worlds: Essays in Cultural Politics*. New York: Methuen, 1987. 154–75.

Stam, Robert and Louise Spence. "Colonialism, Racism and Representation: An Introduction." *Screen* 24.2 (1983): 2–20.

Stevenson, Randall. *Modernist Fiction: An Introdution*. New York: Harvester Wheatsheaf. 1992.

Stewart, Garrett. "Lying as Dying in *Heart of Darkness*." *Heart of Darkness*. By Joseph Conrad. Ed. Robert Kimbrough. 3rd ed. New York: W. W. Norton, 1988. 358–74.

Stocking, George. "The Critique of Racial Formalism." *Race, Culture and Evolution: Essays in the History of Anthropology*. 1968. Chicago: U of Chicago P, 1982. 161–94.

———. "Franz Boas and the Culture Concept." *Race, Culture and Evolution: Essays in the History of Anthropology*. 1968. Chicago: U of Chicago P, 1982. 195–233.

———. "From Physics to Ethnology." *Race, Culture and Evolution: Essays in the History of Anthropology*. 1968. Chicago: U of Chicago P, 1982. 133–60.

———. "Introduction: The Basic Assumptions of Boasian Anthropology." *A Franz Boas Reader: The Shaping of American Anthropology, 1883–1911*. By Franz Boas. 1974. Chicago: U of Chicago P, 1982. 1–20.

Swift, Jonathan. *Gulliver's Travels—The Prose Works of Jonathan Swift: Vol XI*. 1726. Oxford: Shakespeare Head, 1941.

———. "A Modest Proposal." *The Prose Works of Jonathan Swift: Vol XII*. Oxford: Shakespeare Head, 1955. 107–18.

———. "A Proposal for the Universal Use of Irish Manufacture." *The Prose Works of Jonathan Swift: Vol IX*. Oxford: Shakespeare Head, 1948. 13–22.

———. "A Short View of the State of Ireland." *The Prose Works of Jonathan Swift: Vol XII*. Oxford: Shakespeare Head, 1955. 1–12.

———. "The Story of the Injured Lady—In a Letter to Her Friend with His Answer." *The Prose Works of Jonathan Swift: Vol IX*. Oxford: Shakespeare Head, 1948. 1–12.

Tarzan and His Mate. Dir. Cedric Gibbons. With Johnny Weismuller and Maureen O'Sullivan. MGM, 1934.

Taylor, Colonel Meadows. *Confessions of a Thug*. 1839. New Preface by Colonel Taylor. London: Kegan Paul, Trench, Trübner, 1873.

Terdiman, Richard. *Discourse/Counter-Discourse*. Ithaca, NY: Cornell UP, 1989.

Theroux, Paul. *Sir Vidia's Shadow: A Friendship across Five Continents*. Boston: Houghton Mifflin, 1998.

———. "V. S. Naipaul." *Modern Fiction Studies* 30.3 (Autumn 1984): 445–54.

Thornton, Edward. *Illustration of the History and Practice of the Thugs*. London: Allen, 1837.

Tomlinson, John. *Cultural Imperialism*. Baltimore: Johns Hopkins UP, 1991.

Tompkins, Jane. *Sensational Designs*. New York: OUP, 1985.

Torgovnick, Marianna. *Gone Primitive: Savage Intellects, Modern Lives*. Chicago: U of Chicago P, 1990.

Tuker, Sir Francis. *The Yellow Scarf*. London: Dent, 1961.

"Value." *A Dictionary of Marxist Thought*. 2nd ed. Ed. Tom Bottomore. Oxford: Blackwell, 1991. 507–11.

"Value." *Oxford English Dictionary*. 2nd ed. 1989.

Voigt, Milton. *Swift and the Twentieth Century*. Detroit: Wayne State UP, 1964.

Von Gunden, Kenneth. *Postmodern Auteurs: Coppola, Lucas, De Palma, Spielberg and Scorcese*. Jefferson, NC: McFarland, 1991.

Walker, Alice. "Foreword." *Zora Neale Hurston: A Literary Biography*. By Robert Hemenway. Urbana: U of Illinois P, 1977. xi–xviii.

———. "Looking for Zora." ["In Search of Zora Neale Hurston."] 1975. *In Search of Our Mothers' Gardens*. San Diego, CA: Harcourt Brace Johanovich, 1983. 93–116.

Wall, Cheryl A. "Mules and Men and Women: Zora Neale Hurston's Strategies of Narration and Visions of Female Empowerment." *Black American Literature Forum* 23.4 (Winter 1989): 681–90.

Watt, Ian. *Conrad in the Nineteenth Century*. Berkeley: U of California P, 1979.

———. "Conrad's *Heart of Darkness* and the Critics." *North Dakota Quarterly* 57.3 (Summer 1989): 5–15.

Watts, Cedric. "'A Bloody Racist': About Achebe's View of Conrad." *The Yearbook of English Studies* 13 (1983): 196–209.

Webb, Constance. *Richard Wright: A Biography*. New York: G. P. Putnam's Sons, 1968.

Williams, Harold. "Introduction." *Gulliver's Travels—The Prose Works of Jonathan Swift: Vol. XI* . Ed. Herbert Davis. Oxford: Shakespeare Head, 1941. ix–xxvii.

Williams, Raymond. "Ideology." *Marxism and Literature*. Oxford, UK: OUP, 1977.

——. "Materialism." *Keywords*. New York: OUP, 1976. 163–67.

——. *Problems in Materialism and Culture: Selected Essays*. London: Verso, 1980.

Willis, Susan. *Specifying: Black Women Writing the American Experience*. Madison: U of Wisconsin P, 1987.

Wimsatt, William K. and Monroe C. Beardsley. "The Intentional Fallacy." *The Verbal Icon: Studies in the Meaning of Poetry*. By William K. Wimsatt. Lexington: University Press of Kentucky, 1954. 3–18.

Wright, Richard. *American Hunger*. New York: Harper & Row, 1977.

——. *Black Boy*. 1937. New York: Perennial-Harper and Row, 1945.

——. *Black Power: A Record of Reactions in a Land of Pathos*. New York: Harper, 1954.

——. *The Color Curtain: A Report on the Bandung Conference*. London: Dennis Dobson, 1956.

——. "Man, God Ain't Like That." *Eight Men*. Cleveland: World, nd. 163–92.

——. *Native Son*. New York: Grosset & Dunlap, 1940.

——. *The Outsider*. New York: Harper and Row, 1953.

——. "Richard Wright." 1944. *The God That Failed: Six Studies in Communism*. Ed. R. H. S. Crossman. London: Hamilton, 1950.

——. *White Man, Listen!* Garden City, NY: Doubleday, 1957.

Zimmerman, Patricia. "Soldiers of Fortune: Lucas, Spielberg, Indiana Jones and Raiders of the Lost Ark." *Wide Angle* 6.2 (1984): 34–39.

INDEX

SUNY SERIES
EXPLORATIONS IN POSTCOLONIAL STUDIES
EMMANUEL C. EZE, EDITOR

Patrick Colm Hogan, *Colonialism and Cultural Identity: Crises of Tradition in the Anglophone Literatures of India, Africa, and the Caribbean*

Alfred J. Lopez, *Posts and Pasts: A Theory of Postcolonialism*